A CASEBOOK ON

The Declaration
of Independence

In CONGRESS, July 4, 1776.

A DECLARATION

By the REPRESENTATIVES of the

UNITED STATES OF AMERICA,

In GENERAL CONGRESS ASSEMBLED.

WHEN in the Courfe of human Events, it becomes neceffary for one People to diffolve the Political Bands which have connected them with another, and to affume among the Powers of the Earth, the feparate and equal Station to which the Laws of Nature and of Nature's God entitle them, a decent Refpect to the Opinions of Mankind requires that they fhould declare the caufes which impel them to the Separation.

We hold thefe Truths to be felf-evident, that all Men are created equal, that they are endowed by their Creator with certain unalienable Rights, that among thefe are Life, Liberty, and the Purfuit of Happinefs---That to fecure thefe Rights, Governments are inftituted among Men, deriving their juft Powers from the Confent of the Governed, that whenever any Form of Government becomes deftructive of thefe Ends, it is the Right of the People to alter or to abolifh it, and to inftitute new Government, laying its Foundation on fuch Principles, and organizing its Powers in fuch Form, as to them fhall feem moft likely to effect their Safety and Happinefs. Prudence, indeed, will dictate that Governments long eftablifhed fhould not be changed for light and tranfient Caufes; and accordingly all Experience hath fhewn, that Mankind are more difpofed to fuffer, while Evils are fufferable, than to right themfelves by abolifhing the Forms to which they are accuftomed. But when a long Train of Abufes and Ufurpations, purfuing invariably the fame Object, evinces a Defign to reduce them under abfolute Defpotifm, it is their Duty, it is their Duty, to throw off fuch Government, and to provide new Guards for their future Security. Such has been the patient Sufferance of thefe Colonies; and fuch is now the Neceffity which conftrains them to alter their former Syftems of Government. The Hiftory of the prefent King of Great-Britain is a Hiftory of repeated Injuries and Ufurpations, all having in direct Object the Eftablifhment of an abfolute Tyranny over thefe States. To prove this, let Facts be fubmitted to a candid World.

He has refufed his Affent to Laws, the moft wholefome and neceffary for the public Good.

He has forbidden his Governors to pafs Laws of immediate and preffing Importance, unlefs fufpended in their Operation till his Affent fhould be obtained; and when fo fufpended, he has utterly neglected to attend to them.

He has refufed to pafs other Laws for the Accommodation of large Diftricts of People, unlefs thofe People would relinquifh the Right of Reprefentation in the Legiflature, a Right ineftimable to them, and formidable to Tyrants only.

He has called together Legiflative Bodies at Places unufual, uncomfortable, and diftant from the Depofitory of their public Records, for the fole Purpofe of fatiguing them into Compliance with his Meafures.

He has diffolved Reprefentative Houfes repeatedly, for oppofing with manly Firmnefs his Invafions on the Rights of the People.

He has refufed for a long Time, after fuch Diffolutions, to caufe others to be elected; whereby the Legiflative Powers, incapable of Annihilation, have returned to the People at large for their exercife, the State remaining in the mean time expofed to all the Dangers of Invafion from without, and Convulfions within.

He has endeavoured to prevent the Population of thefe States; for that Purpofe obftructing the Laws for Naturalization of Foreigners; refufing to pafs others to encourage their Migrations hither, and raifing the Conditions of new Appropriations of Lands.

He has obftructed the Adminiftration of Juftice, by refufing his Affent to Laws for eftablifhing Judiciary Powers.

He has made Judges dependent on his Will alone, for the Tenure of their Offices, and the Amount and Payment of their Salaries.

He has erected a Multitude of new Offices, and fent hither Swarms of Officers to harrafs our People, and eat out their Subftance.

He has kept among us, in Times of Peace, Standing Armies, without the confent of our Legiflatures.

He has affected to render the Military independent of and fuperior to the Civil Power.

He has combined with others to fubject us to a Jurifdiction foreign to our Conftitution, and unacknowledged by our Laws; giving his Affent to their Acts of pretended Legiflation:

For quartering large Bodies of Armed Troops among us:

For protecting them, by a mock Trial, from Punifhment for any Murders which they fhould commit on the Inhabitants of thefe States:

For cutting off our Trade with all Parts of the World:

For impofing Taxes on us without our Confent:

For depriving us, in many Cafes, of the Benefits of Trial by Jury:

For tranfporting us beyond Seas to be tried for pretended Offences:

For abolifhing the free Syftem of Englifh Laws in a neighbouring Province, eftablifhing therein an arbitrary Government, and enlarging its Boundaries, fo as to render it at once an Example and fit Inftrument for introducing the fame abfolute Rule into thefe Colonies:

For taking away our Charters, abolifhing our moft valuable Laws, and altering fundamentally the Forms of our Governments:

For fufpending our own Legiflatures, and declaring themfelves invefted with Power to legiflate for us in all Cafes whatfoever.

He has abdicated Government here, by declaring us out of his Protection and waging War againft us.

He has plundered our Seas, ravaged our Coafts, burnt our Towns, and deftroyed the Lives of our People.

He is, at this Time, tranfporting large Armies of foreign Mercenaries to compleat the Works of Death, Defolation, and Tyranny, already begun with circumftances of Cruelty and Perfidy, fcarcely paralleled in the moft barbarous Ages, and totally unworthy the Head of a civilized Nation.

He has conftrained our fellow Citizens taken Captive on the high Seas to bear Arms againft their Country, to become the Executioners of their Friends and Brethren, or to fall themfelves by their Hands.

He has excited domeftic Infurrections amongft us, and has endeavoured to bring on the Inhabitants of our Frontiers, the mercilefs Indian Savages, whofe known Rule of Warfare, is an undiftinguifhed Deftruction, of all Ages, Sexes and Conditions.

In every ftage of thefe Oppreffions we have Petitioned for Redrefs in the moft humble Terms: Our repeated Petitions have been anfwered only by repeated Injury. A Prince, whofe Character is thus marked by every act which may define a Tyrant, is unfit to be the Ruler of a free People.

Nor have we been wanting in Attentions to our Britifh Brethren. We have warned them from Time to Time of Attempts by their Legiflature to extend an unwarrantable Jurifdiction over us. We have reminded them of the Circumftances of our Emigration and Settlement here. We have appealed to their native Juftice and Magnanimity, and we have conjured them by the Ties of our common Kindred to difavow thefe Ufurpations, which, would inevitably interrupt our Connections and Correfpondence. They too have been deaf to the Voice of Juftice and of Confanguinity. We muft, therefore, acquiefce in the Neceffity, which denounces our Separation, and hold them, as we hold the reft of Mankind, Enemies in War, in Peace, Friends.

We, therefore, the Reprefentatives of the UNITED STATES OF AMERICA, in General Congress, Affembled, appealing to the Supreme Judge of the World for the Rectitude of our Intentions, do, in the Name, and by Authority of the good People of thefe Colonies, folemnly Publifh and Declare, That thefe United Colonies are, and of Right ought to be, Free and Independent States; that they are abfolved from all Allegiance to the Britifh Crown, and that all political Connection between them and the State of Great-Britain, is and ought to be totally diffolved; and that as Free and Independent States, they have full Power to levy War, conclude Peace, contract Alliances, eftablifh Commerce, and to do all other Acts and Things which Independent States may of right do. And for the fupport of this Declaration, with a firm Reliance on the Protection of divine Providence, we mutually pledge to each other our Lives, our Fortunes, and our facred Honor.

Signed by Order *and in* Behalf *of the* Congress,

JOHN HANCOCK, President.

Attest.

CHARLES THOMSON, Secretary.

Philadelphia: Printed by John Dunlap.

A CASEBOOK ON

The Declaration
of Independence

Edited by

ROBERT GINSBERG

Drexel Institute of Technology

Thomas Y. Crowell Company

New York, Established 1834

Preface

ᚳᚷᛉ ᛉ ᚷᛉᚹ

Essential monument of the American experience and of the experience of mankind, the Declaration of Independence is the most widely known and influential secular document in the history of the world. Conceived in the midst of a great argument over the rights of men, the obligations of the state, and the necessity of revolution, the Declaration has perennially been invoked on the many subsequent occasions when these issues have been debated. These issues are now the subject of intense discussion in America and throughout the world, and thus the Declaration remains contemporary and controversial, worthy of careful study by those who would understand human events and human ideals. The very slogans and taunts heard in our own times echo the phrases made public to the world on July 4, 1776: *arbitrary government, world opinion, free and independent states, the voice of justice, mock trial, armies of foreign mercenaries, consent of the governed, absolute tyranny, equality of men, a free people, right of representation.* If the greatness of the Declaration has been accorded frequent—and sometimes inordinate—praise, the document has also borne a significant history of debunking and sometimes denigration. Men have heralded it as a "sublime manifesto," a "stately and passionate chant of human freedom," the "expression of the American mind," the "magna carta of the race," the "immortal emblem of humanity." But others have labeled it a "juvenile declamation," a piece of "sounding nonsense," a "delusive bundle of fallacies," a "fanfaronade of abstractions," and a "self-evident lie."

This book engages the college student in the issues raised by the Declaration and in the critical controversies it has generated. He is invited to explore the meaning and consequences of the ideas the Declaration embodies; to analyze the argumentative structure of the document, including its logical and rhetorical components; and

v

to appreciate the expressive powers of its style. The student will also be expected to evaluate the variety of critical reactions the Declaration has aroused in the course of the past two centuries.

The twenty-six essays and the five appendices have been selected for their suitability to classroom discussion, to independent reading, and to the writing of original papers. Materials are presented in the appendices that illuminate the background of the Declaration, its composition and revision, and its later history. An extensive bibliography contains entries on historical and textual materials and on critical works that may be consulted by the student who wishes to do further research. The section on Problems for Study and Writing lists questions for discussion and for the preparation of expository themes, critical essays, and research papers.

The text of the Declaration is a literal reprint of the first edition (also reproduced as the frontispiece) from a copy in the New York Public Library. Selections from French and German sources appear here in new translations by the editor, who has also written an essay especially for this volume. The other essays are reprinted from first editions or authoritative texts. The titles of the selections, unless otherwise noted, have been assigned by the editor. The pagination of printed sources is indicated by bracketed figures placed after the last complete word of the selection on its original page. Because of the importance of Jefferson's letters, notes, and compositional materials, these texts are printed directly from the manuscripts. The student may cite them by date, by title, or by the pagination of the present volume. The manuscript Rough Draft of the Declaration is generally cited by its page numbers, which are indicated in brackets in the reprinted text. Typographical errors in the original texts have been corrected, but no attempt has been made to modernize spelling, grammar, and citations, nor to make them consistent throughout the book. The notes originally accompanying the selections have been retained, though occasionally they have been renumbered for convenience, and in all cases they are printed at the foot of the page.

The editor wishes to thank the following institutions for graciously permitting publication of material from their collections: the Library of Congress and the National Archives, Washington; the Historical Society of Pennsylvania, Philadelphia; and the New York Public Library.

Robert Ginsberg

Philadelphia
July, 1966

Contents

ᘓᕽ ✖ ᕽᗏ

A CASEBOOK ON

The Declaration
of Independence

In Congress, July 4, 1776.

A DECLARATION

By the Representatives of the

UNITED STATES OF AMERICA,

In General Congress Assembled.

[I] WHEN in the Course of human Events, it becomes necessary for one People to dissolve the Political Bands which
have connected them with another, and to assume among
the Powers of the Earth, the separate and equal Station to
which the Laws of Nature and of Nature's God entitle
them, a decent Respect to the Opinions of Mankind requires that they should declare the causes which impel them
to the Separation.

[II] WE hold these Truths to be self-evident, that all Men
are created equal, that they are endowed by their Creator
with certain unalienable Rights, that among these are Life,
Liberty, and the Pursuit of Happiness——That to secure
these Rights, Governments are instituted among Men, deriving their just Powers from the Consent of the Governed, that
whenever any Form of Government becomes destructive of
these Ends, it is the Right of the People to alter or to abolish
it, and to institute new Government, laying its Foundation
on such Principles, and organizing its Powers in such Form,
as to them shall seem most likely to effect their Safety and
Happiness. Prudence, indeed, will dictate that Governments
long established should not be changed for light and transient Causes; and accordingly all Experience hath shewn,

FROM the broadside edition published in Philadelphia by John Dunlap, July 4,
1776. Original title. For convenience in referring to the Declaration, the paragraphs and accusations have been numbered in the margin.

that Mankind are more disposed to suffer, while Evils are sufferable, than to right themselves by abolishing the Forms to which they are accustomed. But when a long Train of Abuses and Usurpations, pursuing invariably the same Object, evinces a Design to reduce them under absolute Despotism, it is their Right, it is their Duty, to throw off such Government, and to provide new Guards for their future Security. Such has been the patient Sufferance of these Colonies; and such is now the Necessity which constrains them to alter their former Systems of Government. The History of the present King of Great-Britain is a History of repeated Injuries and Usurpations, all having in direct Object the Establishment of an absolute Tyranny over these States. To prove this, let Facts be submitted to a candid World.

[i]   HE has refused his Assent to Laws, the most wholesome and necessary for the public Good.

[ii]   HE has forbidden his Governors to pass Laws of immediate and pressing Importance, unless suspended in their Operation till his Assent should be obtained; and when so suspended, he has utterly neglected to attend to them.

[iii]   HE has refused to pass other Laws for the Accommodation of large Districts of People, unless those People would relinquish the Right of Representation in the Legislature, a Right inestimable to them, and formidable to Tyrants only.

[iv]   HE has called together Legislative Bodies at Places unusual, uncomfortable, and distant from the Depository of their public Records, for the sole Purpose of fatiguing them into Compliance with his Measures.

[v]   HE has dissolved Representative Houses repeatedly, for opposing with manly Firmness his Invasions on the Rights of the People.

[vi]   HE has refused for a long Time, after such Dissolutions, to cause others to be elected; whereby the Legislative Powers, incapable of Annihilation, have returned to the People at large for their exercise; the State remaining in the mean time exposed to all the Dangers of Invasion from without, and Convulsions within.

[vii]   HE has endeavoured to prevent the Population of these States; for that Purpose obstructing the Laws for Natural-

ization of Foreigners; refusing to pass others to encourage their Migrations hither, and raising the Conditions of new Appropriations of Lands.

[viii]   HE has obstructed the Administration of Justice, by refusing his Assent to Laws for establishing Judiciary Powers.

[ix]   HE has made Judges dependent on his Will alone, for the Tenure of their Offices, and the Amount and Payment of their Salaries.

Judicial Prerogatives

[x]   HE has erected a Multitude of new Offices, and sent hither Swarms of Officers to harrass our People, and eat out their Substance.

[xi]   HE has kept among us, in Times of Peace, Standing Armies, without the consent of our Legislatures.

[xii]   HE has affected to render the Military independent of and superior to the Civil Power.

[xiii]   HE has combined with others to subject us to a Jurisdiction foreign to our Constitution, and unacknowledged by our Laws; giving his Assent to their Acts of pretended Legislation:

[xiv]   FOR quartering large Bodies of Armed Troops among us:

[xv]   FOR protecting them, by a mock Trial, from Punishment for any Murders which they should commit on the Inhabitants of these States:

[xvi]   FOR cutting off our Trade with all Parts of the World:

[xvii]   FOR imposing Taxes on us without our Consent:

[xviii]   FOR depriving us, in many Cases, of the Benefits of Trial by Jury:

[xix]   FOR transporting us beyond Seas to be tried for pretended Offences:

[xx]   FOR abolishing the free System of English Laws in a neighbouring Province, establishing therein an arbitrary Government, and enlarging its Boundaries, so as to render it at once an Example and fit Instrument for introducing the same absolute Rule into these Colonies:

Absolutism Quebec

[xxi]   FOR taking away our Charters, abolishing our most valuable Laws, and altering fundamentally the Forms of our Governments:

[xxii]   FOR suspending our own Legislatures, and declaring themselves invested with Power to legislate for us in all Cases whatsoever.

[xxiii]   HE has abdicated Government here, by declaring us out of his Protection and waging War against us.

[xxiv]   HE has plundered our Seas, ravaged our Coasts, burnt our Towns, and destroyed the Lives of our People.

[xxv]   HE is, at this Time, transporting large Armies of foreign Mercenaries to compleat the Works of Death, Desolation, and Tyranny, already begun with circumstances of Cruelty and Perfidy, scarcely paralleled in the most barbarous Ages, and totally unworthy the Head of a civilized Nation.

[xxvi]   HE has constrained our fellow Citizens taken Captive on the high Seas to bear Arms against their Country, to become the Executioners of their Friends and Brethren, or to fall themselves by their Hands.

[xxvii]   HE has excited domestic Insurrections amongst us, and has endeavoured to bring on the Inhabitants of our Frontiers, the merciless Indian Savages, whose known Rule of Warfare, is an undistinguished Destruction, of all Ages, Sexes and Conditions.

[III]   IN every stage of these Oppressions we have Petitioned for Redress in the most humble Terms: Our repeated Petitions have been answered only by repeated Injury. A Prince, whose Character is thus marked by every act which may define a Tyrant, is unfit to be the Ruler of a free People.

[IV]   NOR have we been wanting in Attentions to our British Brethren. We have warned them from Time to Time of Attempts by their Legislature to extend an unwarrantable Jurisdiction over us. We have reminded them of the Circumstances of our Emigration and Settlement here. We have appealed to their native Justice and Magnanimity, and we have conjured them by the Ties of our common Kindred to disavow these Usurpations, which, would inevitably interrupt our Connections and Correspondence. They too have been deaf to the Voice of Justice and of Consanguinity. We must, therefore, acquiesce in the Necessity, which denounces our Separation, and hold them, as we hold the rest of Mankind, Enemies in War, in Peace, Friends.

[V]   WE, therefore, the Representatives of the UNITED STATES OF AMERICA, in GENERAL CONGRESS, Assembled, appealing to the Supreme Judge of the World for the Rectitude of our Intentions, do, in the Name, and by Authority of the good People of these Colonies, solemnly Publish and Declare, That these United Colonies are, and of Right ought to be, FREE AND INDEPENDENT STATES; that they are absolved from all Allegiance to the British Crown, and that all political Connection between them and the State of Great-Britain, is and ought to be totally dissolved; and that as FREE AND INDEPENDENT STATES, they have full Power to levy War, conclude Peace, contract Alliances, establish Commerce, and to do all other Acts and Things which INDEPENDENT STATES may of right do. And for the support of this Declaration, with a firm Reliance on the Protection of divine Providence, we mutually pledge to each other our Lives, our Fortunes, and our sacred Honor.

Signed by ORDER *and in* BEHALF *of the* CONGRESS,

JOHN HANCOCK, PRESIDENT.

ATTEST.

CHARLES THOMSON, SECRETARY.

The Uncommon Sense of the Americans: Notes on the Declaration

AN ENGLISHMAN

So many pamphlets having been published on the subject of the American rebellion, any farther publications of that kind might be surfeiting; I shall therefore address myself to you in this manner, and desire you to communicate to the public in your paper, some thoughts on the late Declaration of the American Congress.—The Declaration is without doubt of the most extraordinary nature both with regard to sentiment and language; and considering that the motive of it is to assign some justifiable reasons of their separating themselves from G. Britain, unless it had been fraught with more truth and sense, might well have been spared, as it reflects no honour upon either their erudition or honesty.

. . . . .

We hold these truths to be self-evident: That all men are created equal. . . .

In what are they created equal? Is it in size, strength, understanding, figure, moral or civil accomplishments, or situation of life? Every ploughman knows that they are not created equal in any of these. All men, it is true, are equally created: but what is this to the purpose? It certainly is no reason why the Americans should turn rebels, because the people of G. Britain are their fellow-creatures, *i.e.* are created as well as themselves. It may be a reason why they should not rebel, but most indisputably is none why they should.

FROM remarks submitted to the editor of *The Scots Magazine* and published in Vol. XXXVIII (August, 1776), 433–434.

They therefore have introduced their self-evident truth, either through ignorance, or by design, with a self-evident falsehood; since I will defy any American rebel, or any of their patriotic retainers here in England, to point out to me any two men throughout the whole world of whom it may with truth be said, that they are created equal.

. . . . .

That they are endowed by their Creator with certain unalienable rights; That among these are life, liberty, and the pursuit of happiness. . . .

The meaning of these words the Congress appear not at all to understand; among which are life, liberty, and the pursuit of happiness. Let us put some of these words together.—All men are endowed by their Creator with the unalienable right of life. How far they may be endowed with this unalienable right I do not yet say, but, sure I am, these gentry assume to themselves an unalienable right of talking nonsense. Was it ever heard since the introduction of blunders into the world, that life was a man's right? Life or animation is of the essence of human nature, and is that without which one is not a man; and therefore to call life a right, is to betray a total ignorance of the meaning of words. A [433] living man, *i.e.* a man with life, hath a right to a great many things; but to say that a man with life hath a right to be a man with life, is so purely American, that I believe the texture of no other brain upon the face of the earth will admit the idea. Whatever it may be, I have tried to make an idea out of it, but own I am unable. Prior to my having any right at all as a man, it is certain *I* must be a man, and such a man *I* certainly cannot be if I have no life; and therefore if it be said that *I* have a right to life, then the word *I* must signify something without life; and, consequently, something without life must be supposed to have a property, which without life it is not possible it can have.

Well, but they say, all men have not only a right to life, but an unalienable right. The word *unalienable* signifies that which is not alienable, and that which is not alienable is what cannot be transferred so as to become another's; so that their unalienable right is a right which they cannot transfer to a broomstick or a cabbage-stalk; and because they cannot transfer their own lives from themselves to a cabbage-stalk, therefore they think it absolutely necessary that they should rebel; and, out of a decent respect to the opinions of mankind, alleged this as one of the causes which impels them to separate themselves from those to whom they owe obedience.

The next assigned cause and ground of their rebellion is, that every man hath an unalienable right to liberty: and here the words, as it happens, are not nonsense; but then they are not true: slaves there are in America; and where there are slaves, their liberty is alienated.

If the Creator hath endowed man with an unalienable right to liberty, no reason in the world will justify the abridgement of that liberty, and a man hath a right to do every thing that he thinks proper without controul or restraint; and upon the same principle, there can be no such things as servants, subjects, or government of any kind whatsoever. In a word, every law that hath been in the world since the formation of Adam, gives the lie to this self-evident truth, (as they are pleased to term it); because every law, divine or human, that is or hath been in the world, is an abridgement of man's liberty.

Their next self-evident truth and ground of rebellion is, that they have an unalienable right to the pursuit of happiness. The pursuit of happiness an unalienable right! This surely is outdoing every thing that went before. Put it into English: The pursuit of happiness is a right with which the Creator hath endowed me, and which can neither be taken from me, nor can I transfer it to another. Did ever any mortal alive hear of taking a pursuit of happiness from a man? What they possibly can mean by these words, I own, is beyond my comprehension. A man may take from me a horse or a cow, or I may alienate either of them from myself, as I may likewise any thing that I have; but how that can be taken from me, or alienated, which I have not, must be left for the solution of some unborn Oedipus. [434]

꧁ 2 ꧂

An Answer to
the Declaration

JOHN LIND

Short Review of the Declaration

In examining this singular Declaration, I have hitherto confined
myself to what are given as *facts*, and alleged against his Majesty
and his Parliament, in support of the charge of tyranny and usurpation. Of the preamble I have taken little or no notice. The truth is,
little or none does it deserve. The opinions of the modern Americans
on Government, like those of their good ancestors on witchcraft,
would be too ridiculous to deserve any notice, if like them too,
contemptible and extravagant as they be, they had not led to the
most serious evils.

In this preamble however it is, that they attempt to establish a
theory of Government; a theory, as absurd and visionary, as the
system of conduct in defence of which it is established, is nefarious.
Here it is, that maxims are advanced in justification of their enterprises against the British Government. To these maxims, adduced
for *this purpose*, it would be sufficient to say, that they are *repugnant to the British Constitution*. But beyond this they are subversive
of every actual or imaginable kind of Government.

They are about *"to assume,"* as they tell us, *"among the powers of
the earth, that equal and separate* [119] *station to which"*—they
have lately discovered—*"the laws of Nature, and of Nature's God
entitle them."* What difference these acute legislators suppose between the laws of *Nature,* and of *Nature's God,* is more than I can

FROM *An Answer to the Declaration of the American Congress,* 5th ed. (London: T. Cadell, 1776), pp. 119–132. Published anonymously. The marginal
summaries are not reprinted here.

9

take upon me to determine, or even to guess. If to what they now demand they were entitled by any law of God, they had only to produce that law, and all controversy was at an end. Instead of this, what do they produce? What they call self-evident truths. *"All men,"* they tell us, "are created equal." This surely is a new discovery; now, for the first time, we learn, that a child, at the moment of his birth, has the same quantity of *natural* power as the parent, the same quantity of *political* power as the magistrate.

The rights of *"life, liberty,* and *the pursuit of happiness"*—by which, if they mean any thing, they must mean the right to *enjoy* life, to *enjoy* liberty, and to *pursue* happiness—they *"hold to be unalienable."* This they "hold to be among *truths self-evident."* At the same time, to secure these rights, they are content that Governments should be instituted. They perceive not, or will not seem to perceive, that nothing which can be called Government ever was, or ever could be, in any instance, exercised, but at the expence of one or other of those rights.—That, consequently, in as many instances as Government is ever exercised, some one or other of these rights, pretended to be unalienable, is actually alienated.

That men who are engaged in the design of subverting a lawful Government, should endeavour by a cloud of words, to throw a veil over their design; that they should endeavour to beat down the criteria between tyranny and lawful government, is not at all [120] surprising. But rather surprising it must certainly appear, that they should advance maxims so incompatible with their own present conduct. If the right of enjoying life be unalienable, whence came their invasion of his Majesty's province of Canada? Whence the unprovoked destruction of so many lives of the inhabitants of that province? If the right of enjoying liberty be unalienable, whence came so many of his Majesty's peaceable subjects among them, without any offence, without so much as a pretended offence, merely for being suspected not to wish well to their enormities, to be held by them in durance? If the right of pursuing happiness be unalienable, how is it that so many others of their fellow-citizens are by the same injustice and violence made miserable, their fortunes ruined, their persons banished and driven from their friends and families? Or would they have it believed, that there is in their selves some superior sanctity, some peculiar privilege, by which those things are lawful to them, which are unlawful to all the world besides? Or is it, that among acts of coercion, acts by which life or liberty are taken away, and the pursuit of happiness restrained, those only are unlawful, which their delinquency has brought upon them, and which are exercised by regular, long established, accustomed governments?

In these tenets they have outdone the utmost extravagance of all former fanatics. The German Anabaptists indeed went so far as to speak of the right of enjoying life as a right unalienable. To take away life, even in the Magistrate, they held to be unlawful. But they went no farther, it was reserved for an American Congress, to add to the number of unalienable rights, that of enjoying liberty, and pursuing [121] happiness;—that is,—if they mean any thing,—pursuing it wherever a man thinks he can see it, and by whatever means he thinks he can attain it:—That is, that all *penal* laws—those made by their selves among others—which affect life or liberty, are contrary to the law of God, and the unalienable rights of mankind:—That is, that thieves are not to be restrained from theft, murderers from murder, rebels from rebellion.

Here then they have put the axe to the root of all Government; and yet, in the same breath, they talk of "Governments," of Governments "long established." To these last, they attribute some kind of respect; they vouchsafe even to go so far as to admit, that *"Governments, long established, should not be changed for light or transient reasons."*

Yet they are about to *change* a Government, a Government whose establishment is coeval with their own existence as a Community. What causes do they assign? Circumstances which have always subsisted, which must continue to subsist, wherever Government has subsisted, or can subsist.

For what, according to their own shewing, what was their original, their *only original grievance?* That they were actually taxed more than they could bear? No; but that they were *liable* to be so taxed. What is the amount of all the *subsequent* grievances they allege? That they were *actually* oppressed by Government? That Government had *actually* misused its power? No; but that it was *possible* they might be oppressed; *possible* that Government might misuse its powers. Is there any where, can there be imagined any where, *that* Government, where subjects are not liable to be taxed more than they can bear? [122] where it is not possible that subjects may be oppressed, not possible that Government may misuse its powers?

This, I say, is the amount, the *whole sum and substance of all* their grievances. For in taking a general review of the charges brought against his Majesty, and his Parliament, we may observe that there is a studied confusion in the arrangement of them. It may therefore be worth while to reduce them to the several distinct heads, under which I should have classed them at the first, had not the order of the Answer been necessarily prescribed by the order— or rather the disorder—of the Declaration.

The first head consists of Acts of *Government*, charged as so many acts of *incroachment*, so many *usurpations* upon the present King and his Parliaments exclusively, which had been constantly exercised by his Predecessors and their Parliaments.[1]

In all the articles comprised in this head, is there a single power alleged to have been exercised during the present reign, which had not been constantly exercised by preceding Kings, and preceding Parliaments? Read only the commission and instruction for the Council of Trade, drawn up in the 9th of King William III. addressed to Mr. *Locke*, and others.[2] See there what [123] powers were exercised by the King and Parliament over the Colonies. Certainly the Commissioners were directed to inquire into, and make their reports concerning those matters only, in which the King and Parliament had a power of controlling the Colonies. Now the Commissioners are instructed to inquire—into the condition of the Plantations, "as well with regard to the *administration of Government and Justice,* as in relation to the commerce thereof;"—into the means of making "them *most beneficial and useful to England;— into the staples and manufactures, which may be encouraged there;"*—"*into the trades that are taken up and exercised there, which may prove prejudicial to England;"*—"into the means of *diverting them from such trades.*" Farther, they are instructed "*to examine into, and weigh the Acts of the Assemblies* of the Plantations;"—"*to set down the usefulness or mischief to the Crown, to the Kingdom, or to the Plantations their selves.*"—And farther still, they are instructed "*to require an account of all the monies given for public uses by the Assemblies of the Plantations, and how the same are, or have been expended, or laid out.*" Is there now a single Act of

---

[1] Under this head are comprised articles [i. e., accusations] I. II. so far as they are true, III. VII. IX. so far as the last relates to the tenure of the Judges' offices. XI. XII. XIII. XIV. XVII. XVIII. so far as the last relates to the establishment of Courts of Admiralty in general, and the causes, the cognisance of which is attributed to them. XIX. XXII. so far as the latter relates to the Declaration of the power of Parliament to make laws for the Colonies binding in all cases whatsoever.

[2] See Com. Journ. vol. xii. p. 70, 71, 72.

the present reign which does not fall under one or other of these instructions.

The powers then, of which the several articles now before us complain, are supported by usage; were conceived to be so supported *then*, just after the Revolution, at the time these instructions were given; and were they to be supported *only* upon this foot of usage, still that usage being coeval with the Colonies, their tacit consent and approbation, through all the successive periods in which that usage has prevailed, would be implied;—even then the legality of those powers would stand upon the same foot as most of the [124] prerogatives of the Crown, most of the rights of the people;—even then the exercise of those powers could in no wise be deemed usurpations or encroachments.

But the truth is, to the exercise of these powers, the Colonies have not tacitly, but *expressly,* consented; as expressly as any subject of Great Britain ever consented to Acts of the British Parliament. Consult the Journals of either House of Parliament; consult the proceedings of their own Assemblies; and innumerable will be the occasions, on which the legality of these powers will be found to be expressly recognised by Acts of the Colonial Assemblies. For in preceding reigns, the petitions from these Assemblies were couched in a language, very different from that which they have assumed under the present reign. In praying for the non-exercise of these powers, in particular instances, they acknowledged their legality; the right in general was recognised; the exercise of it, in particular instances, was prayed to be suspended on the sole ground of *inexpedience.*

The less reason can the Americans have to complain against the exercise of these powers, as it was under the constant exercise of the self-same powers, that they have grown up with a vigour and rapidity unexampled: That within a period, in which other communities have scarcely had time to take root, they have shot forth exuberant branches. So flourishing is their agriculture, that—we are told— "besides feeding plentifully their own growing multitudes, their annual exports have exceeded a *million:*" So flourishing is their trade, that—we are told—"it has increased far beyond the speculations of the most [125] sanguine imagination." [3] So powerful are they in arms, that we see them defy the united force of that nation, which, but a little century ago, called them into being; which, but a

[3] See Mr. Burke's speeches.

few years ago, in their defence, encountered and subdued almost the united force of Europe.

If the exercise of powers, thus established by usage, thus recognised by express declarations, thus sanctified by their beneficial effects, can justify rebellion, there is not that subject in the world, but who has, ever has had, and ever must have, reason sufficient to rebel: There never was, never can be, established, any government upon earth.

The second head consists of Acts, whose professed object was either the maintenance, or the amendment of their Constitution. These Acts were passed with the view either of freeing from impediments the course of their *commercial* transactions,[4] or of facilitating the administration of justice,[5] or of poising more equally the different powers in their Constitution; [6] or of preventing the establishment of Courts, inconsistent with the spirit of the Constitution.[7]

To state the object of these Acts, is to justify them. Acts of *tyranny* they cannot be: Acts of *usurpation* they *are not;* because no new power is assumed. By former Parliaments, in former reigns, officers of *customs* had been sent to America: Courts of Admiralty had been established there. The [126] increase of trade and population induced the Parliaments, under the present reign, for the *convenience* of the Colonists, and to obviate *their own objections* of delays arising from appeals to England, to establish a Board of Customs, and an Admiralty Court of Appeal. Strange indeed is it to hear the establishment of this Board, and these Courts, alleged as proofs of *usurpation;* and in the same paper, in the same breath, to hear it urged as a head of *complaint,* that his Majesty refused his assent to a much greater exertion of power:—to an exertion of power, which might be dangerous; the establishment of new Courts of Judicature. What in one instance he might have done, to have done in another, cannot be unconstitutional. In former reigns, charters had been altered; in the present reign, the constitution of one charter, having been found inconsistent with the ends of good order and government, was amended.

The third head consists of temporary Acts, passed *pro re natâ,* the object of each of which was to remedy some temporary evil, and the

[4] Article X.
[5] Article XVIII. so far as it relates to the multiplication of the Courts of Admiralty.
[6] Article XXI.   [7] Article VIII.

duration of which was restrained to the duration of the evil itself.[8]

Neither in these Acts was any new power assumed; in some instances only, the objects upon which that power was exercised, were new. Nothing was done but what former Kings and former Parliaments have shewn their selves ready to do, had the same circumstances subsisted. The same circumstances never did subsist before, because, till the present reign, the [127] Colonies never dared to call in question the supreme authority of Parliament.

No charge, classed under this head, can be called a *grievance*. Then only is the subject aggrieved, when, paying *due obedience* to the established Laws of his country, he is not protected in his established rights. From the moment he withholds *obedience,* he forfeits his right to *protection*. Nor can the means, employed to bring him back to obedience, however severe, be called grievances; especially if those means be to cease the very moment that the end is obtained.

The last head consists of Acts of self-defence, exercised in *consequence* of resistance already shewn, but represented in the Declaration as Acts of oppression, tending to provoke resistance.[9] Has his Majesty cut off their trade with all parts of the world? They first attempted to cut off the trade of Great Britain. Has his Majesty ordered their vessels to be seized? They first burnt the vessels of the King. Has his Majesty sent troops to chastise them? They first took up arms against the authority of the King. Has his Majesty engaged the Indians against them? They first engaged Indians against the troops of the King. Has his Majesty commanded their captives to serve on board his fleet? He has only saved them from the gallows. [128]

By some, these acts have been improperly called "*Acts of punishment.*" And we are then asked, with an air of insult, "What! will you punish without a trial, without a hearing?" And no doubt punishment, whether ordinary or extraordinary; whether by *indictment,*

[8] Under this head may be classed Articles IV. V. VI. IX. so far as the last relates to the payment of the Judges by the Crown. XV. XXII. so far as the latter relates to the suspension of their legislatures.

[9] Under this head may be classed Articles XVI. XXIII. XXIV. XXV. XXVI. XXVII. Two other Articles there are, not comprised within any of the four heads, the XX. and XXVIII. The former of these relates to the government of Quebec, with which the revolted Colonies have no more to do, than with the government of Russia: The latter relates to the *humble* petitions they pretend to have presented "in every stage," as they style it, "of the oppressions," under which they pretend to labour. This we have seen to be false. No one humble petition; no one decent representation, have they offered.

impeachment, or bill of *attainder,* should be preceded by judicial examination. But, the acts comprised under this head are not acts of punishment; they are, as we have called them, acts of *self-defence.* And these are not, cannot be, preceded by any judicial examination. An example or two will serve to place the difference between acts of punishment and acts of self-defence in a stronger light, than any definition we can give. It has happened, that bodies of manufacturers have risen, and armed, in order to compel their masters to increase their wages: It has happened, that bodies of peasants have risen, and armed, in order to compel the farmer to sell at a lower price. It has happened, that the civil magistrate, unable to reduce the insurgents to their duty, has called the military to his aid. But did ever any man imagine, that the military were sent to punish the insurgents? It has happened, that the insurgents have resisted the military, as they had resisted the civil magistrate: It has happened, that, in consequence of this resistance, some of the insurgents have been killed:—But did ever any man imagine that those who were thus killed, were therefore *punished?* No more can they be said to be punished, than could the incendiary, who should be buried beneath the ruins of the house, which he had feloniously set on fire. Take an example yet nearer to the present case. When the Duke of Cumberland led the armies of the king, *foreign and domestic,* against the Rebels in Scotland, did any man conceive that he was [129] sent to *punish* the Rebels?—Clearly not.—He was sent to protect dutiful and loyal subjects, who remained in the peace of the King, against the outrages of Rebels, who had broken the peace of the King.—Does any man speak of those who fell at the battle of Culloden, as of men that were *punished?* Would that man have been thought in his senses, who should have urged, that the armies of the King should not have been sent against the Rebels in Scotland, till those very Rebels had been judicially heard, and judicially convicted? Does not every man feel that the fact, the *only* fact, necessary to be known, in order to justify these acts of self-defence, is simply this:—Are men in arms against the authority of the King? —Who does not feel, that to authenticate this fact, demands no judicial inquiry? If when his Royal Highness had led the army under his command into Scotland, there had been no body of men in arms; if, terrified at his approach, they had either laid down their arms and submitted, or had dispersed and retired quietly, each to his own home, what would have been the consequence? The civil magistrate would have searched for and seized upon those who *had* been in arms; would have brought them to a court of justice: That court would have proceeded to examine, and to condemn or to acquit, as evidence was, or was not, given of the guilt of the respective culprits. The Rebels did not submit, they did not lay down their arms, they did not disperse; they resisted the Duke: a battle ensued: some of the Rebels fled, others were slain, others taken. It is upon those only of the *last* class, who were brought before and condemned by Courts of Justice, that *punishment* was inflicted. By what kind of logic then are these acts ranked in the class of grievances? [130]

These are the Acts—these exertions of constitutional, and hitherto, *undisputed* powers, for which, in this audacious paper, a patriot King is traduced—as "a Prince, whose character is marked by every Act which may define a tyrant;" as "unfit to be the ruler of a free people." These are the Acts, these exertions of constitutional, and, hitherto, undisputed powers, by which the Members of the Congress declare their selves and their constituents to be "absolved from all allegiance to the British Crown;" pronounce "all political connection between Great Britain and America to be totally dissolved." With that hypocrisy which pervades the whole of the Declaration, they pretend indeed, that this event is not of their seeking, that it is forced upon them; that they only *"acquiesce in the necessity which denounces their separation from us:"* which compels them hereafter to hold us, as they "hold the rest of mankind; *enemies in war; in peace, friends."*

How this Declaration may strike others, I know not. To me, I own, it appears that it cannot fail—to use the words of a great Orator—"of doing us *Knight's* service." [10] The mouth of faction, we may reasonably presume, will be closed; the eyes of those who saw not, or would not see, that the Americans were long since aspiring at independence, will be opened; the nation will unite as one man, and teach this rebellious people, that it is one thing for them to *say*, the connection, which bound them to us, is *dissolved,* another to *dissolve* it; that to *accomplish* their *independence* is not quite so easy as to *declare* it: *that there is no* [131] *peace with them, but the peace of the King: no war with them, but that war, which offended justice wages against criminals.*—We too, I hope, shall *acquiesce in the necessity* of submitting to whatever burdens, of making whatever efforts may be necessary, to bring this ungrateful and rebellious people back to that allegiance they have long had it in contemplation to renounce, and have now at last so daringly renounced. [132]

[10] Mr. Burke's speech.

ex 3 *ex*

The Declaration in France

Un Banquier de Londres *

Letter, August 16, 1776

I have just received a translation, sir, of the July 4th Act of the General Congress of America. It is unquestionably the greatest event of the campaign, of the war itself, and perhaps of this century. I will transcribe it here in its totality, for none of it must be lost. Such writings and the overthrow of Empire are quite rare— fortunately! [88]

Letter, September 2, 1776

A rumor begins to spread, sir, that the Attorney General will bring suit against the journalists who printed the Declaration of Independence passed on July 4th by the great Congress. If that happens, it appears they will have no lack of defenders. Will they be attacked on all the grievances alleged against the King's administration? They will be able to answer that in four years there hasn't been one grievance that has not been reprinted at least five hundred times in all the public writings; and this is so true that many of the English papers that published this same work excised the grievances, noting that they were only a repetition of what had been seen in the oft reiterated remonstrances of the [89] Colonies. Will one make the boldness of the principles their crime? This would be relative either to royalty in general or to the sovereignty of George III in particular. As to the general rights of Sovereigns, the wisdom with which this article is treated there, has, on the contrary, been admired. Gratitude has been felt towards this people who broke the strongest

---

* FROM "Lettre d'un banquier de Londres à M.———, à Anvers," *Affaires de l'Angleterre et de l'Amérique*, Vol. II (August 16, 1776), p. 88; (September 2, 1776), pp. 89–92. The excerpts appearing here have been translated by the editor. Passages from the Declaration of Independence cited in French by the author are restored in English from the first broadside edition of the Declaration as reprinted in this volume.

tie of human society and in the moment when their despair might have made them forget all considerations, put forward their respect for the opinions of the rest of mankind, who by that very act are invited to cherish them. The truth of this maxim, so precious to the general peace, has been applauded:

Prudence, indeed, will dictate that Governments long established should not be changed for light and transient Causes; and accordingly all Experience hath shewn, that Mankind are more disposed to suffer, while Evils are sufferable, than to right themselves by abolishing the Forms to which they are accustomed.

Congress said *all Men are created equal.* This is an established truth and one that all religions preach to men without cease. They established that men *are endowed by their Creator with certain unalienable rights: That to secure these Rights, Governments are instituted;* and *that whenever any Form of Government becomes destructive of these Ends, it is the Right of the People to alter or to abolish it.* There are three of these ends, [90] two of which are life, or existence, and happiness which is the employ of existence. The very self-interest of Sovereigns with respect to these justifies the assertion of Congress that places them in the fortunate impossibility of arbitrarily denying existence or happiness. In effect, no Subjects, no Kings; no property, no thrones. Up to this point Congress has advanced a strictly true maxim, although only applicable to the single case in which they think themselves and whose kind would not be common to other constitutions. The third end is liberty which is variously modified in different nations. More than one nation would not want or have not wanted the liberty which the English claim to have, and with a view to their greatest happiness they have even surrendered that portion remaining to them to the entire discretion of their Sovereigns. Thus, the axiom of Congress has no more to do with those people, so far as liberty is concerned, than other physical or moral particulars which are peculiar to the English nation.

I see further this assertion in the Act of Congress, that *the Legislative Powers, incapable of Annihilation,* return to their source *the People at large for their exercise.* But far from being able to blame anything about it, one recognizes in it this fundamental maxim of all government, that justice is the first obligation of Sovereigns towards their subjects; [91] and it can only augment the respect and love of the people for the Tribunals to whom this sacred duty is delegated. The right to justice is inseparable from the right to the exercise of existence. Congress, then, has said nothing in this Act which offers affront to the rights of sovereignty in general. [92]

Mirabeau *

The sublime manifesto of the United States of America has been very generally applauded. God forbid that I protest against public opinion in this respect, I, who if not in irons would seek instruction among them and fight for them, but I ask if the powers who have contracted alliances with them have dared to read this manifesto or to examine their conscience after having read it. I ask if there is today any government in Europe, the Swiss and Batavian confederations and the British Isles alone excepted, which judged according to the principles proclaimed by Congress in the Declaration of July 4, 1776, would not have lost its titles. I ask if, of the thirty-two princes of the third race of our kings, there are not more than two-thirds of them who have rendered themselves much more guilty towards their subjects [239] than the kings of Great Britain towards the English colonies. [240]

Condorcet †

The human species had lost its titles; Montesquieu found them and returned them to us.[1] But it is not sufficient for them to be written in the books of philosophers and in the hearts of virtuous men; it is necessary for the ignorant or weak man to be able to read them in the example of a great people.

America has given us that example. The Act which declared its independence is a simple and sublime exposition of these rights so sacred and so long forgotten. In no other nation have they been so well known or conserved in such perfect integrity. [249]

---

[1] Voltaire.

* FROM *Des lettres de cachet et des prisons d'état*, Œuvres, Vol. VII (Paris: Lecointe et Pougin, 1835), pp. 239–240. Originally published in 1782. This excerpt has been translated by the editor.

† FROM *De l'influence de la révolution de l'Amérique sur l'Europe*, Œuvres complètes, ed. Garat and Cabanis, Vol. XI (Paris: Fuchs, An IX [1800–1801]), p. 249. Originally published under a pseudonym in 1786. This excerpt has been translated by the editor.

L'Ami de la Révolution *

But this analysis of the declaration of rights of each of the United States is unnecessary when one considers the magnificent preamble that Congress placed at the head of the Declaration of Independence, proclaimed July 4, 1776. Permit us here this digression. Is there anything more beautiful, more touching, more sublime than this beginning! We cannot resist the pleasure of transcribing it. Those who know it will never grow weary of admiring it; the other readers will be grateful for our having given them the most perfect, the most moving piece of eloquence that may be found not only [238] in the laws of any people but even in the discourses of the most celebrated orators. [239]

. . . . .

Such is this Declaration that the enemies of our Revolution consider seditious and criminal. The courage of the Americans in defending it is an example for us just as their laws are models to be imitated.

This famous Act is itself a declaration of rights, since it establishes a part of the rights and principles which form the base of government.

Man at birth receives inalienable rights from nature. Endowed with the same faculties as all other men, he is their equal; he has a right, like they, to all that may be necessary to his needs. The differences that one notices and that one employs in order to destroy this principle of natural equality (such as inequality of strength, of size, etc.) do not constitute real differences, for the weak or little man has no less right to attend to his preservation, to procure all that he needs, than the big, strong one. In order that men have equal rights it is not necessary that they be of precisely the same weight and stature; otherwise, in the present state of nature, the whole universe would perforce be the domain of a single man, that is, of he who was [242] bigger and stronger than others, each considered individually. [243]

* FROM "Déclaration des droits de l'homme & du citoyen, décrétée par l'assemblée nationale, & sanctionnée par le roi, comparée avec les lois de plusieurs peuples anciens & modernes, & principalement avec les déclarations des États-unis de l'amérique," L'Ami de la révolution, 12th "Philippique" (Paris: Champigny, [1790]), pp. 238–239, 242–243. These excerpts have been translated by the editor.

4

A Juvenile Declamation

JOHN ADAMS

Memorial to the States-General of the United Provinces of the Low Countries, April 19, 1781 *

It is true, that when the British administration, renouncing the ancient character of Englishmen for generosity, justice, and humanity, conceived the design of subverting the political systems of the Colonies; depriving them of the rights and liberties of Englishmen, and reducing them to the worst of all forms of government; starving the people, by blockading their ports, and cutting off their fisheries and commerce; sending fleets and armies to destroy every principle and sentiment of liberty, and to consume their habitations and their lives; making contracts for foreign troops, and alliances with savage nations, to assist them in their enterprise; casting, formally, by act of parliament, three millions of people at once out of the protection of the crown: then, and not till then, did the United States of [396] America, in congress assembled, pass that memorable act, by which they assumed an equal station among the nations.

This immortal declaration, of the 4th of July, 1776, when America was invaded by a hundred vessels of war, and, according to estimates laid before parliament, by fifty-five thousand of veteran troops, was not the effect of any sudden passion or enthusiasm, but a measure which had been long in deliberation among the people, maturely discussed in some hundreds of popular assemblies, and by public writings in all the States; it was a measure which congress did not adopt, until they had received the positive instructions of their constituents in all the States; it was then unanimously adopted by congress, subscribed by all its members, transmitted to the assem-

* FROM *The Works of John Adams,* ed. Charles Francis Adams, Vol. VII (Boston: Charles C. Little and James Brown, 1852), pp. 396–397.

blies of the several States, and by them respectively accepted, ratified and recorded among their archives; so that no decree, edict, statute, placart, or fundamental law of any nation, was ever made with more solemnity, or with more unanimity or cordiality adopted, as the act and consent of the whole people, than this; and it has been held sacred to this day by every State, with such unshaken firmness, that not even the smallest has ever been induced to depart from it, although the English have wasted many millions, and vast fleets and armies, in the vain attempt to invalidate it. [397]

Autobiography, June–July, 1776 *

Not long after this [the events of May 15, 1776] the three greatest Measures of all, were carried. Three Committees were appointed, One for preparing a Declaration of Independence, another for reporting a Plan of a Treaty to be proposed to France, and a third to digest a System of Articles of Confederation to be proposed to the States.—I was appointed on the Committee of Independence, and on that for preparing the form of a Treaty with France: on the Committee of Confederation Mr. Samuel Adams was appointed. The Committee of Independence, were Thomas Jefferson, John Adams, Benjamin Franklin, Roger Sherman and Robert R. Livingston. Mr. Jefferson had been now about a Year a Member of Congress, but had attended his Duty in the House but a very small part of the time and when there had never spoken in public: and during the whole Time I satt with him in Congress, I never heard him utter three Sentences together. The most of a Speech he ever made in my hearing was a gross insult on Religion, in one or two Sentences, for which I gave him immediately the Reprehension, which he richly merited. It will naturally be enquired, how it happened that he was appointed on a Committee of such importance. There were more reasons than one. Mr. Jefferson had the Reputation of a masterly Pen. He had been chosen a Delegate in Virginia, in consequence of a very handsome public Paper which he had written for the House of Burgesses, which had given him the Character of a [335] fine Writer. Another reason was that Mr. Richard Henry Lee was not

* REPRINTED by permission of the publishers from L. H. Butterfield, Editor, *Diary and Autobiography of John Adams,* Vol. III (Cambridge, Mass.: The Belknap Press of Harvard University Press, Copyright, 1961, by The President and Fellows of Harvard College), pp. 335–337. Adams probably wrote these recollections in 1805.

beloved by the most of his Colleagues from Virginia and Mr. Jefferson was sett up to rival and supplant him. This could be done only by the Pen, for Mr. Jefferson could stand no competition with him or any one else in Elocution and public debate. Here I will interrupt the narration for a moment to observe that from all I have read of the History of Greece and Rome, England and France, and all I have observed at home, and abroad, that Eloquence in public Assemblies is not the surest road, to Fame and Preferment, at least unless it be used with great caution, very rarely, and with great Reserve. The Examples of Washington, Franklin and Jefferson are enough to shew that Silence and reserve in public are more Efficacious than Argumentation or Oratory. A public Speaker who inserts himself, or is urged by others into the Conduct of Affairs, by daily Exertions to justify his measures, and answer the Objections of Opponents, makes himself too familiar with the public, and unavoidably makes himself Ennemies. Few Persons can bare to be outdone in Reasoning or declamation or Wit, or Sarcasm or Repartee, or Satyr, and all these things are very apt to grow out of public debate. In this Way in a Course of Years, a Nation becomes full of a Mans Ennemies, or at least of such as have been galled in some Controversy, and take a secret pleasure in assisting to humble and mortify him. So much for this digression. We will now return to our Memoirs. The Committee had several meetings, in which were proposed the Articles of which the Declaration was to consist, and minutes made of them. The Committee then appointed Mr. Jefferson and me, to draw them up in form, and cloath them in a proper Dress. The Sub Committee met, and considered the Minutes, making such Observations on them as then occurred: when Mr. Jefferson desired me to take them to my Lodgings and make the Draught. This I declined and gave several reasons for declining. 1 That he was a Virginian and I a Massachusettensian. 2. that he was a southern Man and I a northern one. 3. That I had been so obnoxious for my early and constant Zeal in promoting the Measure, that any draught of mine, would undergo a more severe Scrutiny and Criticism in Congress, than one of his composition. 4thly and lastly and that would be reason enough if there were no other, I had a great Opinion of the Elegance of his pen and none at all of my own. I therefore insisted that no hesitation should be made on his part. He accordingly took the Minutes and in a day or two produced to me his Draught. Whether I made or suggested any corrections I remember not. The Report was made to the Committee of five, by them examined, [336] but whether altered or corrected in any thing I cannot recollect. But in substance at least it was reported to Congress where, after a severe Criticism, and striking out several of the most oratorical Paragraphs it was adopted on the fourth of July 1776, and published to the World. [337]

Letter to Richard Rush, July 22, 1816 *

Mark my Words; it is Party Faction and Fashion that give Characters; Truth and Justice, are Studiously omitted neglected and forgotten.

> Jefferson is no more my Friend
> Who dares to Independence to pretend
> Which I was born to introduce
> Refin'd it first, and Shew'd its Use.

.   .   .   .   .

P. S. Look in the Journal of Congress 1774 for the Declaration of the Rights of the Colonies, and in the Journal of 1776. Month of May for a Resolution of Independence. Then consider Whether the Declaration of Independence of 4. July 1776 is any thing more than a juvenile declamation founded on those two Documents, Yet those two documents were drawn by the Fingers which now trembling write the Name of   John Adams.

.   .   .   .   .

3d. P. S. My Grand Daughter Says, the Line "Who dares to Independence to pretend" is very bad; and begs me to Substitute "To Independence *he* pretends." But this Amendment does not fully Satisfy me: I therefore propose farther to insert this "Who dares to Independency pretend." But even this I fear, has one Alexandrine Syllable too much.

.   .   .   .   .

6. P. S. Your Father was correct. In 1775 and 1776 I was considered by the Quakers and Proprietarians and by a Majority of the Whiggs of Pensylvania, as a Monster, who advocated Independence. . . .

7. P. S. Among your Fathers Papers will be found a Copy of a

* FROM MS in the Simon Gratz Papers, Historical Society of Pennsylvania.

Declaration of Independence, in 1755 twenty one years before Jeffersons in 1776 in a Letter to Dr Nathan Webb from   John Adams.

Letter to Timothy Pickering, August 6, 1822 *

You inquire why so young a man as Mr. Jefferson was placed at the head of the Committee for preparing a Declaration of Independence? I answer; It was the Frankfort advice, to place Virginia at the head of every thing. Mr. Richard Henry Lee might be gone to Virginia, to his sick family, for aught I know, but that was not the reason of Mr. Jefferson's appointment. There were three committees appointed at the same time. One for the Declaration of Independence, another for preparing articles of Confedration, and another for preparing a treaty to be proposed to France. Mr. Lee was chosen for the Committee of Confederation, and it was not thought convenient that the same person should be upon both. Mr. Jefferson came into Congress, in June, 1775, and brought with him a reputation for literature, science, and a happy talent of [513] composition. Writings of his were handed about, remarkable for the peculiar felicity of expression. Though a silent member in Congress, he was so prompt, frank, explicit, and decisive upon committees and in conversation, not even Samuel Adams was more so, that he soon seized upon my heart; and upon this occasion I gave him my vote, and did all in my power to procure the votes of others. I think he had one more vote than any other, and that placed him at the head of the committee. I had the next highest number, and that placed me the second. The committee met, discussed the subject, and then appointed Mr. Jefferson and me to make the draught, I suppose because we were the two first on the list.

The sub-committee met. Jefferson proposed to me to make the draught. I said, "I will not." "You should do it." "Oh! no." "Why will you not? You ought to do it." "I will not." "Why?" "Reasons enough." "What can be your reasons?" "Reason first—You are a Virginian, and a Virginian ought to appear at the head of this business. Reason second—I am obnoxious, suspected, and unpopular. You are very much otherwise. Reason third—You can write ten times better than I can." "Well," said Jefferson, "if you are decided, I will do as well

* FROM The Works of John Adams, ed. Charles Francis Adams, Vol. II (Boston: Charles C. Little and James Brown, 1850), note, pp. 513–514.

as I can." "Very well. When you have drawn it up, we will have a meeting."

A meeting we accordingly had, and conned the paper over. I was delighted with its high tone and the flights of oratory with which it abounded, especially that concerning negro slavery, which, though I knew his Southern brethren would never suffer to pass in Congress, I certainly never would oppose. There were other expressions which I would not have inserted, if I had drawn it up, particularly that which called the King tyrant. I thought this too personal; for I never believed George to be a tyrant in disposition and in nature; I always believed him to be deceived by his courtiers on both sides of the Atlantic, and in his official capacity only, cruel. I thought the expression too passionate, and too much like scolding, for so grave and solemn a document; but as Franklin and Sherman were to inspect it afterwards, I thought it would not become me to strike it out. I consented to report it, and do not now remember that I made or suggested a single alteration.

We reported it to the committee of five. It was read, and I do not remember that Franklin or Sherman criticized any thing. We were all in haste. Congress was impatient, and the instrument was reported, as I believe, in Jefferson's handwriting, as he first drew it. Congress cut off about a quarter of it, as I expected they would; but they obliterated some of the best of it, and left all that was exceptionable, if any thing in it was. I have long wondered that the original draught has not been published. I suppose the reason is, the vehement philippic against negro slavery.

As you justly observe, there is not an idea in it but what had been hackneyed in Congress for two years before. The substance of it is contained in the declaration of rights and the violation of those rights, in the Journals of Congress, in 1774. Indeed, the essence of it is contained in a pamphlet, voted and printed by the town of Boston, before the first Congress met, composed by James Otis, as I suppose, in one of his lucid intervals, and pruned and polished by Samuel Adams. [514]

5

An Expression of
the American Mind

THOMAS JEFFERSON

Notes on the Proceedings of the Continental
Congress, June–July, 1776

It appearing in the course of these debates* that the colonies of
N. York, New Jersey, Pennsylvania, Delaware, Maryland & South
Carolina were not yet matured for falling from the parent stem, but
that they were fast advancing to that state, it was thought most
prudent to wait a while for them, and to postpone the final decision
to July 1. But that this might occasion as little delay as possible a
committee was appointed to prepare a declaration of independance.
The commee were J. Adams, Dr. Franklin, Roger Sherman, Robert
R. Livingston & myself. Committees were also appointed at the
same time to prepare a plan of confederation for the colonies, and to
state the terms proper to be proposed for foreign alliance. The committee for drawing the declaration of Independance desired me to
do it. It was accordingly done and being approved by them, I reported it to the house on Friday the 28th. of June when it was read
and ordered to lie on the table. On Monday the 1st. of July the
house resolved itself into a commee of the whole & resumed the
consideration of the original motion made by the delegates of Virginia, which being again debated through the day, was carried in

---

* The debates took place on June 8, 10, 1776. The dates bracketed in the text
below are taken from Jefferson's marginal notations.—Ed.

FROM MSS in the Jefferson Papers of the Library of Congress. The text follows
Jefferson's spelling and punctuation, except that the initial word of each sentence has been capitalized and the raised letters in abbreviations have been
printed in modern style.

the affirmative by the votes of N. Hampshire, Connecticut, Massachusets, Rhode island, N. Jersey, Maryland, Virginia, N. Carolina, & Georgia. S. Carolina and Pennsylvania voted against it. Delaware having but two members present, they were divided; the delegates for New York declared they were for it themselves & were assured their constituents were for it, but that their instructions having been drawn near a twelvemonth before, when reconciliation was still the general object, they were enjoined by them to do nothing which should impede that object. They therefore thought themselves not justifiable in voting on either side, and asked leave to withdraw from the question, which was given them. The Commee rose & reported their resolution to the house. Mr Edward Rutlege of S. Carolina then requested the determination might be put off to the next day, as he believed his colleagues, tho' they disapproved of the resolution, would then join in it for the sake of unanimity. The ultimate question whether the house would agree to the resolution of the committee was accordingly postponed to the next day [July 2], when it was again moved and S. Carolina concurred in voting for it. In the mean time a third member had come post from the Delaware counties and turned the vote of that colony in favour of the resolution. Members of a different sentiment attending that morning from Pennsylvania also, their vote was changed, so that the whole 12. colonies, who were authorized to vote at all, gave their voices for it; and within a few days [July 9] the convention of N. York approved of it and thus supplied the void occasioned by the withdrawing of their delegates from the vote.

Congress proceeded the same day [July 2] to consider the declaration of Independance which had been reported & laid on the table the Friday preceding and on Monday referred to a commee of the whole. The pusillanimous idea that we had friends in England worth keeping terms with, still haunted the minds of many. For this reason those passages which conveyed censures on the people of England were struck out, lest they should give them offence. The clause too, reprobating the enslaving the inhabitants of Africa, was struck out in complaisance to South Carolina & Georgia, who had never attempted to restrain the importation of slaves, and who on the contrary still wished to continue it. Our Northern brethren also I believe felt a little tender under those censures; for tho' their people have very few slaves themselves yet they had been pretty considerable carriers of them to others. The debates having taken up the greater parts of the 2d. 3d. & 4th. days of July were, in the evening of the last, closed. The declaration was reported by the commee, agreed to by the house, and signed by every member present except mr Dickinson. As the sentiments of men are known not only by what they receive, but what they reject also I will state the form of the declaration as originally reported: the parts struck out by Congress shall be distinguished by a black line drawn under them; & those inserted by them shall be placed in the margin or in a concurrent column..

Letter to Robert Walsh, December 4, 1818

When the Declaration of Independance was under the consideration of Congress, there were two or three unlucky expressions in it which gave offence to some members. The words 'Scotch and other foreign auxiliaries' excited the ire of a gentleman or two of that country. Severe strictures on the conduct of the British King, in negativing our repeated repeals of the law which permitted the importation of slaves, were disapproved by some Southern gentlemen, whose reflections were not yet matured to the full abhorrence of that traffic. Altho' the offensive expressions were immediately yielded, these gentlemen continued their depredations on other parts of the instrument. I was sitting by Dr. Franklin who percieved that I was not insensible to these mutilations.

Letter to James Madison, August 30, 1823

You have doubtless seen Timothy Pickering's 4th. of July Observations on the Declaration of Independance. If his principles and prejudices personal and political, gave us no reason to doubt whether he had truly quoted the information he alledges to have recieved from Mr. Adams, I should then say that, in some of the particulars, Mr Adams's memory has led him into unquestionable error. At the age of 88. and 47. years after the transactions of Independance, this is not wonderful. Nor should I, at the age of 80, on the small advantage of that difference only, venture to oppose my memory to his, were it not supported by written notes, taken by myself at the moment and on the spot. He says 'the Committee (of 5. to wit, Dr. Franklin, Sherman, Livingston and ourselves) met, discussed the subject, and then appointed him and myself to make the draught; that we, as a subcommittee, met, & after the urgencies of each on the other, I consented to undertake the task; that the draught being made, we, the subcommittee, met, & conned the paper over, and he does not remember that he made or suggested a single alteration.' Now these details are quite incorrect. The Committee of 5. met, no such thing as a subcommittee was proposed, but they unanimously pressed on myself alone to undertake the draught. I consented; I drew it; but before I reported it to the committee, I communicated it *separately* to Dr. Franklin and Mr Adams requesting their corrections; because they were the two members of whose judgments and amendments I wished most to have the benefit before presenting it to the Committee; and you have seen the original paper now in my hands, with the corrections of Doctor Franklin and Mr Adams interlined in their own hand writings. Their alterations were two or three only, and merely verbal. I then wrote a fair copy, reported it to the Committee, and from them, unaltered to Congress. This personal communication and consultation with Mr Adams he has misremembered into the actings of a sub-committee. Pickering's observations, and Mr Adams's in addition, 'that it contained no new ideas, that it is a commonplace compilation, it's sentiments hacknied in Congress for two years before, and it's essence contained in Otis's pamphlet,' may all be true. Of that I am not to be the judge. Richd. H. Lee charged it as copied from Locke's treatise on government. Otis's pamphlet I never saw, & whether I had gathered my ideas from reading or reflection I do not know. I know only that I turned to neither book or pamphlet while writing it. I did not consider it as any part of my charge to invent new ideas altogether & to offer no sentiment which had ever been expressed before. Had Mr Adams been so restrained, Congress would have lost the benefit of his bold and impressive advocations of the rights of revolution. For no man's confident & fervid addresses, more than Mr Adams's, encoraged and supported us thro' the difficulties surrounding us, which, like the ceaseless action of gravity, weighed on us by night and by day. Yet, on the same ground, we may ask what of these elevated thoughts was new, or can be affirmed never before to have entered the conceptions of man? Whether also the sentiments of independance, and the reasons for declaring it which makes so great a portion of the instrument had been hacknied in Congress for two years before the 4th. of July 76. or this dictum also of Mr Adams be another slip of memory, let history say. This however I will say for Mr Adams, that he supported the declaration with zeal & ability, fighting fearlessly for every word of it. As to myself, I thought it a duty to be, on that occasion, a passive auditor of the opinions of others, more impartial judges than I could be, of it's merits or demerits. During the debate I was sitting by Dr. Franklin, and he observed that I was writhing a little under the acrimonious criticisms on some of it's parts; and it was on that occasion that, by way of comfort, he told me the story of John Thompson the Hatter, and his new sign. Timothy thinks the instrument the better for having a fourth of it expunged. He would have thought it still better had the other three fourths gone out also, all but the single sentiment (the only one he approves) which recommends friendship to his dear England, whenever she is willing to be at peace with us. His insinuations are that altho' 'the high tone of the instrument was in unison with the warm feelings of the times, this sentiment of habitual friendship to England should never be forgotten, and that the duties it enjoins should *especially* be borne in mind on every celebration of this anniversary.' In other words, that the Declaration, as being a libel on the government of England, composed in times of passion, should now be buried in utter oblivion to spare the feelings of our English friends and Angloman fellow citizens. But it is not to wound them that we wish to keep it in mind; but to cherish the principles of the instrument in the bosoms of our own citizens: and it is a heavenly comfort to see that these principles are yet so strongly felt as to render a circumstance so trifling as this little lapse of memory of Mr Adams worthy of being solemnly announced and supported at an anniversary assemblage of the nation on it's birthday. In opposition however to Mr Pickering, I pray God that these principles may be eternal, and close the prayer with my affectionate wishes for yourself of long life health and happiness.

Letter to Henry Lee, May 8, 1825

But with respect to our rights and the acts of the British government contravening those rights, there was but one opinion on this side of the water. All American whigs thought alike on these subjects. When forced therefore to resort to arms for redress, an appeal to the tribunal of the world was deemed proper for our justification. This was the object of the Declaration of Independance. Not to find out new principles, or new arguments, never before thought of, not merely to say things which had never been said before; but to place before mankind the common sense of the subject; [in] terms so plain and firm as to command their assent, and to justify ourselves in the independant stand we [were co]mpelled to take. Neither aiming at originality of principle or sentiment, nor yet copied from any particular and previous writing, it was intended to be an expression of the American mind, and to give to that expression the proper tone and spirit called for by the occasion. All it's authority rests then on the harmonising sentiments of the day, whether expressed in conversns, in letters, printed essays or in the elementary books of public right, as Aristotle, Cicero, Locke, Sidney &c. The historical documents which you mention as in your possession, ought all to be found, and I am persuaded you will find, to be corroborative of the facts and principles advanced in that Declaration.

Letter to Roger O. Weightman, June 24, 1826

Respected Sir

The kind invitation I recieve from you on the part of the citizens of the city of Washington, to be present with them at their celebration of the 50th. anniversary of American independance; as one of the surviving signers of an instrument, pregnant with our own, and the fate of the world, is most flattering to myself, and heightened by the honorable accompaniment proposed for the comfort of such a journey. It adds sensibly to the sufferings of sickness, to be deprived by it of a personal participation in the rejoicings of that day. But acquiescence is a duty, under circumstances not placed among those we are permitted to controul. I should indeed, with peculiar delight, have met and exchanged there, congratulations personally, with the small band, the remnant of that host of worthies, who joined with us, on that day, in the bold and doubtful election we were to make, for our country, between submission, or the sword; and to have enjoyed with them the consolatory fact that our fellow citizens, after half a century of experience and prosperity, continue to approve the choice we made. May it be to the world what I believe it will be, (to some parts sooner, to others later, but finally to all,) the Signal of arousing men to burst the chains, under which Monkish ignorance and superstition had persuaded them to bind themselves, and to assume the blessings & security of self government. The form which we have substituted restores the free right to the unbounded exercise of reason and freedom of opinion. All eyes are opened, or opening to the rights of man. The general spread of the light of science has already laid open to every view the palpable truth that the mass of mankind has not been born, with saddles on their backs, nor a favored few booted and spurred, ready to ride them legitimately, by the grace of god. These are grounds of hope for others. For [our]selves let the annual return of this day, for ever refresh our recollections of these r[ights,] and an undiminished devotion to them.

6

Against the King

DANIEL WEBSTER

With all its merits, there are those who have thought that there was one thing in the declaration to be regretted; and that is, the asperity and apparent anger with which it speaks of the person of the king; the industrious ability with which it accumulates and charges upon him, all the injuries which the colonies had suffered from the mother country. Possibly some degree of injustice, now or hereafter, at home or abroad, may be done to the character of Mr. Jefferson, if this part of the declaration be not placed in its proper light. Anger or resentment, certainly, much less personal reproach and invective, could not properly find place, in a composition of such high dignity, and of such lofty and permanent character.

A single reflection on the original ground of dispute, between England and the colonies, is sufficient to remove any unfavorable impression, in this respect.

The inhabitants of all the colonies, while colonies, admitted themselves bound by their allegiance to the king; but they disclaimed, altogether, the authority of parliament; holding themselves, in this respect, to resemble the condition of Scotland and Ireland, before the respective unions of those kingdoms with England, when they acknowledged allegiance to the same king, but each had its separate legislature. The tie, therefore, which our revolution was to break, did not subsist between us and the British parliament, or between us and the [28] British government, in the aggregate; but directly between us and the king himself. The colonies had never admitted themselves subject to parliament. That was precisely the point of the original controversy. They had uniformly denied that parliament had authority to make laws for them. There was, therefore, no sub-

FROM *A Discourse in Commemoration of the Lives and Services of John Adams and Thomas Jefferson* (Boston: Cummings, Hilliard and Company, 1826), pp. 28–30.

jection to parliament to be thrown off.[1] But allegiance to the king did exist, and had been uniformly acknowledged; and down to 1775 the most solemn assurances had been given that it was not intended to break that allegiance, or to throw it off. Therefore, as the direct object, and only effect of the declaration, according to the principles on which the controversy had been maintained, on our part, was to sever the tie of allegiance which bound us to the king, it was properly and necessarily founded on acts of the crown itself, as its justifying causes. Parliament is not so much as mentioned, in the whole instrument. When odious and oppressive acts are referred to, it is done by charging the king with confederating, [29] with others, 'in pretended acts of legislation;' the object being, constantly, to hold the king himself directly responsible for those measures which were the grounds of separation. Even the precedent of the English revolution was not overlooked, and in this case, as well as in that, occasion was found to say that the king had *abdicated* the government. Consistency with the principles upon which resistance began, and with all the previous state papers issued by congress, required that the declaration should be bottomed on the misgovernment of the king; and therefore it was properly framed with that aim and to that end. The king was known, indeed, to have acted, as in other cases, by his ministers, and with his parliament; but as our ancestors had never admitted themselves subject either to ministers or to parliament, there were no reasons to be given for now refusing obedience to their authority. This clear and obvious necessity of founding the declaration on the misconduct of the king himself, gives to that instrument its personal application, and its character of direct and pointed accusation. [30]

[1] This question, of the power of parliament over the colonies, was discussed with singular ability, by Gov. Hutchinson on the one side, and the house of representatives of Massachusetts on the other, in 1773. The argument of the House is in the form of an answer to the governor's message, and was reported by Mr. Samuel Adams, Mr. Hancock, Mr. Hawley, Mr. Bowers, Mr. Hobson, Mr. Foster, Mr. Phillips, and Mr. Thayer. As the power of the parliament had been acknowledged, so far at least as to affect us by laws of trade, it was not easy to settle the line of distinction. It was thought however to be very clear, that the charters of the colonies had exempted them from the general legislation of the British parliament. See Massachusetts State Papers, p. 351.

✺ 7 ✺

Criticism on the Declaration

of Independence as

a Literary Document

RICHARD ELY SELDEN

Seventy years having passed away, since this celebrated production was published, it will not be deemed disrespectful to its signers,
or invidious toward any order of partisans, if we bring to its examination the same rigid impartiality, allowable in criticising passages
of Longinus or a composition of Aristotle.

As it may be said of the Declaration, that it accomplished the
purposes for which it was designed, all unfavorable observations are
as supererogatory, as were the sinister reflections of Buonaparte on
the disposition of the British forces at Waterloo—a triumphant reply
to all which consisted in the brief assertion of the respondants, "we
beat you." So it may be rejoined with like propriety; for as much as
it was the end to be attained, and not the means to attain that end
which became important on the day of that eventful battle; it is
true, neither the glory of the victory is diminished, or the consolations of the vanquished increased, by the imperfection of the means
used. But so far as an analogy exists in the two cases, it bears on the
political aim and sequences of the Declaration of Independence;
upon which topic I do not propose at present to remark. Its literary
merits and demerits are a different, and as I think, a fair subject of
critical examination. To this aspect, and to this alone, do I invite the
attention of all those whose curiosity or peculiarities lead them to

FROM Criticism on the Declaration of Independence as a Literary Document,
by Mon Droit (New York: 1846), pp. 3–8, 10–15, 17–20, 22–28, 30–31.

37

make a distinction between what is good and bad, proper and improper.

The document proposed for consideration, has every where and at all times received the plaudits and huzzas of the multitude. The question comes now to be considered, whether upon a careful review, it deserves the approbation of the scholar. Whether we ought to have a more exalted idea of some of the actors in the drama of the revolution, in consequence of this production, or a [3] less one, is certainly a legitimate subject of inquiry. But that matter can only be settled by a close inspection of the document itself. I understand to be sure, that great men will not always bear close inspection; but who ever claims to be a great writer, or for whomsoever that reputation is claimed, their works must abide that test, or their claims must fall.

These brief preliminaries being all I deem clearly necessary upon commencing the subject, I invite the examination of my readers to the first paragraph. Supposing it to be familiar to every one, or if not, that it is in every one's law book where reference can be had to it any moment, I will not quote it entire.[1] My observations upon this passage will be brief, because the purpose of it for the most part, seems to be for an opening of the subject, and for an harmless soother of asperities expected to follow.

"When in the course of human events" it appears *expedient* "for one people to dissolve the political bands which have connected them with an other," I admit it would not be improper for that people to declare the causes which made that expediency apparent to them. But I entirely deny the propriety of a similar declaration

---

[1] Since this criticism has grown to dimensions far exceeding any thing I purposed at the commencement, it has occurred to me, that it would be convenient to the reader, to have the first, and so much of the second paragraph, as I have commented on, inserted in a note. I accordingly subjoin them here, as they stand in the last edition of our statutes.

"When in the course of human events, it becomes necessary for one people to dissolve the political bands which have connected them with another, and to assume, among the powers of the earth, the separate and equal station *to* which the laws of nature and of nature's God entitle them, a decent respect to the opinions of mankind requires, that they should declare the causes, which impel them to the separation."

"We hold these truths to be self-evident—That all men are created equal; that they are endowed by their Creator with certain unalienable rights; that among these are life, liberty, and the pursuit of happiness. That to secure these rights, governments are instituted among men, deriving their just powers from the consent of the governed," &c.

This is I believe, verbatim et literatim; except that I have italicized the preposition "*to*" that its ungrammatical position may be more obvious.

"when in the course of human events it becomes *necessary* for one people to dissolve the political bands" that have connected them with an other. That necessity knows no law, is a thoroughly established maxim—that it knows no apologies—can neither make them or receive them, is as evident as the maxim of which it is but another version. More strenuously should I deny the propriety of a declaration of causes, when a necessity (necessity is obligatory if it is any thing) obliges them "to *assume* among the powers of the earth, the separate and equal station *to* which the laws of nature and of nature's God entitle them."

A mere philological criticism was no part of my design; perhaps then I ought to apologise for noticing the queer position of the preposition "*to*," in the lines last quoted. To assume a station, which the laws of nature entitled them to occupy; would have been *natural*, and perhaps easy: but "to assume a station *to* which the laws of nature and of nature's God entitle them," it [4] occurs to me, would have been an exploit as awkward in the performance as it is in the grammar.

It is the ideas however,[2] and not the mode in which they are expressed that I purpose to examine. To these let us return, with all the indulgent tenderness for our national character, consistent with truth. If a gentleman in a ball-room had broken his thigh, so that it became necessary in the course of events, for him to assume a recumbent position; would a decent respect to the company he was in require, that he should declare the causes why he could not dance? I

[2] The ideas set forth are these; that *necessity* obliged them to do a certain act; which act also nature entitled them to perform. That there are such a class of acts is true. Nature entitles us (gives us the privilege) to sleep, to eat, &c., and other acts, cognate, correspondent or correlative. It may be said also, that nature obliges (compels) us to do these things. But *acts* of this sort are extremely limited. They are such as belong to man as an animal, and not to him as a rational being. A man with a bad cold, is entitled by the laws of nature to sneeze; and as he can not very well help doing it; it may be alledged that necessity obliges him to do it. To go into a declaration of causes why we sleep or eat, or do other cognate or correlavant acts, would appear particularly superfluous in our day; and I can hardly be made to understand, why it was not as much of a superfluity seventy years ago. No *decent* respect, to the opinions of mankind, would require a declaration of causes for such acts. Nor do I think a decent apology can be made for stating them, if indeed they are causes of a character ascribed to them. The document subsequently goes into a statement of causes, and very good ones they are too, but of a character as different from the one alledged of them by the author, as facts ever are from falsehoods. They are made by the recital, to consist wholly in the magisterial and judicial cruelties of the British government.

do not make this comparison for the sake of its mirth but simply as a convenient parallel to illustrate the anti-climax of this peculiar species of gravity.

"To declare the causes" which impel to certain acts, that had just been stated to arise from necessity and the laws of nature and of nature's God, favors the impression, that the writer had forgotten at the close of his sentence, the ideas he had advanced at the beginning. It reminds me of the edifying exposition of a sick man to his physician. "Oh doctor," said the patient, "necessity obliges me to send for you." Well, said the physician, what is the matter? "Oh Sir! matter enough; my throat is all stopped up—can't breathe—head aches ready to split, with terrible pains in the side and back; besides I a'nt very well myself."

The distinction we ought to make, between the "laws of nature" and the "laws of nature's God," the writer, doubtless, were he living, would be able to explain. But being dead, we are left to conjecture what the difference is. I will put the best construction upon it, and suppose, by "the laws of nature" the writer meant that physical arrangement of the globe, by which an ocean separated us from the ruling power, making the propriety of an independent government, more obvious on that account. And by the expression "laws of nature's God" he contemplated those ever springing aspirations in the heart of man, to possess all the liberty he could get, and power too. If this was the meaning, it suffers only for the want of an interpretation. If it was not, the latter clause is merely an useless expansion of the first—a mode of expression admissible in the paroxysms of frantic eloquence on a fourth of July; but entirely out of place in a grave piece of writing.³ [5]

³ When we reduce the rhetoric of the first paragraph to its plain truth, it amounts to about this: the "laws of nature," meant simply a *will*, to resent certain injuries—the "necessity," a *will* to do nothing else but resent them. The entire expression "laws of nature and of nature's God," furnishes no idea more than the simple word *nature* would furnish.

Instances of these metaphorical expansions, however, in their appropriate place, are sometimes exceedingly felicitous. The famous example—'sink or swim, live or die, survive or perish,"—when we consider the time, place, and circumstances, in which it was uttered, is in the highest degree beautiful. It is obvious enough to be sure, that these several expressions are but a repetition of the same idea; nevertheless, the want of additional ideas in the words uttered, is more than compensated by the testimony they furnish of the superabundant and overflowing patriotism of the speaker. But a similar expansion inserted in a King's speech from the throne, would be as singularly infelicitous as it is happy in the speech of an ardent orator. I have frequently observed, that brilliant and devout men, in the exercise of prayer, use these

The expression "human events" I submit to the taste of the cultivated reader. *Affairs,* may be human or inhuman; divine or diabolical. An "event" may be great or small, &c. But can humanity or inhumanity be predicated of "events?" To be sure, human beings are actors frequently, in the scenes which when completed we call "events." Does that fact however, make them *human?* A pestilence —famine—the rise and fall of empires and wars are events. Does the connection of human affairs with any of these events, make the *event* human? The error of the writer is however very small; consisting merely in attaching the same idea to the word "events" which a scholar would have attached to *affairs.*

Events are abstractions; in the mind of the pagan more or less connected with *fate:* and in the view of the christian with Divine Providence. In either case they are understood to be supra-human. Truth, may be divine; but can it with strict propriety be called *human?* A human truth would be nearly as inappreciable as a divine lie. Human beings may tell the truth; that does not make the truth *human;* because it is what exists irrespective of the man or of his veracity. So of events. They are passed, or are transpiring, or foreshadow their coming, and all this irrespective of man. Events, therefore are not human. "To err, is human."

My remarks upon the first paragraph, having been protracted far beyond any expectation or previous design; it may be proper to state here, that I do not meditate a querulous critic upon the whole piece. So far from that, I look upon the Declaration as possessing literary merit of a high order. It is too late to deny it, if one had the disposition. A composition that for seventy years can carry such a burthen of defects as this has, must possess great strength somewhere. I had rather carry the gates of Gaza than such a load. And since it was once discovered, that the great strength of a giant lay in his hair, let no neophite suppose, as a corresponding paradox, that the vigor of the composition under review, lies concealed in the unintelligible generalities at the beginning, or the sounding nonsense at the end. Whoever possesses sufficient acumen to distinguish flourishes of rhetoric from facts, will perceive (as he reads the passages that follow the [6] one commencing thus—"The history of the

---

metaphorical expansions with a very fine effect indeed. The scriptures furnish many specimens of inimitable beauty. Job, in particular, abounds in this trope. Its use is justified, and in fact sanctified on certain occasions. Where enthusiasm, devotion or ardor, are allowable, there this species of metaphor is admissible. But where facts are of more value than rhetoric, it is as much out of place as it would be in a note of hand or bill of exchange.

present king of Great Britain, is a history of repeated injuries and usurpations") that the bold, honest, straightforward recital of facts that follow, is a different affair altogether, both in style and sentiment from the verbiage that precedes it. But more of this in its appropriate place.

The second paragraph of the Declaration, is the one on which I purpose to extend my reflections; both because it is oftenest quoted, and as I think, most unhappily calculated to create the same confusion of ideas in the reader, that the mind of its writer unquestionably was troubled with. If I am charged with microscopic views, I shall treat the charge as captious, unless its author is able to show, that a different lens would lead to different conclusions.

We will quote so much of it here as I purpose to comment upon; that the reader of these pages may refer to it as often as occasion requires.

"We hold these truths to be self-evident—that all men are created equal; that they are endowed by their Creator with certain unalienable rights; that among these are life, liberty, and the pursuit of happiness; that to secure these rights governments are instituted among men," &c.

It is to be observed that the preceding paragraph had closed with the sentiment, "that a decent respect to the opinions of mankind required that they should declare the causes which impelled them" to certain acts. Now it occurs to me, that a decent respect to the hearers or readers of the document would have impelled its author immediately to declare those "causes." So far however from such a sequence, the author drops the subject of "causes" and goes into a statement of views, having not the least relation to what had preceded, nor any necessary connection with what was to follow. While the mind of the reader is occupied in vigorous efforts to discover the verity of the author's self-evident truths, he can hardly fail to forget that there was any necessity for a declaration of causes, or in fact any causes to declare. But this defect in the composition is doubtless pardonable, it is so common, and known to arise from the juvenile desire on the part of an author, to exhibit himself instead of his subject. [7]

Let us see what the author holds to. Says he "we hold these truths to be self-evident," &c.—going on to make a statement of them. Is it not obvious to remark, that what is self-evident, needs no attestation? Is it not a needless piece of supererogation to declare, what in the same breath is affirmed to be evident without a declaration?

What is self-evident, is, what is known. To inform men of what they knew before, seems but a slow way of increasing knowledge: nevertheless, the author of this part of the Declaration of Independence thought proper to undertake it. The measure of his success in this peculiar method of instruction, is a matter yet to be determined.[4]

The verb "hold" in the sentence under review, is used in its metaphorical sense, and is undoubtedly appropriate, so far as the philology of the passage is concerned. But to hold, to what one cannot get away from, does not appear to me a greater virtue, than to let go what one cannot keep. At any rate, it is not a virtue I would recommend a friend to make any parade about. In modern times "self-evident truths" would not escape observation, if they were not held. But in "the times that tried men's" logic, it appears that what was self-evident could not be brought to notice without considerable pains. However, holding to self-evident truths, may yet come in fashion. . . . [8]

. . . . .

A self-evident *truth*, is what no man can avoid knowing. If a knowledge of it can be avoided, it ceases to be self-evident. A self-evident proposition, is one that invariably carries conviction with the mere statement. In mathematics, propositions of this nature, are not necessarily ludicrous. But in ethics, this mirth mooving quality is unalterably connected with every statement. [10]

. . . . .

Leaving for the present the absurdity of stating, what in the same breath, it is conceded no man can avoid knowing, to the consolations of its own company; let us see what is the first famous truth the author of the Declaration affirms to be self-evident. Why! "that all men are created equal!!" If the professor of mathematics in Yale College, should gravely announce to his pupils, the following theo-

---

[4] To make a man a present of his own face, would be a specimen of generosity of the same value, as presenting him an example of what was self-evident. If a gentleman should propose to introduce me to myself, for the purpose of enlarging the circle of my acquaintance, I should consider his politeness of the same kind with that which would exert itself to increase my knowledge, by informing me of what I knew before. What was self-evident, I must have known; to suppose to the contrary, presupposes my powers inadequate to comprehend a *statement*. If the thing to be stated, was what I knew, then there was no *use* for the statement. If it was what I did not know, then it was not *self*-evident. I think this logic, must be sufficient to show, that a statement of self-evident truths, is altogether a piece of gratuitous nonsense.

rem—"I hold this truth to be self-evident—that all geometrical figures are exactly similar," he would place his reputation for veracity and acumen, in the same position I conceive the author of the Declaration to occupy. And if his pupils should give a gaping credence to his asseverations, I should look also upon them, as entitled to the same degree of respect, which the applauders of these passages in the Declaration deserve.

Would it be disrespectful to inquire of the author, if living, by what authority he made this statement? For how are we to believe him possessed of this extraordinary piece of knowledge, when no other man does or can know it without a special revelation? If the author had prepared our minds for his marvellous statement, by informing us that he held the truth he was about to utter, as *re-vealed,* then no doubt, we should all be willing to concede to him, the same measure of respect we invariably pay to a Mormon; but since he entirely neglected so to prepare our minds, we cannot think him entitled to that measure of respect. [11]

The truths which are of vital importance to man, are those revealed in the scriptures. A necessity for this revelation, under the circumstances of the case, arose from the fact, that those truths were not only not self-evident, but they were incapable of a demonstration. . . .

If the statement "all men are created equal," had been found among the passages of scripture, which reveal to us the information, "that the day is set when God will judge the world in righteousness,"—had the statement been invested with the sanctity such company would give it; then indeed should I have yielded my assent to its truth, not as a matter of reason, but of faith: and [12] not then without the reflection that my faith in that particular, was indeed a virtue, as difficult to practise as any other connected with self-denial.

But the passage under consideration is invested with no sanctity commending it to our faith; neither does it possess a speciousness that commends it to our reason. It is neither more nor less than an uninspired and presumptous asseveration, upon a subject that no man can possibly know any thing about.

We draw our inferences from facts as they exist, or from facts as they are presented to us. And what are those facts? Under every conceivable contingency—under circumstances unlimited in their dissimilitude and inequality, are men born; under all these do they continue to live; and under them also they die. Whether all men are *created* equal (using the verb in its true and literal sense) can be known only to their Creator. And since there is no revelation on that point, it is as impossible for man to know any thing about it, as it is to beget himself.

But admitting the word to be used in an expanded or figurative sense; and that the creation alluded to, is to man as he is, or as he appears. How are the facts more applicable then? Still, from forms of surpassing beauty, through a long series of gradations to the most offensive deformity—from minds of the purest radiance, through like gradations, to those of the obscurity, fog and confusion of his, whose profitless aphorisms are under review—from the extremest verge of what is lovely and desirable, to the limit of all that is odious in complexion, condition or circumstance are men created. These are facts, as palpable as the continent on which we stand. No reasoning, no study, faith or patience can make them or unmake them. These are the facts, and there are no other. One might as soon reason the Andes from their foundations, as reason us out of knowledge we cannot avoid possessing.

What apology then, is there to be found for the man, who, in the face of all these facts, and against the convictions of a conscience, if he had one, took occasion upon the going forth of a solemn public document, to parade the absurd crudity of his own "that he held it to be a self-evident truth, that all men were created equal?" What national dignity have we gained for our consolation, or what national honor for our comfort, for thus publishing to the world in our first and gravest document, this [13] swelling axiom, as contemptible for its inapplicability, as for its falsehood? Neither the Divine government, nor any human government, with which history or experience have made us acquainted, have treated men as created equal, or as being equal; and for the best of all reasons. It is an impossibility. The attempt would confound all distinctions between right and wrong, good and bad, useful and useless. The human government that should attempt it, would attempt its own nullification. It might as well attempt the task of singing the dirge at its own funeral.

Nevertheless, it is not improper that men should be contemplated as equals, and treated as such in several particulars. Courts of justice, and governments too, may be instituted for this purpose among others. It is not, however, their whole duty. It is certainly as much a part of that duty, and as an agreeable a function of it, to create inequalities between the good and bad, as to level them under different circumstances.

Supposing the author of the Declaration had asserted among *his*

self-evident truths, that he held the heavens to be made of brass!!
Certainly there are more appearances at times to justify such assertion, than there ever was to justify those he has made. Would any
man have practised under such a belief? Would any man have
shaped his conduct to that contingency? And if they did not, would
not their conduct be satisfactory evidence that they did not believe
the assertion? Men have not altered their conduct since the marvelous developement "that all men are created equal." The author of
the statement never shaped his to that end. This is as good testimony as can ever be got, that neither he, nor any one else, ever
practically believed the statement true. And it is to be questioned,
whether theoretically, the author, or any other, ever gave credence
to it. For it is quite difficult for me to conceive how a man can have
a belief, upon a subject, upon which he can have no knowledge.
That difficulty, I apprehend, is irremoveable. If the assertion had
been, that all men are created unequal, we might with some
propriety have put credence in it; because a great multitude of
analogies lead to that supposition. We have what amounts to some
knowledge on that point. But when the assertion is, "that all men are
created equal," we possess no fact, circumstance, analogy or revelation, that touches the [14] subject; consequently we can have no
knowledge, and of course, no belief. The author of this statement
could have had no belief in its truth, because he possessed no
knowledge in the premises, that is not common to us. There is no
possible apology for his making it, but lunacy. [15]

. . . . .

In conclusion of my remarks on this part of the subject, there is
one point of negative testimony, which I admit, so far as it goes,
favors the supposition, that the declaration under review is self-
evident. It is this. What is self-evident, cannot be shown to be true,
by demonstration clearer than itself. I allow therefore, the expression "all men are created equal," to be self-evident, if evident at all;
for it is clearly incapable of any proof whatever.

The second truth affirmed to be self-evident is expressed thus—
"that they (i.e. all men) are endowed by their Creator with certain
unalienable rights; that among these are life, liberty and the pursuit
of happiness."

To *alien*, is to dispose of, part with, put away. What is *unalienable*, is what cannot be disposed of, parted with, or put away, either
by the possessor, or by any one else: for if it can, it ceases to be

unalienable. Life is affirmed to be one of these possessions. If it were true that no man could alienate (dispose of) his own life or any one's else, it would prove an immense comfort to braggarts. They could parade their patriotism and bravery without serious risk. Wars too, would cease to be attended with those losses, which have hitherto been accounted their chief terror. For myself I had supposed that life was alienable: and I apprehend the author of the very sentence under remark, thought so; for before he closes this famous declaration, he pledges his "life," among other things. To pledge what one cannot dispose of, amounts to no higher virtue, than to give away what one does not own. If life were unalienable, the pledge so sonorously paraded at the close of the Declaration, would be as worthless as a Virginia abstraction, or an abstract Virginian.

Moreover, if life is unalienable, there can be no more evidence of true patriotism. No man can part with his, for the good of his country. The Declaration that contains the self-evident truth that life was unalienable, was published the 4th July, 1776. The battle of Bunker Hill, where Warren, and many brave warriors had alienated their lives for the benefit of their country, had taken place in June, of the previous year. Montgomery also, with his [17] companions in glory, had the same year alienated their lives under the ramparts of Quebec, for the same purpose. The patriots, likewise, who were slain at Lexington, had done the same thing. They sleep in their graves, each one with the sweet hope of immortal joy for his bed-fellow; and when they awake, they will find that their smiling companion had awoke before them.

It seems fortunate for the posthumous fame of these glorious old warriors, that they effected this impossible *alienation,* and secured their renown, a little before the *self-evident truth* made it evident they could do no such thing.

To pretend a distinction between the *right* to life, and life itself, is but making darkness visible. The alienation of life, under certain circumstances, has ever been considered one of the most exalted actions a human being is capable of performing. The alienation effected on mount calvary, has attracted the admiration of half mankind, for more than eighteen hundred years. Every battle field, from Marathon to Saratoga; every page of history, every day's experience, furnish us with but too much, and too lamentable testimony, that life is alienable. The assertion therefore that life is an unalienable endowment, is not only not self-evident, but is a specimen of sophistry unsupported by any known fact, and incapable of the shadow of proof.

It is indeed not improper to suppose, that our first parent, when he came from the forming hand of his Creator, was endowed with an unalienable right to life. But he, with that perverseness, common to all his race, succeeded in alienating the affections of his Maker. As a just retribution for his perversity, the glorious endowment of a right to life, was taken away from him, and the endowment of a right to die substituted in its place. This endowment, has clave to his posterity with an unalienability that has never been broken, though every device that the ingenuity of man could invent, has been tried to effect that alienation.

If the author of the Declaration had asserted, that all men were endowed by their Creator with an unalienable right to die, he would have come as much nearer the fact, than he has, by all the distance there is between falsehood and truth. [18]

. . . . .

To be endowed with a right to live, and yet at the same time can not live—that is to say, a right to life, and yet not in possession—is not an endowment of any practical value. An abstract right to life, which some one has taken away from us is worth less than the carcass of a dead cat. The Creator, I apprehend, has higher occupation than making such endowments. Moreover, the right to live, would seem to conflict very much with the right to die. I doubt whether the two rights can coexist. That we have the latter, is made evident by testimony as magnificent in quantity, as it is melancholy in detail. The truth is, the right to life is in the *possession*. It is inseparable. If it were; if a man had a right to life after he had been dispossessed; I know of no process he could institute for its recovery. Where would he stand, while he vindicated his right? What court could he get to entertain his cause, except that of Radamanthus? Ordinary dead men, in such an emergency would want the aid of a live lawyer. Could they find one to go before the courts in the next world, to vindicate a dead man's *right to life?* But supposing he should recover judgment by default; what sheriff would bring him back to this world, and put him in possession of his lost property?

To be sure, man has a self-evident right to life while he lives. I do not dispute that. But it would take an immense amount of sophistry to prove his right to it after that time; or that the right was worth any thing if it could be proved. I think therefore it has been shown that the *right* to life and life, are one and inseparable; consequently the expression, "unalienable right to life" amounts to nothing more than "unalienable life"—the word "rights" adding no appreciable idea to the expression, or being of any practical use, except in sound—sound signifying nothing. [19]

We come now to an examination of the expression "right to liberty." It is true in this case, the right, under certain circumstances, may be worth something without the possession: and in that particular the word as applicable to "liberty," has some meaning, but as applicable to "life" none; and herein in part consists the cheat of the sophistry under review. The right to liberty, in a given case, may be valuable just in proportion to the chances of obtaining actual possession. But an abstract right to what one has not got, and what there is no probability of his getting, seems worth no more than a *right* to be disappointed. To suppose our Creator makes endowments of that sort, is a presumption I would not like to answer for. "All men" includes black men!! Perhaps the reader ought to be informed that the above, is a self-evident truth; otherwise he might possibly doubt its verity. The value then, of this *right* to liberty, which a South Carolina slave is endowed with, (if all men are,) may be calculated more easily than a nullifier can calculate the value of the Union. The value of this right, to the poor slave, according to my mathematics, is just the value nullification adds to that Union. The truth is, the *value* of the right, without the possession, exists only in theory, not in fact. To be endowed with a right to think, without being endowed with any mind to think with, would be just such another endowment—just such an one as the author of the Declaration must have contemplated, if he had any distinct idea of the subject. To this complexion it must come at last.

The point to be proved then was this, that the *right* to liberty, though nominally appreciable as a thing separate from the possession, is not in ninety-nine cases in a hundred, worth more than the *right* to life without the possession. To all practical intents and useful purposes, the word "rights" as connected with liberty, may be dropped from the text, and the idea will in fact be as little impaired, as I have shown it would be by omitting it before the word "life." The whole idea there was to be communicated, so far as life and liberty are concerned, might have been expressed without the word "rights" and would have stood thus—"endowed by their Creator with unalienable life, liberty," &c. If my reasoning on this subject has not been fair, I should not know how to appreciate that which was. [20]

. . . . .

The third item with which we are endowed, and which is affirmed to possess the same fixed attributes as the others, is the "*right* to the pursuit of happiness!!" The idea, if there was one attached to this expression, is too remote and vague for criticism. The attempt to weigh an abstraction in scales, or moonshine in a balance, would require the same manipulations as an attempt to calculate the value of an idea which its author could not express. The most favorable construction I can put upon it is, that no idea was meant to be communicated. The passage was particularly designed for southern ears; therefore sound, not sense, was required. It was more euphonious to terminate the clause with these sounds, than to stop where the idea stopped; hence they were added.

A sarcastic Frenchman once said, "the chief use of language is to conceal ideas." That was not the chief use of it in the case before us; for it does not appear there was any idea to conceal. Pursuit of happiness!! *Right* to the pursuit of happiness!!! The same logic, which I am sure made it satisfactory to the reader, that the *right* to life must coexist with the possession—that they are one and inseparable—is applicable in the present case. To be endowed with an abstract *right* to the pursuit of happiness, and yet endowed with no ability to pursue, is in all respects as barren a privilege as the right to life when one is not [22] in possession. As dead men tell no tales, I do not know how we are to get any witnesses of a man's right to life after he is dispossessed; so the right to the pursuit of happiness, must be proved by the pursuit, if proved at all. The right, and the possession, must be contemplated as one, if indeed it is a subject concrete enough for contemplation. I shall so treat it from obvious necessity.

Some men's pursuit of happiness consists in picking our pockets; others in taking our lives; a third makes his pursuit of happiness consist in getting the two first convicted of their pursuits; and in getting them alienated of their unalienable rights to liberty and life. Success in the latter pursuit is quite after my notion of what ought to take place. But these antagonist and ever conflicting rights!! Are they divine endowments? Rights! nullifying and devouring each other!!! The rights of the Kilkenny cats to fight till there was nothing left but their tails, were just such rights.

Such, Oh Progressive Democracy! is the length and the breadth, the weight, the superfices, substance and sum-total of the sounding sophistry in this part of the Declaration of Independence. If in our first and most solemn public document we parade such stuff as this—if we quote it, utter it, laud it, is it to be wondered at, that other nations should scoff at our pretensions, and mock when our vain-glory cometh? Our patriotic nation seems determined to have a magnificent opinion of itself, at all hazards and in despite every obstacle. No amount of folly in our state papers, or of nonsense in our public speeches and diplomacy, is adequate to alter that opinion. But what views of our sense or sanity, is all this ostentatious setting forth of unintelligible aphorisms and inappreciable generalities, calculated to create in our cotemporaries? Oh that we were endowed with an unalienable disposition to divest ourselves of vanity and lies. I would give more for such an endowment, than for all the abstract rights this side the moon.

The third self-evident truth asserted, is expressed thus—"that to secure these rights" (meaning those we have just been contemplating) "governments are instituted among men, deriving their just powers from the consent of the governed," &c. Rights! with which we are endowed by our Creator, and in a manner [23] withal, that makes them self-evidently unalienable, a sane man would suppose, were about as secure as any thing could well be made on this side the grave. Who would want a human government, to secure, what in the same breath is alledged, a Divine one had secured, so as make the loss of it self-evidently impossible?

Had the writer of the Declaration *believed* his two first self-evident truths! he could not avoid knowing that there was no possible use for his third one. Rights, possessing the remarkable characteristics affirmed of these, must be objects as fixed as the sun. That luminary does not abide in its place, by any stronger security, than an "unalienable" endowment of its Creator. Consequently there is no more need of a human government to secure what is unalienable in us, than there is to secure what is unalienable in the sun. The pyramid of Cheops is not endowed with an unalienable privilege of existence, so far as we know, and is therefore indefinitely more transitory than the rights spoken of; nevertheless I apprehend, three or even four self-evident flourishes of rhetoric, would not add enough to its stability to pay for the breath that uttered them. The earth likewise on which we stand, is not fixed in its sphere with the irremovability affirmed of these rights. It is therefore more liable to drop from beneath our feet, than our unalienable rights are, to slip from our possession. If that contingency should occur, and leave this amazing nation to get along as well as it could without it, the government would not probably find it out; for it appears that as yet it has never been able to discover what was "self-evident!!" A government instituted to secure the earth from dropping away from us, would not have a more laborious vocation, than one instituted to secure us in rights that could not possibly be taken away. In fine, a government instituted to secure us in a knowledge of what was self-evident; would have the same marvelous employment, as one instituted to secure us in rights that are unalienable.

The most astonishing thing about these passages of the Declaration is, that such an immense quantity of nonsense could be got into so small a compass. . . . [24]

My conviction increases as I proceed in the examination of this document, that its author had no distinct ideas on the subject he was writing about; or if he had, he possessed no faith in the truth of his own assertions. Certainly I have no disposition to undervalue any thing connected with the credit or renown of our country; but would rather pertinaciously insist upon every thing connected therewith as great and good, if I thought I could possibly maintain such a position. But in the face of this filial affection I must say, a more crude and profitless jumble of words, than fills the passages in the fore part of the Declaration, is no where to be found in any State document north of Mason and Dixon's line.

The first and most fatal mistake of its author, as I conceive, lay in his attempt to *make* truths. As if the truth was something that could be made. The first prerequisite and vital quality of truth, is, that it is something which *exists*. Men may tell it, or neglect to tell it. But the attempt to make it, is evidence, that what they purposed to make, did not exist; consequently it could not be the truth. Visionaries like the author under review, and most persons of some learning without any thorough discipline of mind, are very fond of these attempts to *make* important truths. They succeed in making a statement. Afterwards on looking round for facts in its support, finding none, nevertheless its author [25] never seems to alter his opinions of its value. (Let them find the facts, or make them, who are interested in having it true.) The value of a statement consists in its truth: unless the design was to deceive. In that case its value is a minus quantity to all who are deceived.

The question may be put to me here, with as much force perhaps as in any other place—if this document is the miserable specimen of sophistry you suppose, how comes it to pass, that such men as Franklin, Roger Sherman and other northern men of unquestionable acumen—how comes it they should have put their signatures to it? For the same reason that made them adopt the constitution—a strong imperious necessity. A necessity vehement and inappeasable, demanded of them the adoption of some constitution of government. The same necessity narrowed their choice to the one they did adopt or none. It was the best of two alternatives, notwithstanding its great and almost fatal blemishes. So with regard to the Declaration—the blood at Lexington had been spilt, Warren and his companions had fallen at Bunker Hill, Montgomery at Quebec—it was a time of trouble, when every face gathered blackness, and every town felt distresses daily. The full time was come when the leaders must declare what they purposed to do; and so pressing was the emergency, as to narrow their choice to the Declaration as it stands or none. They signed it notwithstanding its defects, and in so doing did as I myself would have done.

But the signers had some apology for this act, besides the rigorous necessity that pressed them. There was some excellent things about it, as I trust it is yet possible to show. It is not the taste or the genius of the signers that I impugn. Their part in it was what emergent circumstances compelled. An apology for them is manifest; not so with the writer. His part in the premises was the work of the closet—of premeditation and preparation. He therefore is not entitled to any indulgence for the crude nonsense it exhibits.

If the question occurs to any one, how the same tree bringeth forth good fruit and evil fruit? my response will be simply because there are two trees. The composition is evidently the production of two minds. Upon a close and critical examination of this [26] instrument—the style of its ideas and expressions, I have come to a settled conviction on that point. The same amount of testimony necessary to convince me, that the whitest children of our country are the offspring of the blackest inhabitants, would be required to prove to my satisfaction, that the clear straight forward statements in the body of the document, were the production of the same mind as the verbiage that precedes them. The difference in solidity between ramparts of stone, and the mists of the morning, is but a trifle more conspicuous, than the difference between the thoughts to be expressed and the mode of expressing them, observable in the two parts of this production. The clear, strong-minded and honest man, when he has any thing to declare, takes the method which becomes conspicuous in the document, where it says "The history of the present King of Great Britain, is a history of repeated injuries and usurpations," &c.—the man whose mind is forty-nine parts fog, and fifty-one self-conceit will invariably employ the style, mystification and pompous nonsense of the passages we have been reviewing.

Moreover, from many analogies I am inclined to the opinion, that one of these minds had been invigorated by the discipline of a higher latitude; the other enervated by the lassitude of a lower—one from the land of facts and truth, the other from the land of abstractions and vain philosophy. The mind of the higher latitude begins to manifest itself in the Declaration, as soon as we begin to find any truth in it, or any appreciable idea. The sentences in the second paragraph, following those I have commented on, are intelligible. I think it reasonable to suppose therefore, that no southern mind produced them. This intelligibility increases apace till the composition comes to the recital of facts, when that intelligibility is complete. We come now to statements that carry conviction with them—to ideas that cannot be misunderstood and facts that no man can dispute. Not only what truth or honesty there is in its Declaration; but all the strength, beauty and value lie in this plain, unambitious narrative.

"See how a plain tale will put you down," says a fine writer. He, and those who heard him knowing well, that the force of language consisted in the force of the facts recited; and sublimity in the brevity wherewith the truth is set forth. [27]

On reading the Declaration, my interest continues unabated from the beginning of the recital of facts, through all that part of it which was evidently the production of a northern mind. At the last paragraph but one, that interest rises to excitement. I venture the opinion, that a specimen of more touching pathos than is there set forth, is not to be found in any State paper, of this country or of any other. That, is the way in which a strongminded man speaks, when he feels himself wronged, and his purpose has become fixed to redress that wrong.

We see no more of the soft latitude in this production until we come to the concluding clause of the last sentence: there it bursts forth again with its "peculiar" rhetoric and unmistakable characteristics.

As the passage is often quoted—as it is more frequently in the mouths of the mock orators and quack patriots than any other, we will subject it to the same considerate and fair criticism, we have applied to its cognate and fellow passages in the first part of the document. I will quote so much of it here as I purpose to inspect.— "We mutually pledge to each other our lives, our fortunes, and our sacred honor."!! If this is not bathos, what is? If here is not a specimen of anti-climax, in the place of a supposed sublime asseveration —laughable but from our respect to the circumstances, where can we find one? If after a man had pledged his fortune, he should propose to increase the security by pledging his movable estate, we should hardly think him sane enough to make any pledge at all. "All that a man hath will he give for his life" saith a far wiser writer than the one we are reviewing. Life is by so much the most valuable of all our possessions, that in its common meaning, it is used as comprehending every thing else that belongs to us. Life, in the sense in which it is used in the passage before us, is not confined to mere animal vitality; it comprehends all that goes to make up the man. It includes his qualities of soul, as much as it does the blood in his veins. But if we take the passage as it stands, we must conclude that when they pledged their lives, they made a reservation of honor; as if that attribute was something which did not necessarily belong to *their* lives: for afterwards, as if upon second thought, they pledge that too. [28]

. . . . .

The expression "our lives, our fortunes and our sacred honor," I cannot but contemplate as verbiage of the poorest sort. Nothing is added to the idea after the word "lives." Had the sentence of which we have quoted a part, been written thus—"and for the support of this Declaration, with a firm reliance on the protection of Divine providence, we mutually pledge to each other our lives" it would have expressed all the meaning it does as it stands. But sound!! sound!! the Jupiter-tonans and the ding-dong it would not have had. These, to chivalric ears, are of more consequence than sense; therefore those insipid and profitless appendages are affixed to a sentence, which but for them would have been sublime.

Men in the strong agonies of death, make no parade of rhetoric,

And in the trying emergencies of life, public or private, when the strain of rigorous necessity brings us to as straight a condition; a brevity as rigid as the condition we are in, is the first, last, and [30] sole characteristic of our speech. In the emergency which constrained our leading men at the time of the Declaration, we should suppose they would have pledged all they had to pledge at once; and so they would undoubtedly have done, if left to the promptings of their own good sense; but the document makes them dribble out the items they propose to pledge one by one; and the mind in contemplating the worth of the separate parts, loses sight of the value of the whole. [31]

⚛ 8 ⚛

The Most False and Dangerous of All Political Errors

JOHN C. CALHOUN

Taking the proposition ["all men are born free and equal"] literally, (it is in that sense it is understood,) there is not a word of truth in it. It begins with "all men are born," which is utterly untrue. Men are not born. Infants are born. They grow to be men. And concludes with asserting that they are born "free and equal," which is not less false. They are not born free. While infants they are incapable of freedom, being destitute alike of the capacity of thinking and acting, without which there can be no freedom. Besides, they are necessarily born subject to their parents, and remain so among all people, savage and civilized, until the development of their intellect and physical capacity enables them to take care of themselves. They grow to all the freedom, of which the condition in which they were born permits, by growing to be men. Nor is it less false that they are born "equal." They are not so in any sense in which it can be regarded; and thus, as I have asserted, there is not a word of truth in the whole proposition, as expressed and generally understood.

If we trace it back, we shall find the proposition differently expressed in the Declaration of Independence. That asserts that "all men are created equal." The form of expression, though less dangerous, is not less erroneous. All men are not created. According to the

FROM Speech on the Oregon Bill, June 27, 1848, *Appendix to the Congressional Globe*, 30th Cong., 1st Sess. (Washington: Blair & Rives, 1848), p. 872. The title is taken from a passage in Calhoun's Speech.

Bible, only two, a man and a woman, ever were, and of these one was pronounced subordinate to the other. All others have come into the world by being born, and in no sense, as I have shown, either free or equal. But this form of expression being less striking and popular, has given way to the present, and under the authority of a document put forth on so great an occasion, and leading to such important consequences, has spread far and wide, and fixed itself deeply in the public mind. It was inserted in our Declaration of Independence without any necessity. It made no necessary part of our justification in separating from the parent country, and declaring ourselves independent. Breach of our chartered privileges, and lawless encroachment on our acknowledged and well-established rights by the parent country, were the real causes, and of themselves sufficient, without resorting to any other, to justify the step. Nor had it any weight in constructing the governments which were substituted in the place of the colonial. They were formed of the old materials and on practical and well-established principles, borrowed for the most part from our own experience and that of the country from which we sprang. [872]

9

Created Equal?

ABRAHAM LINCOLN and
STEPHEN A. DOUGLAS

A. Lincoln at Chicago, Ill., June 10, 1858

We hold this annual celebration * to remind ourselves of all the good done in this process of time of how it was done and who did it, and how we are historically connected with it; and we go from these meetings in better humor with ourselves—we feel more attached the one to the other, and more firmly bound to the country we inhabit. In every way we are better men in the age, and race, and country in which we live for these celebrations. But after we have done all this we have not yet reached the whole. There is something else connected with it. We have besides these men—descended by blood from our ancestors—among us perhaps half our people who are not descendants at all of these men, they are men who have come from Europe—German, Irish, French and Scandinavian—men that have come from Europe themselves, or whose ancestors have come hither and settled here, finding themselves our equals in all things. If they look back through this history to trace their connection with those days by blood, they find they have none, they cannot carry them-

* Fourth of July—Ed.

SELECTIONS A, B, C, E, and F are reprinted from *The Illinois Political Campaign of 1858: A Facsimile of the Printer's Copy of His Debates with Senator Stephen Arnold Douglas as Edited and Prepared for Press by Abraham Lincoln* ([Washington:] The Library of Congress, [1958]), pp. 45, 47, 77, 79, 89, 165, 167. The *Facsimile* is of the scrapbook in which Lincoln pasted the newspaper reports of the debates on one side of the page. The audience responses transcribed by the reporters were crossed out by Lincoln in preparing the debates for publication, but they are restored in brackets in this reprinting. Selection D is reprinted from *The Collected Works of Abraham Lincoln*, Roy P. Basler, Editor, Marion Dolores Pratt and Lloyd A. Dunlap, Associate Editors, Vol. II (New Brunswick, N.J.: Rutgers University Press, 1953), pp. 546–547, by permission of the Abraham Lincoln Association.

selves back into that glorious epoch and make themselves feel that they are part of us, but when they look through that old Declaration of Independence they find that those old men say that "We hold these truths to be self-evident, that all men are created equal," and then they feel that that moral sentiment taught in that day evi- ences their relation to those men, that it is the father of all moral principle in them, and that they have a right to claim it as though they were blood of the blood, and flesh of the flesh of the men who wrote that Declaration, [loud and long continued applause] and so they are. That is the electric cord in that [45] Declaration that links the hearts of patriotic and liberty-loving men together, that will link those patriotic hearts as long as the love of freedom exists in the minds of men throughout the world. [Applause.]

Now, sirs, for the purpose of squaring things with this idea of "don't care if slavery is voted up or voted down," for sustaining the Dred Scott decision [A voice—"Hit him again"], for holding that the Declaration of Independence did not mean anything at all, we have Judge Douglas giving his exposition of what the Declaration of Independence means, and we have him saying that the people of America are equal to the people of England. According to his con- struction, you Germans are not connected with it. Now I ask you in all soberness, if all these things, if indulged in, if ratified, if con- firmed and endorsed, if taught to our children, and repeated to them, do not tend to rub out the sentiment of liberty in the country, and to transform this Government into a government of some other form. Those arguments that are made, that the inferior race are to be treated with as much allowance as they are capable of enjoying; that as much is to be done for them as their condition will allow. What are these arguments? They are the arguments that kings have made for enslaving the people in all ages of the world. You will find that all the arguments in favor of king-craft were of this class; they always bestrode the necks of the people, not that they wanted to do it, but because the people were better off for being ridden. That is their argument, and this argument of the Judge is the same old serpent that says you work and I eat, you toil and I will enjoy the fruits of it. Turn in whatever way you will—whether it come from the mouth of a King, an excuse for enslaving the people of his country, or from the mouth of men of one race as a reason for enslaving the men of another race, it is all the same old serpent, and I hold if that course of argumentation that is made for the purpose of convincing the public mind that we should not care about this, should be granted, it does not stop with the negro. I should like to know if taking this old Declaration of Independence, which declares that all men are equal upon principle and making exceptions to it where will it stop. If one man says it does not mean a negro, why not another say it does not mean some other man? If that declaration is not the truth, let us get the Statute book, in which we find it and tear it out! Who is so bold as to do it! [Voices—"me," "no one," &c.] If it is not true let us tear it out! [cries of "no, no,"] let us stick to it then, [cheers] let us stand firmly by it then. [Applause.] [47]

B. *Douglas at Springfield, Ill., July 17, 1858*

Hence, you find that Mr. Lincoln and myself come to a direct issue on this whole doctrine of slavery. He is going to wage a war against it everywhere, not only in Illinois but in his native State of Kentucky. And why? Because he says that the Declaration of Independence contains this language: "We hold these truths to be self-evident, that all men are created equal; that they are endowed by their Creator with certain inalienable rights; that among these are life, liberty and the pursuit of happiness," and he asks whether that instrument does not declare that all men are created equal. ["Not niggers."] Mr. Lincoln then goes on to say that that clause of the Declaration of Independence includes negroes. ["I say not."] Well, if you say not I do not think you will vote for Mr. Lincoln. [Laughter, and the same voice, "I'll be d—d if I do."] Mr. Lincoln goes on to argue that the language "all men" included the negroes, Indians and all inferior races.

In his Chicago speech he says in so many words that it includes the negroes, that they were endowed by the Almighty with the right of equality with the white man, and therefore that that right is divine—a right under the higher law; that the law of God makes them equal to the white man, and therefore that the law of the white man cannot deprive them of that right. This is Mr. Lincoln's argument. He is conscientious in his belief. I do not question his sincerity, I do not doubt that he, in his conscience, believes that the Almighty made the negro equal to the white man. He thinks that the negro is his brother. [Laughter.] I do not think that the negro is any kin of mine at all. [Laughter and cheers.] And here is the difference between us. I believe that the Declaration of Independence, in the words "all men are created equal," was intended to allude only to the people of the United States, to men of European birth or descent, being white men, that they were created equal, and hence that Great Britain had no right to deprive them of their political and religious privileges; but the signers of that paper did not intend to include the Indian or the negro in that declaration, ["never," &c.,] for if they had would they not have been bound to abolish slavery in every state and colony from that day. ["Certainly," and cheers.] Remember, too, that at the time the Declaration was put forth every one of the thirteen colonies were slaveholding colonies; every man who signed that Declaration represented slaveholding constituents. ["Hurrah for Douglas."] Did those signers mean by that act to charge themselves and all their constituents with having violated the law of God, in holding the negro in an inferior condition to the white man? ["No, certainly not."] And yet, if they included negroes in that term they were bound, as conscientious men, that day and that hour, not only to have abolished slavery throughout the land, but to have conferred political rights and privileges on the negro, and elevated him to an equality with the white man. ["They did not do it."] I know [77] they did not do it, and the very fact that they did not shows that they did not understand the language they used to include any but the white race. Did they mean to say that the Indian, on this continent, was created equal to the white man, and that he was endowed by the Almighty with inalienable rights— rights so sacred that they could not be taken away by any constitution or law that man could pass? Why, their whole action towards the Indian showed that they never dreamed that they were bound to put him on an equality. I am not only opposed to negro equality, but I am opposed to Indian equality. I am opposed to putting the coolies, now importing into this country, on an equality with us, or putting the Chinese or any inferior race on an equality with us. I hold that the white race, the European race, I care not whether Irish, German, French, Scotch, English, or to what nation they belong, so they are the white race, to be our equals, ["Good, that's the doctrine," and cheers.] and I am for placing them, as our fathers did, on an equality with us. [Cheers.] Emigrants from Europe and their descendants constitute the people of the U.S. [Renewed applause.] The declaration of independence only included the white people of the U.S. ["Not the negro."] [79]

C. Lincoln at Springfield, Ill., July 17, 1858

One more thing. Last night Judge Douglas tormented himself with horrors about my disposition to make negros perfectly equal with white men in social and political relations. He did not stop to show that I have said any such thing, or that it legitimately follows from any thing I have said, but he rushes on with his assertions. I adhere to the Declaration of Independence. If Judge Douglas and his friends are not willing to stand by it, let them come up and amend it. Let them make it read that all men are created equal except negroes. Let us have it decided, whether the Declaration of Independence, in this blessed year of 1858, shall be thus amended. In his construction of the Declaration last year he said it only meant that Americans in America were equal to Englishmen in England. Then, when I pointed out to him that by that rule he excludes the Germans, the Irish, the Portuguese, and all the other people who have come amongst us since the Revolution, he reconstructs his construction. In his last speech he tells us it meant Europeans.

I press him a little further, and ask if it meant to include the Russians in Asia? or does he mean to exclude that vast population from the principles of our Declaration of Independence? I expect ere long he will introduce another amendment to his definition. He is not at all particular. He is satisfied with any thing which does not endanger the nationalizing of negro slavery. It may draw white men down, but it must not lift negroes up. Who shall say, "I am the superior, and you are the inferior?"

My declarations upon this subject of negro slavery may be misrepresented, but can not be misunderstood. I have said that I do not understand the Declaration to mean that all men were created equal in all respects. They are not our equal in color; but I suppose that it does mean to declare that all men are equal in some respects; they are equal in their right to "life, liberty, and the pursuit of happiness." Certainly the negro is not our equal in color—perhaps not in many other respects; still, in the right to put into his mouth the bread that his own hands have earned, he is the equal of every other man, white or black. In pointing out that more has been given you, you can not be justified in taking away the little which has been given him. All I ask for the negro is that if you do not like him, let him alone. If God gave him but little, that little let him enjoy. [89]

D. Lincoln at Lewistown, Ill., August 17, 1858

The Declaration of Independence was formed by the representatives of American liberty from thirteen States of the confederacy—twelve of which were slaveholding communities. We need not discuss the way or the reason of their becoming slaveholding communities. It is sufficient for our purpose that *all of them* greatly deplored the evil and that they placed a provision in the Constitution which they supposed would gradually remove the disease by cutting off its source. This was the abolition of the slave trade. So general was conviction—the public determination—to abolish the African slave trade, that the provision which I have referred to as being placed in the Constitution, declared that it should *not* be abolished prior to the year 1808. A constitutional provision was necessary to prevent the people, through Congress, from putting a stop to the traffic immediately at the close of the war. Now, if slavery had been a good thing, would the Fathers of the Republic have taken a step calculated to diminish its beneficent influences among themselves, and snatch the boon wholly from their posterity? These communities, by their representatives in old Independence Hall, said to the whole world of men: "We hold these truths to be self evident: that all men are created equal; that they are endowed by their Creator with certain unalienable rights; that among these are life, liberty and the pursuit of happiness." This was their majestic interpretation of the economy of the Universe. This was their lofty, and wise, and noble understanding of the justice of the Creator to His creatures. [Applause.] Yes, gentlemen, to *all* His creatures, to the whole great family of men. In their enlightened belief, nothing stamped with the Divine image and likeness was sent into the world to be trodden on, and degraded, and imbruted by its fellows. They grasped not only the whole race of man then living, but they reached forward and seized upon the farthest posterity. They erected a beacon to guide their children and their children's children, and the countless myriads who should inhabit the earth in other ages. Wise statesmen as they were, they knew the tendency of prosperity to breed tyrants, and so they established these great self-evident truths, that when in the distant future some man, some faction, some interest, should set up the doctrine that none but rich men, or none but white men, were entitled to life, liberty and the pursuit of happiness, their posterity might look up again to the

Declaration of Independence and take courage to renew the battle which their fathers began—so that truth, and justice, and mercy, and all the humane and Christian virtues might not be [546] extinguished from the land; so that no man would hereafter dare to limit and circumscribe the great principles on which the temple of liberty was being built. [Loud cheers.]

Now, my countrymen [Mr. Lincoln continued with great earnestness,] if you have been taught doctrines conflicting with the great landmarks of the Declaration of Independence; if you have listened to suggestions which would take away from its grandeur, and mutilate the fair symmetry of its proportions; if you have been inclined to believe that all men are *not* created equal in those inalienable rights enumerated by our chart of liberty, let me entreat you to come back. Return to the fountain whose waters spring close by the blood of the Revolution. Think nothing of me—take no thought for the political fate of any man whomsoever—but come back to the truths that are in the Declaration of Independence. You may do anything with me you choose, if you will but heed these sacred principles. You may not only defeat me for the Senate, but you may take me and put me to death. While pretending no indifference to earthly honors, I *do claim* to be actuated in this contest by something higher than an anxiety for office. I charge you to drop every paltry and insignificant thought for any man's success. It is nothing; I am nothing; Judge Douglas is nothing. *But do not destroy that immortal emblem of Humanity—the Declaration of American Independence.* [547]

E. Douglas at Galesburg, Ill., October 7, 1858

I tell you that this Chicago doctrine of Lincoln's—declaring that the negro and the white man are made equal by the Declaration of Independence and by Divine Providence—is a monstrous heresy. [That's so, and terrific applause.] The signers of the Declaration of Independence never dreamed of the negro when they were writing that document. They referred to white men, to men of European birth and European descent, when they declared the equality of all men. I see a gentleman there in the crowd shaking his head. Let me remind him that when Thomas Jefferson wrote that document he was the owner, and so continued until his death, of a large number of slaves. Did he intend to say in that Declaration that his negro slaves, which he held and treated as property, were created his equals by Divine law, and that he was violating the law of God every day of his life by holding them as slaves? ["No, no."] It must be borne in mind that when that Declaration was put forth every one of the thirteen colonies were slaveholding colonies, and every man who signed that instrument represented a slaveholding constituency. Recollect, also, that no one of them emancipated his slaves, much less put them on an equality with himself, after he signed the Declaration. On the contrary, they all continued to hold their negroes as slaves during the revolutionary war. Now, do you believe —are you willing to have it said—that every man who signed the Declaration of Independence declared the negro his equal, and then was hypocrite enough to continue to hold him as a slave, in violation of what he believed to be the divine law. ["No, no."] And yet when you say that the Declaration of Independence includes the negro, you charge the signers of it with hypocrisy.

I say to you, frankly, that in my opinion this government was made by our fathers on the white basis. It was made by white men for the benefit of white men and their posterity forever, and was intended to be administered by white men in all time to come. [That's so, and cheers.] [165]

F. Lincoln at Galesburg, Ill., October 7, 1858

The Judge has alluded to the Declaration of Independence, and insisted that negroes are not included in that Declaration; and that it is a slander upon the framers of that instrument, to suppose that negroes were meant therein; and he asks you: Is it possible to believe that Mr. Jefferson, who penned the immortal paper, could have supposed himself applying the language of that instrument to the negro race, and yet held a portion of that race in slavery? Would he not at once have freed them? I only have to remark upon this part of the Judge's speech, (and that, too, very briefly, for I shall not detain myself, or you, upon that point for any great length of time,) that I believe the entire records of the world, from the date of the Declaration of Independence up to within three years ago, may be searched in vain for one single affirmation, from one single man, that the negro was not included in the Declaration of Independence. I think I may defy Judge Douglas to show that he ever said so, that Washington ever said so, that any President ever said so, that any member of Congress ever said so, or that any living man upon the whole earth ever said so, until the necessities of the present policy of the Democratic party, in regard to slavery, had to invent that affirmation. [Tremendous applause.] And I will remind Judge Douglas and this audience, that while Mr. Jefferson was the owner of slaves, as undoubtedly he was, in speaking upon this very subject, he used the strong language that "he trembled for his country when he remembered that God was just;" and I will offer the highest premium in my power to Judge Douglas if he will show that he, in all his life, ever uttered a sentiment at all akin to that of Jefferson. [Great applause and cries of "Hit him again," "good," "good."] [167]

The Meaning of
the Declaration

ROBERT G. INGERSOLL

Fellow-citizens.—You have just heard read the grandest, the bravest, and the profoundest political document that was ever signed by man. It is the embodiment of physical and moral courage and of political wisdom. I say of physical courage, because it was a declaration of war against the most powerful nation then on the globe; a declaration of war by thirteen weak, unorganized colonies; a declaration of war by a few people, without military stores, without wealth, without strength, against the most powerful kingdom on the earth; a declaration of war made when the British navy, at that day the mistress of every sea, was hovering along the coast of America, looking after defenceless towns and villages to ravage and destroy. It was made when thousands of English soldiers were upon our soil, and when the principal cities of America were in the possession of the enemy. And so, I say, all things considered, it was the bravest political document ever signed by man. And if it was physically brave, the moral courage of the document is almost infinitely beyond the physical. They had the courage not only, but they had the almost infinite wisdom to declare that all men are created equal. Such things had occasionally been said by some political enthusiasts in the olden time, but for the first time in the history of the world, the representatives of a nation, the representatives of a real living, breathing, hoping people, declared that all men are created equal. With one blow, with one stroke of the pen, they struck down all the

FROM *Our National Centennial Jubilee: Orations, Addresses, and Poems Delivered on the Fourth of July, 1876, in the Several States of the Union,* ed. Frederick Saunders (New York: E. B. Treat, 1877), pp. 694–696. Original title.

cruel, heartless barriers that aristocracy, that priestcraft, that king-craft had raised between man and man. They struck down with one immortal blow, that infamous spirit of caste that makes a god [694] almost a beast, and a beast almost a god. With one word, with one blow, they wiped away and utterly destroyed all that had been done by centuries of war—centuries of hypocrisy—centuries of injustice.

What more did they do? They then declared that each man has a right to live. And what does that mean? It means that he has the right to make his living. It means that he has the right to breathe the air, to work the land, that he stands the equal of every other human being beneath the shining stars; entitled to the product of his labor —the labor of his hand and of his brain.

What more? That every man has the right to pursue his own happiness in his own way. Grander words than these have never been spoken by man.

And what more did these men say? They laid down the doctrine, that governments were instituted among men for the purpose of preserving the rights of the people. The old idea was that people existed solely for the benefit of the state—that is to say, for kings and nobles.

And what more? That the people are the source of political power. That was not only a revelation, but it was a revolution. It changed the ideas of the people with regard to the source of political power. For the first time it made human beings men. What was the old idea? The old idea was that no political power came from, nor in any manner belonged to, the people. The old idea was that the political power came from the clouds; that the political power came in some miraculous way from heaven; that it came down to kings, and queens, and robbers. That was the old idea. The nobles lived upon the labor of the people; the people had no rights; the nobles stole what they had and divided with the kings, and the kings pre-tended to divide what they stole with God Almighty. The source, then, of political power was from above. The people were responsi-ble to the nobles, the nobles to the kings, and the .people had no political rights whatever, no more than the wild beasts of the forest. The kings were responsible to God: not to the people. The kings were responsible to the clouds; not to the toiling millions they robbed and plundered.

And our forefathers, in this declaration of independence, reversed this thing, and said, No; the people, they are the source of [695] political power, and their rulers, these presidents, these kings, are but the agents and servants of the great, sublime people. For the first time, really, in the history of the world, the king was made to get off the throne and the people were royally seated thereon. The people became the sovereigns, and the old sovereigns became the servants and the agents of the people. It is hard for you and me now to imagine even the immense results of that change. It is hard for you and for me at this day to understand how thoroughly it had been ingrained in the brain of almost every man, that the king had some wonderful right over him; that in some strange way the king owned him; that in some miraculous manner he belonged, body and soul, to somebody who rode on a horse, with epaulettes on his shoulders and a tinsel crown upon his brainless head. [696]

The Strategy of Composition

WILHELM ONCKEN

Thomas Jefferson of Virginia prepared the draft [of the Declaration of Independence]; Benjamin Franklin, back from England since autumn, 1775, John Adams, Roger Sherman, and Robert Livingston were members of the drafting committee. The author and signers of the document had a very clear picture of the situation and its problems and they accordingly acted with far more sober reflection than the enthusiasts in France believed—what the latter read with rapture they also deemed a deed of purest enthusiasm. From Jefferson's personal notes we gather [719] the reasons advanced during the preliminary deliberations of Congress for the pressing necessity of a Declaration of Independence.[1] The effectiveness of these did not follow from consideration of England, with whom indeed they were already in the midst of war, nor from thoughts of sweeping the still hesitant middle Colonies to immediate union. It followed rather from the consideration that so long as the Americans themselves do nothing to prevent continued appearance as plain "rebels," neither on land nor at sea would they have the protection of international law, nor could they enter into diplomatic relations with any European power, much less form an alliance with them.

That a declaration of Independence alone could render it consistent with European delicacy, for European powers to treat with us, or even to receive an Ambassador from us:

[1] H. A. Washington, *The Writings of Thomas Jefferson* (New York: 1853), I (Autobiography), pp. 16–17.

TRANSLATED by the editor from *Das Zeitalter Friedrichs des Großen, Allgemeine Geshichte*, 3rd Ser., Vol. VIII, Pt. II (Berlin: G. Grote'sche Verlagsbuchman by Oncken are restored in English from H. A. Washington's edition of Jefferson's *Writings*. The passages by Raynal and Turgot translated into German by Oncken are rendered into English directly from the French.

That till this, they would not receive our vessels into their ports, nor acknowledge the adjudications of our courts of admiralty to be legitimate, in cases of capture of British vessels:

That though *France* and *Spain* may be jealous of our rising power, they must think [720] it will be much more formidable with the addition of Great Britain; and will therefore see it their interest to prevent a coalition; but should they refuse, we shall be but where we are; whereas without trying, we shall never know whether they will aid us or not: °

That the present campaign may be unsuccessful, and therefore we had better propose an alliance while our affairs wear a hopeful aspect:

That to wait the event of this campaign will certainly work delay, because, during the summer, France may assist us effectually, by cutting off those supplies of provisions from England and Ireland, on which the enemy's armies here are to depend; or by setting in motion the great power they have collected in the West Indies, and calling our enemy to the defence of the possessions they have there:

That it would be idle to lose time in settling the terms of alliance, till we had first determined we would enter into alliance:

That it is necessary to lose no time in opening a trade for our people, who will want clothes, and will want money too, for the payment of taxes:

And that the only misfortune is, that we did not enter into alliance with France six months sooner, as, besides opening her ports for the vent of our last year's produce, she might have marched an army into Germany, and prevented the petty princes there, from selling their unhappy subjects to subdue us.

The evident force of these considerations was the decisive factor, and now the meaning of the passage with which the Declaration of July 4 concludes, becomes clear:

We, therefore, the representatives of the United States of America in General Congress assembled, appealing to the supreme judge of the world for the rectitude of our intentions, do in the name, and by the authority of the good people of these colonies, solemnly publish and declare, that these united colonies are, and of right ought to be free and independent states; that they are absolved from all allegiance to the British crown, and that all political connection between them and the state of Great Britain is, and ought to be, totally dissolved, and that as free and independent states, they have full power to *levy war, conclude peace, contract* [721] *alliances, establish commerce,* and to do all other acts and things which independent states may of right do.[2]

° Italics supplied by Oncken.—Ed.
[2] [Italics supplied by Oncken.] The entire text with the alterations of the draft is in *Writings of Thomas Jefferson,* I, pp. 19–26.

In declaring themselves free and independent states, the rebellious Colonies claimed the rights of a belligerent power capable of making alliances, and in designating their renunciation of England as irrevocable, they meant to give a pledge to the French and Spanish Crowns which was the necessary prerequisite to any open alliance with them. We will later see with amazement what value France placed on this pledge, as she subsequently embarked on the war against England.

The Declaration—never would America again become a province of the King of England—was intended for the *governments* plagued with fear that the reunited power of England and America could one day snatch away their last colonies in the new world. The further content of the Declaration was meant for the *peoples*, and it struck quite happily the tone that promised the greatest effect upon their collaborators, namely *the French.*

Here right at the beginning they speak in solemn priestly tones:

When, in the course of human events, it becomes necessary for one people to dissolve the political bands which have connected them with another, and to assume among the powers of the earth the separate and equal station to which the laws of nature and of nature's God entitle them, a decent respect to the opinions of mankind requires that they should declare the causes which impel them to the separation.

We hold these truths to be self evident: that all men are created equal; that they are endowed by their creator with [certain] inalienable rights; that among these are life, liberty, and the pursuit of happiness; that to secure these rights, governments are instituted among men, deriving their just powers from the consent of the governed; that whenever any form of government becomes destructive of these ends, it is the right of the people to alter or to abolish it, and to institute new government, laying its foundation on such principles, and organizing its powers in such form, as to them shall seem most likely to effect their safety and happiness.

The natural right of men to equality, the natural right of nations to liberty, the dream of Rousseau, the intellectual yearning of the entire young generation that inflamed its pathos: here it was publicly claimed for the first time in a great controversy between nations and [722] formulated with the certainty of a universally valid law. It was not the audible soliloquy of enthusiastic visionaries; it was the will, the solemn vow of a contending nation, enunciated by simple colonists who knew nothing of the heartaches that oppressed the peoples of old Europe. The effect was indescribable; in seething France it worked with volcanic might. A single voice may attest it for us. In his work, *American Revolution,* Abbé Raynal speaks of the author and signers of this Declaration:

Would that I had received the genius and eloquence of the celebrated orators of Athens and Rome! With what grandeur, with what enthusiasm would I not speak of the generous men who by their patience, wisdom, and courage erected this great edifice! Hancock, Franklin, the two Adamses were the greatest actors in this intriguing episode, but they were not the only ones. Posterity will know them all. Their famous names will be transmitted to it by a more felicitous pen than mine. Marble and bronze will reveal them to the most remote centuries. Upon seeing them, the friend of liberty will feel his eyes fill with tears of delight, his heart tremble with joy. Below the bust of one of them has been written: HE TORE LIGHTNING FROM HEAVEN AND THE SCEPTER FROM TYRANTS. All will share with him the last words of this tribute.

Heroic country, my advanced age does not permit me to visit you. Never will I find myself in the midst of the worthy dignitaries of your Areopagus; never will I be present at the deliberations of your Congress. I will die without having seen the abode of tolerance, manners, law, virtue, and liberty. A free and sacred earth will not cover my ashes, though I do desire it; and my last words will be wishes addressed to heaven for your prosperity.[3]

Following the appeal to human rights in the text, is evidence of frequent encroachments upon these rights of the Americans. If this had actually happened, the fault, as we have seen, was not that of any individual will but of the active *national will of England* in Parliament, the world then first learning to what extent it had become subservient to the *commercial interests* of the merchants and manufacturers. Whoever saw liberty and tyranny struggling with one another here, could, like Turgot, attach only *one* observation to the preceding, that is,—as indeed Ireland's tale of woe already demonstrated—that

The tyranny of a people is the most cruel and intolerable of all tyrannies, one that leaves the least resource to the oppressed; because a despot, after all, is stopped by his own interest, he is checked by remorse or [723] public opinion, but a multitude takes nothing into account, never feels remorse, and attributes glory to itself when it merits the greatest shame.[4]

Now we know quite well the despotic temper of George III and the extreme personal interest he had taken on the one hand in the prosecution of John Wilkes, and on the other in the punitive laws

---

[3] *Révolution de l'Amérique* ([Stockholm:] 1781), pp. 86–87.
[4] Turgot, Letter to Dr. Price *sur les constitutions américaines,* March 28, 1778, *Œuvres,* II, p. 806.

against America; nevertheless, it was the grossest misconception, or rather disavowal, first of English constitutional law and then of the most well-known facts of contemporary history, when in the Declaration of Independence King George III was uniquely and exclusively accused as originator and executor of the 28 diverse species of genocidal crime. Only once, quite incidentally, was he thought of as doing this in conjunction "with others," i.e., Parliament, but never was there a thought of the whole duly-resolved *Law* in accordance with which his Ministers and Governors acted, and whose execution was, indeed, thoroughly frustrated by the opposition and defensiveness of the Americans. Here liberty makes a stand against despotism, the despot being not a king but an entire people, the people of England who outside of Parliament had no constitutional will, but who had sanctioned as explicitly as possible through their elections the avowed will of the country on this question in Parliament. Out of consideration for the small number of friends of America in Parliament, a very pointed passage was omitted from Jefferson's draft against the "unfeeling English brethren" who through continued re-election supported the "disturbers of harmony" with America in their injustice, and who finally are sending over not just soldiers of English blood but Scotch and foreign mercenaries.[5] But even if this had remained, the design of the whole would not thereby have been altered; there still remains standing the crying inaccuracy that instead of a people and their legislative body a king was accused who according to the most admitted tenets of English constitutional law could do no wrong at all—and yet the Americans wished to be good Englishmen, and their jurists had, as we are expressly told, devoted an exceedingly assiduous study to Blackstone's Commentaries.[6] This obscuring of the accused party was an artifice of demagogy, above all splendidly calculated for the hatred of despots in a France fresh from the school of Rousseau and Montesquieu. It would have been considerably more effective if under the alleged offenses of King George a very special one, [724] treated by Jefferson with extremely forceful language, had met with good reception:

He has waged cruel war against human nature itself, violating its most sacred rights of life and liberty in the persons of a distant people who

[5] Jefferson, I, pp. 24–25.
[6] *Cf.* pp. 658*ff.* In his Speech of March 22, 1775, Edmund Burke said that one of the largest booksellers in England had informed him that there were just about as many copies of Blackstone's Commentaries in print in America as in England. From the American side this was corroborated by Shea, *Life and Epoch of Alexander Hamilton* (Boston: 1879), p. 88.

never offended him, captivating and carrying them into slavery in another hemisphere, or to incur miserable death in their transportation thither. This piratical warfare, the opprobrium of INFIDEL powers, is the warfare of the CHRISTIAN king of Great Britain. Determined to keep open a market where MEN should be bought and sold, he has prostituted his negative for suppressing every legislative attempt to prohibit or to restrain this execrable commerce. And that this assemblage of horrors might want no fact of distinguished die, he is now exciting those very people to rise in arms among us, and to purchase that liberty of which he has deprived them, by murdering the people on whom he also obtruded them: thus paying off former crimes committed against the LIBERTIES of one people, with crimes he urges them to commit against the LIVES of another.

A scorching critique of *negro slavery*, a solemn proscription of the *slave trade* in its first manifesto, would not merely have done honor to the United States, it was really quite indispensable in a document which began with expression of the "self-evident truth" that "all men are created equal" and their right to life, liberty, and the pursuit of happiness is "inalienable," especially if one was warranted, as Jefferson at least assumed, in allowing all the crimes in the list of wicked acts of the King of England to culminate in this one. We know, unfortunately, how little the royalty of England was an accomplice in the genesis and growth of this affliction,[7] and how the guilt of George III for the continuance of the latter was understood quite differently by Jefferson's countrymen as he was now to learn. The entire passage had to be expunged, as he said in his memoirs,

in complaisance to South Carolina and Georgia, who had never attempted to restrain the importation of slaves, and who, on the contrary, still wished to continue it. Our northern brethren also, I believe, felt a little tender under those censures; for though their people had very few slaves themselves, yet they had been pretty considerable carriers of them to others.[8]

The appeal to human rights was thus only a weapon against England and a means to win over the opinion of nations, but it certainly was not itself meant to furnish the legal basis for the constitutional life of America. Since the Americans could not appeal to written law, they referred to the unwritten natural law of the philosophers; to this artifice they appended the other that all their grievances and accusations were erected exclusively against that personage of England who according to the plainest doctrines of English constitutional law could not at all be accused and also was

---

[7] *Cf.* p. 639.   [8] Jefferson, I, p. 19.

no more guilty in this affair [725] than the Ministers and both Houses of Parliament. Both were calculated to the mental state of France, where two strong feelings prevailed: one was enthusiasm for human rights, the other hatred of despots and love of liberty. The calculated effect was not wanting, but that it was calculated and how very much so, people in France did not suspect; only one man had to learn how little the "heroes of liberty" themselves felt the enthusiasm they infused others with: he was Beaumarchais. [726]

The Ethics of the

Declaration of Independence

R. M. BLACK

On the face of it, the Declaration is a strongly purposive document which the results of the century past will in the main be held to have justified.

Ethically considered, the Declaration makes pretence to the statement of four principles, which are, in order, the principle of equality, the principle of government by consent, the principle of independence, and the principle of prudence.

"Prudence will dictate that governments, long established, should not be changed for light and transient causes; and, accordingly, all experience hath shown that mankind are more disposed to suffer, while evils are sufferable, than to right themselves by abolishing the forms to which they are accustomed." But the principle of independence will dictate that, "when a long train of abuses and usurpations, pursuing invariably the same object, evinces a design to reduce them under absolute despotism, it is their right, it is their duty, to throw off such government, and to provide new guards for their future security." These principles are, perhaps, too well recognized in theory to require comment. Also evident is it that life, liberty, and the pursuit of happiness are unalienable: one cannot transfer his own nor receive another's. At the most the despot can but destroy them. If secured or perpetuated to any one, it can only be to the individual who possesses them already. To secure them, "governments are instituted among men, deriving their just powers from the consent [138] of the governed." That is, according to the Declaration, government is a common act whereto many individuals

FROM *Annals of the American Academy of Political and Social Science*, II (July, 1891), 138–144. Original title.

agree, and have a rightful voice by reason of their equality: which leads us to the first and altogether the most remarkable principle enunciated, "that all men are created equal." And this principle is the real ethical groundwork of the Declaration.

To most minds, or to a well-constituted perception at least, it would seem as if no truth could be more self-evident than that all men are created *un*-equal. On principles of causation we should also expect this to be so: for unequal conditions of parentage, birth, environment, rearing, and experience attend us all. Even allowing for the principle that plurality of causes may produce like effects, the results in the case of a numerous humanity must be various. In truth, the principle of singularity, of oddity, of numerical identity, combined with absolute idiosyncrasy, is the indelibly wrought character of every man.

Paying regard, then, only to the principle of absolute non-equality in man as expressing his true character, it is still in point to ask, What would be meant, as applied to men unequal in every particular and in total character, by the statement that "they are endowed by their Creator with certain unalienable rights; that among these are life, liberty, and the pursuit of happiness?"

First, as to the right to life. If it be true that all men are unequal *in toto*, and unequal in every particular, it follows that the life which is a man's is likewise unequal to the life of any other. The life, therefore, to which he has a right is the peculiar, individual life which is his already. For, furthermore, life apart from individuals, that is, from any individual, would be no life at all. There is no common boon of life, common as the air is common, externally to the individual. To get a taste of "life," in the vulgar sense, is to experience the things, fashions, activities, and amusements that are common. But life itself, being [139] individual to the person, a right to it can be clearly defined only as a right to be what one peculiarly is or may be.

Again, as to the rights to liberty and the pursuit of happiness. Each man being of unequalled nature, a right to liberty or the pursuit of happiness must likewise be defined as a right appertaining to that unequalled nature. Happiness indeed may be sought in common modes of living or possession. But the *pursuit*, or the bending of the active powers of the man toward an intended object, is a peculiarly personal and idiosyncratic process. And the right to it, as to liberty, can be defined clearly only as a right for what one peculiarly is or may be.

"To secure these rights," the Declaration proceeds, "governments are instituted among men." By implication, therefore, government is not for the purpose of securing happiness directly, nor good for the greatest number directly, for, furthermore, it would violate the principle of unalienable rights, for government, for any man or set of men, to dictate or assume to judge what is good or happiness for any other man or set of men. The security of personal life, liberty, and pursuits is then its first aim. It is needless to remark here upon the fact that laws affecting conduct, which at first sight would seem to transgress this principle and abridge the rights of individuals, have for their real object the better security of those rights.

Government, or a method of treatment to secure those rights, includes conversely the right of every man to be treated as a peculiar and individual entity. And at this point, though having started out with a principle apparently anomalous to the Declaration, we penetrate to the very core of its purpose, for it is every man—that is, all men equally—to whom belongs the right to be treated each as an absolutely unequalled entity, the inwardness of whose personality is a mystery alike inviolable and beyond our ken. To make use of a paradox, all men are equal, because no two are equal; all are equally unequal, equal [140] only by reason of the prevalence of this universal principle of non-equality. Were two or any number really equal then there would be a basis of classification whereby the inequality of the remainder might be distinguished. But classifications and class distinctions as applied to men, every soul of whom is in essence an original classifier, are but as scales that fall from him, and fade into insignificance before the miracle of his being. The tremendous ethical import of the Declaration is that in effect it sets up the strictly and peculiar character of prince and commoner alike, and even of the fool, as a sacred object to which all customs and traditions, all accessory marks and distinctions of power and possession, must of right give place.

When the representatives in Congress declared "that all men are created equal," it is doubtful if the true ground of the Declaration was defined, defined at least in a manner clearly obvious to all. It was the dictum of profound judgment, no doubt, but under exigent circumstances. The leaders had felt the break with England coming; they had anticipated the form the opposition would take; their attitude on this occasion was the frequent attitude of reformers who, long speechless victims, feeling rather than defining the wrongs they suffer, gradually have come to the full consciousness that the remedy lies solely in the overthrow of existing systems, and, finally, with the determined purpose to accomplish the revolution at all hazards, are ever wont to rest in justification of their action on a basis of principles affirmed to be patent to the knowledge of all men in the exercise of right reason. The principle of equality was affirmed instinctively rather than philosophically, and their declaration of it was creative rather than explanatory. They hit upon it as the principle needed to justify their end, rather than justified it or deduced their purpose from it. Certainly, they could not claim independence on the ground of superiority to England, though the latter claimed it over them. But they happily escaped the error of small minds, which is to adopt the tactics of [141] the enemy, and so, in the very act of opposing them, virtually to succumb to their methods. As the basis of an independent movement, they fortunately hit upon an independent principle, whose success was a distinct advance in the evolution of government. They could claim equality with their English brethren without shocking the intelligence of the world, and probably the real principle which justified America to civilized Europe, and, aside from considerations of policy, gained for her recognition abroad, was the conclusion which followed from the declaration of her *equality with England,* rather than the deeper principle of universal equality as applied to all persons whatsoever.

That the conception of the equality of men had not ripened into the perception of the real ground of that equality, at least in popular knowledge, is further evidenced by the fact that the principle was held in abeyance for nearly a century, while the essential manhood of an enslaved race was denied recognition. And though civil statutes of to-day recognize it, the principle of equality has hardly as yet penetrated the confines of the body social, wherein the injustice done it is of a more insidious description, which statutory remedies are inadequate to cure. Much less has it found its way to its final vantage place among the common ethical motives which govern the daily conduct of men toward men—a condition of things which Utopian schemes of universal benefactions will do well to consider. But the revolutionists, feeling the injury of unequal treatment, were driven by circumstances to adopt a conception of mankind in accordance with which the evil might be abolished. Here the conception of equality, being *for the purpose of treatment,* presented no difficulty; it meant the equal rights, privileges, protection, justice, and liberty to which, as compared with English subjects, they felt themselves entitled. The equalities and inequalities of the time were those of caste. To be equal with another meant to be treated with the same consideration, and, conversely, to have equal station and rank was [142] practically to be equal. This latter view is probably the nearest approach we can make to the spirit of the prime dictum of the Declaration, and its correctness is confirmed by the fact that the representatives of the colonies were met with the avowed purpose of considering principles of government. The whole instrument is, therefore, to be interpreted in the light of that purpose which at the time eclipsed all others. For the purpose of government it was that men were equal, that is, though they be not equal at all, yet are they to be governed with equality.

Recalling now the ethical ground of this principle of equality, which makes it eternally a true one, that every person is a unique and unequalled entity, we may see how the very fact of inequality in persons gives rise to the principle of equality of treatment, the rights to life, liberty, and the pursuit of happiness being admitted as defined at the outset without discussion. For, without knowing fully what you are, I desire to treat you with respect to these rights. Beyond the qualities which are evident, I know that you are an individual whose personality is an inscrutable mystery. However deeply I sympathize with you, or however shrewdly I diagnose you or, as they say, "size you up," nevertheless if I treat you according to my summation of your qualities only, I do you the basest injustice, and deal with you as an inferior thing, which my knowledge comprehends and is superior to. But the character of a man and my knowledge of him can be proportioned only as a surd to another quantity. If I treat a man according to my comprehension of him only, how do I know that I am not trespassing upon his right of life, liberty, or pursuits? How can I avoid thus trespassing, but by making it a universal principle of conduct to accord to every man that treatment which has regard also for the individual *inequality* of his nature? It results, therefore, that, although all differ and are unequal, yet in one transcendent respect I am, if I admit these rights, ethically [143] bound to treat all *as* equal, compassing no limitation nor detriment to life, liberty, or the pursuit of happiness.

So much in exposition of the ethical basis of the Declaration. I attempt no argument in its favor, believing that, however imperfectly legislation may embody it, the principle involved will not fail ever to commend itself to the intelligent judgment of a free people.
[144]

13

The Declaration of
Independence in the Light
of Modern Criticism

MOSES COIT TYLER

III

It can hardly be doubted that some hindrance to a right estimate of the Declaration of Independence is occasioned by either of two opposite conditions of mind, both of which are often to be met with among us: on the one hand, a condition of hereditary, uncritical awe and worship of the American Revolution and of this state paper as its absolutely perfect and glorious expression; on the other hand, a later condition of cultivated distrust of the Declaration, as a piece of writing lifted up into inordinate renown by the passionate and heroic circumstances of its origin, and ever since then extolled beyond reason by the blind energy of patriotic enthusiasm. Turning from the former state of mind,—which obviously calls for no further comment,—we may note, as a partial illustration of the latter, that American confidence in the supreme intellectual merit of this all-famous document received a serious wound, some forty years ago, from the hand of Rufus Choate, when, with a courage greater than would now be required for such an act, he characterized it as made up of "glittering and sounding generalities of natural right." [1] What the great advocate then so unhesitantly suggested, many a [498]

[1] "Letter of Rufus Choate to the Whigs of Maine," 1856.

FROM *The Literary History of the American Revolution, 1763–1783*, Vol. I (New York: G. P. Putnam's Sons, 1897), pp. 498–521. An earlier version of Tyler's essay appeared under the title used here.

thoughtful American since then has at least suspected,—that this famous proclamation, as a piece of political literature, cannot stand the test of modern analysis; that it belongs to the immense class of over-praised productions; that it is, in fact, a stately patchwork of sweeping propositions of somewhat doubtful validity; that it has long imposed upon mankind by the well-known effectiveness of verbal glitter and sound; that, at the best, it is an example of florid political declamation belonging to the sophomoric period of our national life—a period which, as we flatter ourselves, we have now outgrown.

Nevertheless, it is to be noted that, whatever authority the Declaration of Independence has acquired in the world, has been due to no lack of criticism, either at the time of its first appearance or since then,—a fact which seems to tell in favor of its essential worth and strength. From the date of its original publication down to the present moment, it has been attacked again and again, either in anger or in contempt, by friends as well as by enemies of the American Revolution, by liberals in politics as well as by conservatives. It has been censured for its substance, it has been censured for its form: for its misstatements of fact, for its fallacies in reasoning; for its audacious novelties and paradoxes, for its total lack of all novelty, for its repetition of old and threadbare statements, even for its downright plagiarisms; finally, for its grandiose and vaporing style.

IV

One of the earliest and ablest of its assailants was Thomas Hutchinson, the last civil governor of the colony of Massachusetts, who, being stranded in London by the political storm which had blown him thither, published there, in the autumn of 1776, his "Strictures upon the Declaration of the Congress at Philadelphia" [2]; wherein, with an [499] unsurpassed knowledge of the origin of this controversy, and with an unsurpassed acumen in the discussion of it, he traverses the entire document, paragraph by paragraph, for the purpose of showing that its allegations in support of American Independence are "false and frivolous." [3]

A better written, and, upon the whole, a more effective arraignment of the great Declaration, was the celebrated pamphlet by an

---

[2] His pamphlet is dated October 15, 1776. The copy of it now before me, the property of Cornell University, is the very copy presented "To Sir Francis Bernard, Bart., From the Author."

[3] "Strictures," etc., 3.

English barrister, John Lind, "An Answer to the Declaration of the American Congress,"—a pamphlet evidently written at the instigation of the ministry, and sent abroad under its approval. Here, again, the manifesto of Congress is subjected to a searching criticism, in order to show that the theory of government put forward in its preamble is "absurd and visionary"[4]; that its political maxims are not only "repugnant to the British constitution" but "subversive of every actual or imaginable kind of government"[5]; and that its specific charges against the king and parliament are "calumnies,"[6]— since they allege as usurpations and as encroachments certain acts of government under George the Third identical in character with those which had been "constantly exercised by his predecessors and their parliaments," and which had been on many occasions recognized as constitutional by the American colonial assemblies.[7] It is doubtful if any disinterested student of history, any competent judge of reasoning, will now deny to this pamphlet the praise of making out a strong case against the historical accuracy and the logical soundness of many parts of the Declaration of Independence.

Undoubtedly, the force of such censures is for us much broken by the fact, that those censures proceeded from men who were themselves partisans in the Revolutionary controversy and bitterly hostile to the whole movement which the Declaration was intended to justify. Such is not the case, however, with the leading modern English critics of the [500] same document, who, while blaming in severe terms the policy of the British government toward the Thirteen Colonies, have also found much to abate from the confidence due to this official announcement of the reasons for our secession from the empire. For example, Earl Russell, after frankly saying that the great disruption proclaimed by the Declaration of Independence, was a result which Great Britain had "used every means most fitted to bring about," such as "vacillation in council, harshness in language, feebleness in execution, disregard of American sympathies and affections," also pointed out that "the truth of this memorable Declaration" was "warped" by "one singular defect," namely, its exclusive and excessive arraignment of George the Third "as a single and despotic tyrant," much like Philip the Second to the people of the Netherlands.[8]

This temperate criticism from an able and a liberal English states-

4 "An Answer," etc., 119.   5 Ibid.   6 Ibid. 5.   7 Ibid. 123–130.
8 Russell, Lord John, "Memorials and Correspondence of Charles James Fox,"
i. 151–152.

man of the present century, may be said to touch the very core of the problem as to the historic justice of our great indictment of the last king of America; and there is deep significance in the fact, that this is the very criticism upon the document, which, as John Adams tells us, he himself had in mind when it was first submitted to him in committee, and even when, shortly afterwards, he advocated its adoption by Congress. After mentioning certain things in it with which he was delighted, he adds: "There were other expressions which I would not have inserted if I had drawn it up,—particularly that which called the king tyrant. I thought this too personal; for I never believed George to be a tyrant in disposition and in nature. I always believed him to be deceived by his courtiers on both sides of the Atlantic, and, in his official capacity only, cruel. I thought the expression too passionate, and too much like scolding, for so grave and solemn a document; but, as Franklin and Sherman were to inspect it afterwards, I [501] thought it would not become me to strike it out. I consented to report it." [9]

A more minute and a more poignant criticism of the Declaration of Independence has been made in recent years by still another English writer of liberal tendencies, who, however, in his capacity as critic, seems here to labor under the disadvantage of having transferred to the document which he undertakes to judge, much of the extreme dislike which he has for the man who wrote it,—whom, indeed, he regards as a sophist, as a demagogue, as quite capable of inveracity in speech, and as bearing some resemblance to Robespierre "in his feline nature, his malignant egotism, and his intense suspiciousness, as well as in his bloodyminded, yet possibly sincere, philanthropy." [10] In the opinion of Professor Goldwin Smith, our great national manifesto is written "in a highly rhetorical strain" [11]; "it opens with sweeping aphorisms about the natural rights of man,

[9] "The Works of John Adams," ii. 514 n. The distinction here made by John Adams between the personal and the official character of George III., is quite pointless in its application to the Declaration of Independence; since it is of the King's official character only that the Declaration speaks. Moreover, John Adams's testimony in 1822 that he "never believed George to be a tyrant in disposition and in nature," is completely destroyed by John Adams's own testimony on that subject as recorded at an earlier period of his life. For example, in 1780, in a letter to M. Dumas, he thus speaks of George III.—"Europe, in general, is much mistaken in that character; it is a pity that he should be believed to be so amiable; the truth is far otherwise. *Nerone neronior* is nearer the truth." Ibid. vii. 327.

[10] Goldwin Smith, in "The Nineteenth Century," No. 131, January, 1888, p. 109.

[11] "The United States. An Outline of Political History," 88.

at which political science now smiles, and which . . . might seem strange when framed for slave-holding communities by a publicist who himself held slaves" [12], while, in its specifications of facts, it "is not more scrupulously truthful than are the general utterances" [13] of the statesman who was its scribe. Its charges that the several offensive acts of the king, besides "evincing a design to [502] reduce the colonists under absolute despotism," "all had as their direct object the establishment of an absolute tyranny," are simply "propositions which history cannot accept." [14] Moreover, the Declaration "blinks the fact that many of the acts, styled steps of usurpation, were measures of repression which, however unwise or excessive, had been provoked by popular outrage." [15] "No government could allow its officers to be assaulted and their houses sacked, its loyal lieges to be tarred and feathered, or the property of merchants sailing under its flag to be thrown by lawless hands into the sea." [16] Even "the preposterous violence and the manifest insincerity of the suppressed clause" against slavery and the slave-trade, "are enough to create suspicion as to the spirit in which the whole document was framed." [17]

V

Finally, as has been already intimated, not even among Americans themselves has the Declaration of Independence been permitted to pass on into the enjoyment of its superb renown, without much critical disparagement at the hands of statesmen and historians. No doubt Calhoun had its preamble in mind, when he declared that "nothing can be more unfounded and false" than "the prevalent opinion that all men are born free and equal"; for "it rests upon the assumption of a fact which is contrary to universal observation." [18] Of course, all Americans who have shared to any extent in Calhoun's doctrines respecting human society, could hardly fail to agree with him in regarding as fallacious and worthless those general propositions in the Declaration which seem to constitute its logical starting point, as well as its ultimate defense. [503]

Perhaps, however, the most frequent form of disparagement to which Jefferson's great state paper has been subjected among us, is that which would minimize his merit in composing it, by denying to it the merit of originality. For example, Richard Henry Lee sneered

[12] Ibid. 87–88.   [13] "The Nineteenth Century," No. 131, p. 111.
[14] "The United States," etc., 88.   [15] Ibid.
[16] "The Nineteenth Century," No. 131, p. 111.   [17] Ibid.
[18] "A Disquisition on Government," in "The Works of John C. Calhoun," i. 57.

at it as a thing "copied from Locke's treatise on government." [19]
The author of a life of Jefferson, published in the year of Jefferson's
retirement from the presidency, suggests that the credit of having
composed the Declaration of Independence "has been perhaps more
generally, than truly, given by the public" to that great man.[20]
Charles Campbell, the historian of Virginia, intimates that some
expressions in the document were taken without acknowledgment
from Aphra Behn's tragi-comedy, "The Widow Ranter, or, The History of Bacon in Virginia." [21] John Stockton Littell describes the
Declaration of Independence as "that enduring monument at once
of patriotism, and of genius and skill in the art of appropriation,"—
asserting that "for the sentiments and much of the language" of it,
Jefferson was indebted to Chief Justice Drayton's charge to the
grand jury of Charleston delivered in April, 1776, as well as to the
declaration of independence said to have been adopted by some
citizens of Mecklenburg County, North Carolina, in May, 1775.[22]
Even the latest and most critical editor of the writings of Jefferson
calls attention to the fact, that a glance at the declaration of rights,
as adopted by Virginia on the 12th of June, 1776, "would seem to
indicate the source from which Jefferson derived a most important
and popular part" of his famous production.[23] By no one, however,
has the charge of a lack of originality been pressed with so much
decisiveness as by John Adams, who took evident pleasure in speaking of it as a document in which were merely [504] "recapitulated"
previous and well-known statements of American rights and
wrongs,[24] and who, as late as in the year 1822, deliberately wrote
that "there is not an idea in it but what had been hackneyed in
Congress for two years before. The substance of it is contained in
the declaration of rights and the violation of those rights, in the
journals of Congress, in 1774. Indeed, the essence of it is contained
in a pamphlet, voted and printed by the town of Boston, before the
first Congress met, composed by James Otis, as I suppose, in one of
his lucid intervals, and pruned and polished by Samuel Adams." [25]

[19] "The Writings of Thomas Jefferson," H. A. Washington ed., vii. 305.
[20] Stephen Cullen Carpenter, "Memoirs of Thomas Jefferson," i. 11.
[21] "History of Virginia," 317.
[22] "Graydon's Men and Times of the American Revolution," 323 n.
[23] Paul Leicester Ford, "The Writings of Thomas Jefferson," i. Introd. xxvi.
[24] "The Works of John Adams," ii. 377.
[25] Ibid. 514 n. Thus, the ingenuous reader has the happiness of seeing the
eternal fitness of things complied with, and the chief intellectual merit of the
Declaration of Independence brought back to the place where it belongs, and
there divided between the town of Boston, James Otis, and the Adams family.

VI

Perhaps nowhere in our literature would it be possible to find a criticism brought forward by a really able man against any piece of writing, less applicable to the case, and of less force or value, than is this particular criticism by John Adams and others, as to the lack of originality in the Declaration of Independence. Indeed, for such a paper as Jefferson was commissioned to write, the one quality which it could not properly have had—the one quality which would have been fatal to its acceptance either by the American Congress or by the American people—is originality. They were then at the culmination of a tremendous controversy over alleged grievances of the most serious kind—a controversy that had been fiercely raging for at least twelve years. In the course of that long dispute, every phase of it, whether as to abstract right or constitutional privilege or personal procedure, had been presented in almost every conceivable form of speech. At last, they had resolved, in view of all this experience, no longer to prosecute the controversy as [505] members of the empire: they had resolved to revolt, and casting off forever their ancient fealty to the British crown, to separate from the empire, and to establish themselves as a new nation among the nations of the earth. In this emergency, as it happened, Jefferson was called upon to put into form a suitable statement of the chief considerations which prompted them to this great act of revolution, and which, as they believed, justified it. What, then, was Jefferson to do? Was he to regard himself as a mere literary essayist, set to produce before the world a sort of prize dissertation,—a calm, analytic, judicial treatise on history and politics with a particular application to Anglo-American affairs,—one essential merit of which would be its originality as a contribution to historical and political literature? Was he not, rather, to regard himself as, for the time being, the very mouthpiece and prophet of the people whom he represented, and as such required to bring together and to set in order, in their name, not what was new, but what was old; to gather up into his own soul, as much as possible, whatever was then also in their souls—their very thoughts and passions, their ideas of constitutional law, their interpretations of fact, their opinions as to men and as to events in all that ugly quarrel; their notions of justice, of civic dignity, of human rights; finally, their memories of wrongs which seemed to them intolerable, especially of wrongs inflicted upon them during those twelve years by the hands of insolent and brutal men, in the name of the king, and by his apparent command?

Moreover, as the nature of the task laid upon him made it necessary that he should thus state, as the reasons for their intended act, those very considerations both as to fact and as to opinion which had actually operated upon their minds, so did it require him to do so, to some extent, in the very language which the people themselves, in their more formal and deliberate utterances, had all along been using. In the development of political life in England and America, there had already been created a vast literature of [506] constitutional progress,—a literature common to both portions of the English race, pervaded by its own stately traditions, and reverberating certain great phrases which formed, as one may say, almost the vernacular of English justice, and of English aspiration for a free, manly, and orderly political life. In this vernacular the Declaration of Independence was written. The phraseology thus characteristic of it, is the very phraseology of the champions of constitutional expansion, of civic dignity and of progress, within the English race ever since Magna Charta; of the great state papers of English freedom in the seventeenth century, particularly the Petition of Right in 1629, and the Bill of Rights in 1689; of the great English charters for colonization in America; of the great English exponents of legal and political progress,—Sir Edward Coke, John Milton, Algernon Sidney, John Locke; finally, of the great American exponents of political liberty and of the chief representative bodies, whether local or general, which had convened in America from the time of the Stamp Act Congress until that of the Congress which resolved upon our Independence. To say, therefore, that the official Declaration of that resolve is a paper made up of the very opinions, beliefs, unbeliefs, the very sentiments, prejudices, passions, even the errors in judgment and the personal misconstructions—if they were such—which then actually impelled the American people to that mighty act, and that all these are expressed in the very phrases which they had been accustomed to use, is to pay to that state paper the highest tribute as to its fitness for the purpose for which it was framed.

Of much of this, also, Jefferson himself seems to have been conscious; and perhaps never does he rise before us with more dignity, with more truth, than when, late in his lifetime, hurt by the captious and jangling words of disparagement then recently put into writing by his old comrade, to the effect that the Declaration of Independence "contained no new ideas, that it is a commonplace compilation, its sentiments hackneyed in Congress for two years before, and its [507] essence contained in Otis's pamphlet," Jefferson quietly replied that perhaps these statements might "all be true: of that I am not to be the judge. . . . Whether I had gathered my ideas from reading or reflection, I do not know. I know only that I turned to neither book nor pamphlet while writing it. I did not consider it as any part of my charge to invent new ideas altogether, and to offer no sentiment which had ever been expressed before." [26]

Before passing from this phase of the subject, however, it should be added that, while the Declaration of Independence lacks originality in the sense just indicated, in another and perhaps in a higher sense, it possesses originality—it is individualized by the character and the genius of its author. Jefferson gathered up the thoughts and emotions and even the characteristic phrases of the people for whom he wrote, and these he perfectly incorporated with what was already in his own mind, and then to the music of his own keen, rich, passionate, and enkindling style, he mustered them into that stately and triumphant procession wherein, as some of us still think, they will go marching on to the world's end.

There were then in Congress several other men who could have written the Declaration of Independence, and written it well— notably, Franklin, either of the two Adamses, Richard Henry Lee, William Livingston, and, best of all—but for his own opposition to the measure—John Dickinson; but had any one of these other men written the Declaration of Independence, while it would have contained, doubtless, nearly the same topics and nearly the same great formulas of political statement, it would yet have been a wholly different composition from this of Jefferson's. No one at all familiar with his other writings as well as with the writings of his chief contemporaries, could ever have had a moment's doubt, even if the fact were not already notorious, [508] that this document was by Jefferson. He put into it something that was his own, and that no one else could have put there. He put himself into it,—his own genius, his own moral force, his faith in God, his faith in ideas, his love of innovation, his passion for progress, his invincible enthusiasm, his intolerence of prescription, of injustice, of cruelty, his sympathy, his clarity of vision, his affluence of diction, his power to fling out great

[26] "The Writings of Thomas Jefferson," H. A. Washington ed., vii. 305. This was written to Madison, 30 August, 1823, and should be compared with Madison's letter in reply, 6 September, 1823: "Letters and Other Writings of James Madison," iii. 336–337.

phrases which will long fire and cheer the souls of men struggling against political unrighteousness. And herein lies its essential originality, perhaps the most precious, and indeed almost the only, originality ever attaching to any great literary product that is representative of its time. He made for himself no improper claim, therefore, when he directed that upon the granite obelisk at his grave should be carved the words,—"Here was buried Thomas Jefferson, author of the Declaration of Independence."[27]

VII

If the Declaration of Independence is now to be fairly judged by us, it must be judged with reference to what it was intended to be—namely, an impassioned manifesto of one party, and that the weaker party, in a violent race quarrel; of a party resolved, at last, upon the extremity of revolution, and already menaced by the inconceivable disaster of being defeated in the very act of armed rebellion against the mightiest military power on earth. This manifesto, then, is not to be censured because, being avowedly a statement of its own side of the quarrel, it does not also contain a moderate and judicial statement of the opposite side; or because, being necessarily partisan in method, it is likewise both partisan and vehement in tone; or because it bristles with accusations against the enemy so fierce and so unqualified as now to seem in some respects overdrawn; or because it resounds with certain great aphorisms about the [509] natural rights of man, at which, indeed, political science cannot now smile except to its own discomfiture and shame —aphorisms which are likely to abide in this world as the chief source and inspiration of heroic enterprises among men for self-deliverance from oppression.

Taking into account, therefore, as we are bound to do, the circumstances of its origin, and especially its purpose as a solemn and piercing appeal to mankind, on behalf of a small and weak nation against the alleged injustice and cruelty of a great and powerful one, it still remains our duty to enquire whether, as has been asserted in our time, history must set aside either of the two central charges embodied in the Declaration of Independence.

The first of these charges affirms that the several acts complained of by the colonists, evinced "a design to reduce them under absolute despotism," and had as their "direct object the establishment of an

[27] Randall, "The Life of Thomas Jefferson," iii. 563.

absolute tyranny" over the American people. Was this, indeed, a groundless charge, in the sense intended by the words "despotism" and "tyranny,"—that is, in the sense commonly given to those words in the usage of the English-speaking race? According to that usage, it was not an oriental despotism that was meant, nor a Greek tyranny, nor a Roman, nor a Spanish. The sort of despot, the sort of tyrant, whom the English people, ever since the time of King John and especially during the period of the Stuarts, had been accustomed to look for and to guard against, was the sort of tyrant or despot that could be evolved out of the conditions of English political life. Furthermore, he was not by them expected to appear among them at the outset in the fully developed shape of a Philip or an Alva in the Netherlands. They were able to recognize him, they were prepared to resist him, in the earliest and most incipient stage of his being—at the moment, in fact, when he should make his first attempt to gain all power over his people by assuming the single power to take their property without their consent. Hence it was, as Edmund Burke pointed out in the house [510] of commons only a few weeks before the American Revolution entered upon its military phase, that in England "the great contests for freedom . . . were from the earliest times chiefly upon the question of taxing. Most of the contests in the ancient commonwealths turned primarily on the right of election of magistrates, or on the balance among the several orders of the state. The question of money was not with them so immediate. But in England it was otherwise. On this point of taxes the ablest pens and most eloquent tongues have been exercised, the greatest spirits have acted and suffered. . . . They took infinite pains to inculcate, as a fundamental principle, that in all monarchies the people must in effect themselves, mediately or immediately, possess the power of granting their own money, or no shadow of liberty could subsist. The colonies draw from you, as with their life-blood, these ideas and principles. Their love of liberty, as with you, fixed and attached on this specific point of taxing. Liberty might be safe or might be endangered in twenty other particulars without their being much pleased or alarmed. Here they felt its pulse; and as they found that beat, they thought themselves sick or sound." [28]

Accordingly, the meaning which the English race on both sides of the Atlantic were accustomed to attach to the words "tyranny" and "despotism," was a meaning to some degree ideal: it was a meaning

[28] Speech on moving his "Resolutions for Conciliation with the Colonies," March 22, 1775. "The Works of Edmund Burke," ii. 120–121.

drawn from the extraordinary political sagacity with which that race is endowed, from their extraordinary sensitiveness as to the use of the taxing-power in government, from their instinctive perception of the commanding place of the taxing-power among all the other forms of power in the state, from their perfect assurance that he who holds the purse with the power to fill it and to empty it, holds the key of the situation,—can maintain an army of his own, can rule without consulting parliament, can silence criticism, can crush opposition, can [511] strip his subjects of every vestige of political life; in other words, he can make slaves of them, he can make a despot and a tyrant of himself. Therefore, the system which in the end might develop into results so palpably tyrannic and despotic, they bluntly called a tyranny and a despotism in the beginning. To say, therefore, that the Declaration of Independence did the same, is to say that it spoke good English. Of course, history will be ready to set aside the charge thus made in language not at all liable to be misunderstood, just so soon as history is ready to set aside the common opinion that the several acts of the British government, from 1763 to 1776, for laying and enforcing taxation in America, did evince a somewhat particular and systematic design to take away some portion of the property of the American people without their consent.

The second of the two great charges contained in the Declaration of Independence, while intimating that some share in the blame is due to the British parliament and to the British people, yet fastens upon the king himself as the one person chiefly responsible for the scheme of American tyranny therein set forth, and culminates in the frank description of him as "a prince whose character is thus marked by every act which may define a tyrant." Is this accusation of George the Third now to be set aside as unhistoric? Was that king, or was he not, chiefly responsible for the American policy of the British government between the years 1763 and 1776? If he was so, then the historic soundness of the most important portion of the Declaration of Independence is vindicated.

Fortunately, this question can be answered without hesitation, and in few words; and for these few words, an American writer of to-day, conscious of his own bias of nationality, will rightly prefer to cite such as have been uttered by the ablest English historians of our time, who have dealt with the subject. Upon their statements alone it must be concluded, that George the Third ascended his throne with the fixed purpose of resuming to the crown [512] many of those powers which by the constitution of England did not then belong to it, and that in this purpose, at least during the first twenty-five years of his reign, he substantially succeeded,—himself determining what should be the policy of each administration, what opinions his ministers should advocate in parliament, and what measures parliament itself should adopt. "The king desired," says Sir Erskine May, "to undertake personally the chief administration of public affairs, to direct the policy of his ministers, and himself to distribute the patronage of the crown. He was ambitious not only to reign, but to govern." "Strong as were the ministers, the king was resolved to wrest all power from their hands, and to exercise it himself." "But what was this, in effect, but to assert that the king should be his own minister? . . . The king's tactics were fraught with danger, as well to the crown itself, as to the constitutional liberties of the people." [29]

Already, prior to the year 1778, according to Lecky, the king had "laboriously built up" in England a "system of personal government"; and it was because he was unwilling to have this system disturbed, that he then refused, "in defiance of the most earnest representations of his own minister and of the most eminent politicians of every party . . . to send for the greatest of living statesmen at the moment when the empire appeared to be in the very agonies of dissolution. . . . Either Chatham or Rockingham would have insisted that the policy of the country should be directed by its responsible ministers, and not dictated by an irresponsible sovereign." This refusal of the king to adopt the course which was called for by the constitution, and which would have taken the control of the policy of the government out of his hands, was, according to the same great historian, an act "the most criminal in the whole reign of George the Third, . . . as criminal as [513] any of those acts which led Charles the First to the scaffold." [30]

Even so early as the year 1768, according to John Richard Green, "George the Third had at last reached his aim." In the early days of the ministry which began in that year, "this influence was felt to be predominant. In its later and more disastrous days it was supreme; for Lord North, who became the head of the ministry on Grafton's retirement in 1770, was the mere mouthpiece of the king. 'Not only did he direct the minister,' a careful observer tells us, 'in all impor-

---

[29] These sentences occur in the chapter on "The Influence of the Crown during the Reign of George III.," in Sir Erskine May's "Constitutional History of England," i. 11, 12, 14–15.

[30] "A History of England in the Eighteenth Century," iv. 457–458.

tant matters of foreign and domestic policy, but he instructed him as to the management of debates in parliament, suggested what motions should be made or opposed, and how measures should be carried. He reserved for himself all the patronage, he arranged the whole cast of the administration, settled the relative place and pretensions of ministers of state, law officers, and members of the household, nominated and promoted the English and Scotch judges, appointed and translated bishops and deans, and dispensed other preferments in the church. He disposed of military governments, regiments, and commissions, and himself ordered the marching of troops. He gave and refused titles, honors, and pensions.' All this immense patronage was steadily used for the creation and maintenance of a party in both houses of parliament attached to the king himself. . . . George was, in fact, sole minister during the fifteen years which followed; and the shame of the darkest hour of English history lies wholly at his door." [31]

Surely, until these tremendous verdicts of English history shall be set aside, there need be no anxiety in any quarter as to the historic soundness of the two great accusations which together make up the principal portion of the Declaration of Independence. In the presence of these verdicts, also, even the passion, the intensity of language, in [514] which those accusations are uttered, seem to find a perfect justification. Indeed, in the light of the most recent and most unprejudiced expert testimony, the whole document, both in its substance and in its form, seems to have been the logical response of a nation of brave men to the great words of the greatest of English statesmen, as spoken in the house of commons precisely ten years before: "This kingdom has no right to lay a tax on the colonies.[32] . . . Sir, I rejoice that America has resisted. Three millions of people so dead to all the feelings of liberty as voluntarily to submit to be slaves, would have been fit instruments to have made slaves of the rest." [33]

VIII

It is proper for us to remember that what we call criticism, is not the only valid test of the genuineness and worth of any piece of writing of great practical interest to mankind: there is, also, the test of actual use and service in the world, in direct contact with the

---

[31] "A Short History of the English People," 736–737.
[32] "The Celebrated Speech of a Celebrated Commoner," London, 1766, p. 5.
[33] Ibid. 12.

common sense and the moral sense of large masses of men, under various conditions, and for a long period. Probably no writing which is not essentially sound and true has ever survived this test.

Neither from this test has the great Declaration any need to shrink. Probably no public paper ever more perfectly satisfied the immediate purposes for which it was sent forth. From one end of the country to the other, and as fast as it could be spread among the people, it was greeted in public and in private with every demonstration of approval and delight.[34] To a marvelous degree, it quickened the friends of the Revolution for their great task. "This Declaration," wrote one of its signers but a few days after it had been [515] proclaimed, "has had a glorious effect—has made these colonies all alive." [35] "With the Independency of the American States," said another political leader a few weeks later, "a new era in politics has commenced. Every consideration respecting the propriety or impropriety of a separation from Britain is now entirely out of the question. . . . Our future happiness or misery, therefore, as a people, will depend entirely upon ourselves." [36] Six years afterward, in a review of the whole struggle, a great American scholar expressed his sense of the relation of this document to it, by saying, that "into the monumental act of Independence," Jefferson had "poured the soul of the continent." [37]

Moreover, during the century and a quarter since the close of the Revolution, the influence of this state paper on the political character and the political conduct of the American people has been great beyond all calculation. For example, after we had achieved our own national deliverance, and had advanced into that enormous and somewhat corrupting material prosperity which followed the adoption of the constitution, the development of the cotton interest, and the expansion of the republic into a trans-continental power, we fell, as is now most apparent, under an appalling national temptation,— the temptation to forget, or to repudiate, or to refuse to apply to the case of our human brethren in bondage, the very principles which

[34] Frank Moore, in his "Diary of the American Revolution," i. 269–285, has given extracts from the American newspapers for July and August, 1776, describing the official and popular demonstrations in many of the States at the first reading of the Declaration.

[35] William Whipple, of New Hampshire, in Force, "American Archives," 6th series, i. 368.

[36] Jonathan Elmer, of New Jersey, given in Moore, "Diary of the American Revolution," i. 279–280.

[37] Ezra Stiles, president of Yale College, in Connecticut election sermon, for 1783, p. 46.

we ourselves had once proclaimed as the basis of every rightful government, and as the ultimate source of our own claim to an untrammeled national life. The prodigious service rendered to us in this awful moral emergency by the Declaration of Independence was, that its public repetition, at least once every year, in the hearing of vast throngs of the American [516] people, in every portion of the republic, kept constantly before our minds, in a form of almost religious sanctity, those few great ideas as to the dignity of human nature, and the sacredness of personality, and the indestructible rights of man as mere man, with which we had so gloriously identified the beginnings of our national existence, and upon which we had proceeded to erect all our political institutions both for the nation and for the States. It did, indeed, at last become very hard for us to listen each year to the preamble of the Declaration of Independence, and still to remain the owners and users and catchers of slaves; still harder, to accept the doctrine that the righteousness and prosperity of slavery was to be taken as the dominant policy of the nation. The logic of Calhoun was as flawless as usual, when he concluded that the chief obstruction in the way of his system, was the preamble of the Declaration of Independence. Had it not been for the inviolable sacredness given by it to those sweeping aphorisms about the natural rights of man, it may be doubted whether, under the vast practical inducements involved, Calhoun might not have succeeded in winning over an immense majority of the American people to the support of his compact and plausible scheme for making slavery the basis of the republic. It was the preamble of the Declaration of Independence which elected Lincoln, which sent forth the Emancipation Proclamation, which gave victory to Grant, which ratified the Thirteenth Amendment.

Moreover, we cannot doubt that the permanent effects of the great Declaration on the political and even the ethical ideals of the American people are wider and deeper than can be measured by our experience in grappling with any single political problem; for they touch all the spiritual springs of American national character, and they create, for us and for all human beings, a new standard of political justice and a new principle in the science of government. "Much ridicule, a little of it not altogether undeserved," says a brilliant English scholar of our time, who is also [517] nobly distinguished in the sphere of English statesmanship, "has been thrown upon the opening clause of the Declaration of Independence, which asserts the inherent natural right of man to enjoy life and liberty, with the means of acquiring and possessing property, and pursuing and obtaining happiness and safety. Yet there is an implied corollary in this which enjoins the highest morality that in our present state we are able to think of as possible. If happiness is the right of our neighbor, then not to hinder him but to help him in its pursuit, must plainly be our duty. If all men have a claim, then each man is under an obligation. The corollary thus involved is the corner-stone of morality. It was an act of good augury thus to inscribe happiness as entering at once into the right of all, and into the duty of all, in the very head and front of the new charter, as the base of a national existence, and the first principle of a national government. The omen has not been falsified. The Americans have been true to their first doctrine. They have never swerved aside to set up caste and privilege, to lay down the doctrine that one man's happiness ought to be an object of greater solicitude to society than any other man's, or that one order should be encouraged to seek its prosperity through the depression of any other order. Their example proved infectious. The assertion in the New World, that men have a right to happiness and an obligation to promote the happiness of one another, struck a spark in the Old World. Political construction in America immediately preceded the last violent stage of demolition in Europe." [38]

We shall not here attempt to delineate the influence of this state paper upon mankind in general. Of course, the emergence of the American Republic as an imposing world-power is a phenomenon which has now for many years attracted the attention of the human race. Surely, no slight effect must have resulted from the fact that, among all civilized peoples, the one American document best known, is [518] the Declaration of Independence,[39] and that thus the spectacle of so vast and beneficent a political success has been everywhere associated with the assertion of the natural rights of man. "The doctrines it contained," says Buckle, "were not merely welcomed by a majority of the French nation, but even the government itself was unable to withstand the general feeling." [40] "Its effect in hastening the approach of the French Revolution . . . was indeed most remarkable." [41] Elsewhere, also, in many lands, among many peoples, it has been appealed to again and again as an inspira-

[38] John Morley, "Edmund Burke: A Historical Study," 161–162.
[39] The editor of the latest edition of "The Writings of Thomas Jefferson," i. Introd. xxv., does not shrink from calling it "the paper which is probably the best known that ever came from the pen of an individual."
[40] "History of Civilization in England," 846.   [41] Ibid. 847.

tion for political courage, as a model for political conduct; and if, as the brilliant English historian just cited has affirmed, "that noble Declaration . . . ought to be hung up in the nursery of every king, and blazoned on the porch of every royal palace," [42] it is because it has become the classic statement of political truths which must at last abolish kings altogether, or else teach them to identify their existence with the dignity and happiness of human nature.

IX

It would be unfitting, in a work like the present, to treat of the Declaration of Independence without making more than an incidental reference to its purely literary character.

Very likely, most writings—even most writings of genuine and high quality—have had the misfortune of being read too little. There is, however, a misfortune—perhaps, a greater misfortune—which has overtaken some literary compositions, and these not necessarily the noblest and the best,—the misfortune of being read too much. At any rate, the writer of a piece of literature which has been neglected, need not be refused the consolation he may get from reflecting that he is, at least, not the writer of a piece of literature which has become hackneyed. Just this is the [519] sort of calamity which seems to have befallen the Declaration of Independence. Is it, indeed, possible for us Americans, near the close of the nineteenth century, to be entirely just to the literary quality of this most monumental document—this much belauded, much bespouted, much beflouted document?—since, in order to be so, we need to rid ourselves, if we can, of the obstreperous memories of a lifetime of Independence Days, and to unlink and disperse the associations which have somehow confounded Jefferson's masterpiece with the rattle of fire-crackers, with the flash and the splutter of burning tar-barrels, and with that unreserved, that gyratory and perspiratory, eloquence now for more than a hundred years consecrated to the return of our fateful Fourth of July.

Had the Declaration of Independence been, what many a revolutionary state paper is, a clumsy, verbose, and vaporing production, not even the robust literary taste and the all-forgiving patriotism of the American people could have endured the weariness, the nausea, of hearing its repetition, in ten thousand different places, at least once every year, for so long a period. Nothing which has not su-

[42] Ibid. 846.

preme literary merit has ever triumphantly endured such an ordeal, or ever been subjected to it. No man can adequately explain the persistent fascination which this state-paper has had, and which it still has, for the American people, or for its undiminished power over them, without taking into account its extraordinary literary merits—its possession of the witchery of true substance wedded to perfect form:—its massiveness and incisiveness of thought, its art in the marshaling of the topics with which it deals, its symmetry, its energy, the definiteness and limpidity of its statements,[43] its [520] exquisite diction—at once terse, musical, and electrical; and, as an essential part of this literary outfit, many of those spiritual notes which can attract and enthrall our hearts,—veneration for God, veneration for man, veneration for principle, respect for public opinion, moral earnestness, moral courage, optimism, a stately and noble pathos, finally, self-sacrificing devotion to a cause so great as to be herein identified with the happiness, not of one people only, or of one race only, but of human nature itself.

Upon the whole, this is the most commanding and the most pathetic utterance, in any age, in any language, of national grievances and of national purposes; having a Demosthenic momentum of thought, and a fervor of emotional appeal such as Tyrtæus might have put into his war-songs. Indeed, the Declaration of Independence is a kind of war-song; it is a stately and a passionate chant of human freedom; it is a prose lyric of civil and military heroism. We may be altogether sure that no genuine development of literary taste among the American people in any period of our future history can result in serious misfortune to this particular specimen of American literature. [521]

[43] Much has been said of the generalities, whether glittering or otherwise, of the Declaration; yet they who have most objected to its teachings seem to have found them sufficiently specific and distinct. Its famous assertion that "all men are created equal," has been complained of as liable to be misconstrued; "but," as a recent biographer of Jefferson cleverly says, "no intelligent man has ever misconstrued it, except intentionally." John T. Morse, Jr., "Thomas Jefferson," 40.

The Political Principles
of the Declaration

WILLIAM F. DANA

"When forced, therefore, to resort to arms for redress, an appeal to the tribunal of the world was deemed proper for our justification. This was the object of the Declaration of Independence."—*Jefferson to Henry Lee, May 8, 1825.*

I

The Declaration of Independence, rightly or not, has often been criticised, as lacking in originality. John Adams, concurring in a slur of Timothy Pickering, said of it:—

"As you justly observe, there is not an idea in it but what had been hackneyed in Congress for two years before. The substance of it is contained in the declaration of rights, and the violation of those rights, in the Journals of Congress, in 1774.[1] Indeed, the essence of it is contained [319] in a pamphlet, voted, and printed by the town of Boston,[2] before

[1] Declaration of Rights and Grievances, October 14, 1774. It is this state paper, which aroused Dr. Johnson's wrath, and occasioned the tract, "Taxation No Tyranny." "It were a curious, but an idle speculation," says the Doctor, "to inquire, what effect these dictators of sedition expect from the dispersion of their Letter among us. If they believe their own complaints in hardship, and really dread the danger which they describe, they will naturally hope to communicate the same perceptions to their fellow-subjects. But probably in America, as in other places, the chiefs are incendiaries, that hope to rob in the tumults of a conflagration, and toss brands among a rabble passively combustible. Those who wrote the Address though they have shown no great extent of profundity of mind, are yet probably wiser than to believe it; but they have been taught by some master of mischief, how to put in motion the engine of political electricity; to attract by the sounds of Liberty and Property, to repel by those of Popery and Slavery; and to give the great stroke by the name of Boston."

[2] Boston Town Records, November 20, 1772. Samuel Adams, and not James Otis, was the author. 1 Well's Life and Public Services of Samuel Adams, 501,

FROM *Harvard Law Review*, XIII (January, 1900), 319–343.

the first Congress met, composed by James Otis, as I suppose, in one of his lucid intervals, and pruned and published by Samuel Adams." [3]

And again:—

"These two declarations, the one of rights and the other of violations,[4] which are printed in the Journals of Congress for 1774, were two years afterwards recapitulated in the Declaration of Independence, on the Fourth of July, 1776." [5]

And yet again in a more querulous vein:—

"The declaration of independence of 4 July, 1776, contained nothing but the Boston declaration of 1772 [6] and the Congress declaration of 1774.[7] Such are the caprices of fortune. This declaration of rights was drawn by the little John Adams. The mighty Jefferson, by the declaration of independence of 4 July, 1776, carried away the glory of the great and the little. J.A. 1813." [8]

Richard Henry Lee, who, in obedience to instructions from the Virginia Convention, moved the Resolution of Independence [9] in

---

note. Jefferson denies ever having seen the pamphlet. Jefferson to Madison, August 30, 1823, 1 Randall's life of Jefferson, 186.
  [3] Adams to Pickering, August 6, 1822, 2 Adams's Life and Works, 512, 514.
  [4] Declaration of Rights and Grievances, *supra.*
  [5] Autobiography, 2 Adams's Life and Works, 377.
  [6] Boston Town Records, November 20, 1772.
  [7] Declaration of Rights and Grievances, *supra.*
  [8] MS. note to Discourses on Davila, 6 Life and Works, 221, 278. This jealousy of Adams is very characteristic, but in the present instance, seems certainly justifiable. He had borne the brunt of the debate, which resulted in the adoption of the Resolution (July 2), and the Declaration (July 4), of Independence; was older than Jefferson by seven years; had been in Congress continuously, while Jefferson had not; and, undoubtedly, at this time, was a more prominent figure than Jefferson. It is questionable, indeed, whether the members of Congress fully realized the importance that history would attach to the report of the Committee upon the Declaration, and whether they did not themselves singularly underrate the relative value in this respect of the Resolution (July 2), and the Declaration (July 4). Adams could never master his irritation at Jefferson's fame. He writes, in a letter to Benjamin Rush, May 1, 1807: "Jefferson has acquired such glory by his declaration of independence in 1776, that I think I may boast of my declaration of independence in 1755 [a letter written to Nathan Webb], twenty-one years older than his." 9 Adams's Life and Works, 591, 592.
  [9] This Resolution was in these words: "That these United Colonies are, and of right ought to be free and independent States; that they are absolved from all allegiance to the British Crown; and that all political connection between them and the State of Great Britain is, and ought to be, totally dissolved." 6 Force's American Archives (4th series), 1699. Jefferson's conclusion to his original draft of the Declaration was: "We, therefore, the Representatives of the United States of America in General Congress assembled, do, in the Name and by the Authority of the good People of these States, reject and renounce all Allegiance and Sub-

[320] Congress, possibly from no higher motives, ascribed the doctrines of the Declaration to Locke.[10] And so far has this disparagement gone, that charges, even, have been made of plagiarism from the spurious North Carolina Mecklenburg Resolves, of May 20, 1775.[11]

II

Attempts of this character, hitherto, one and all have signally failed, as they have deserved to fail. Except as a matter of historical, or biographical interest, it makes no difference whether the Declaration was a copy, or an original; for, as Jefferson, in his letter to Madison, of August 30, 1823, submitting Adams's criticisms upon the Declaration, well says, it was not "any part of my [321] [his] charge to invent new ideas altogether, and to offer no sentiment which had ever been expressed before." [12] The complete answer to such carp-

---

jection to the Kings of Great Britain, and all others who may hereafter claim by, through or under them; We utterly dissolve all political Connection which may have heretofore subsisted between us and the People or Parliament of Great Britain; and finally we do assert and declare these Colonies to be free and independent States," etc. 2 Ford's Writings of Jefferson, 57 and 58. This was changed, so as to conform to the phraseology of the Resolution of July 2, 1776, which, as appears from the above copy thereof, makes no reference to the People or Parliament of Great Britain, but only to the Crown.

[10] "Richard Henry Lee charged it as copied from Locke's treatise on government." Jefferson to Madison, August 30, 1823, 1 Randall's Life of Jefferson, 186.

[11] For references to a discussion of these, see 6 Winsor's Narrative and Critical History of America, 256. They first came to light in the Raleigh Register, April 30, 1819. Adams was much taken aback. He writes to Jefferson, June 22, 1819: "May I enclose you one of the greatest curiosities and one of the deepest mysteries that ever occurred to me? It is in the 'Essex Register' of June 5th, 1819. It is entitled the 'Raleigh Register Declaration of Independence.' How is it possible that this paper should have been concealed from me to this day? Had it been communicated to me in the time of it, I know, if you do not know, that it would have been printed in every whig newspaper upon this continent. You know, that, if I had possessed it, I would have made the hall of Congress echo and re-echo with it fifteen months before your Declaration of Independence." 10 Adams's Life and Works, 380. Jefferson, in his reply to Adams, July 9, 1819, while not expressly denying the authenticity of the Mecklenburg Declaration, states his strong incredulity upon the point: "But what has attracted my particular notice, is the paper from Mecklenburg county, of North Carolina, published in the 'Essex Register,' which you were so kind as to enclose in your last, of June the 22d. And you seem to think it genuine. I believe it spurious. I deem it to be a very unjustifiable quiz, like that of the volcano, so minutely related to us as having broken out in North Carolina, some half dozen years ago, in that part of the country, and perhaps in that very county of Mecklenburg, for I do not remember its precise locality." 3 Randall's Life of Jefferson, 572.

[12] 1 Randall's Life of Jefferson, 186. Jefferson, in this letter, also, strikes out at Pickering, who had read the Declaration of Independence, at Salem, July 4,

ing is the one here given by Jefferson himself, and indorsed by Madison in his reply, of September 6:—

"Nothing can be more absurd than the cavil that the declaration contains known, and not new truths. The object was to assert, not to discover truths, and to make them the basis of the Revolutionary act. The merit of the Draught, therefore, could only consist in a lucid communication of human rights, in a condensed enumeration of the reasons for such an exercise of them, and in a style and tone appropriate to the great occasion, and to the spirit of the American people." [13]

Or, in the words of Webster:—

"It has sometimes been said, as if it were a derogation from the merits of this paper, that it contains nothing new; that it only states grounds of proceedings, and presses topics of argument, which had often been stated and pressed before. But it was not the object of the Declaration to produce anything new. It was not to invent reasons for independence, but to state those which governed the Congress. For great and sufficient causes, it was proposed to declare independence; and the proper business of the paper to be drawn, was to set forth those causes, and justify the authors of the measure, in any event of fortune, to the country and to posterity. The cause of American independence, moreover, was now to be presented to the world, in such manner, if it might so be, as to engage its sympathy, to command its respect, to attract its admiration; and [322] in an assembly of most able and distinguished men, Thomas Jefferson had the high honor of being the selected advocate of this cause. To say that he performed his great work well, would be doing him injustice. To say

---

1823, and on that occasion, had given to the public the contents of Adams's letter. Pickering, in a patronizing way, spoke of the "high tone" of the Declaration, and of the "improvement" that it had undergone by "reduction" to "three fourths of its original size." He then went out of his way to commend the Treaty of Peace of 1783 with Great Britain, wherein "the contending parties acknowledged the hand of Divine Providence in disposing the hearts of both 'to forget all past misunderstandings and differences,'" and further to point out the "exact correspondence" of this "solemn profession" with "the fine sentiment happily expressed by Mr. Jefferson in the Declaration of Independence concerning our British Brethren, 'to hold them, as we hold the rest of mankind, enemies in war, in peace friends.'" 4 Life of Timothy Pickering, 463. Jefferson retaliated: "Timothy" [such is his disrespectful appellation] "thinks the instrument the better for having a fourth of it expunged. He would have thought it still better, had the other three fourths gone out also, all but the single sentiment (the only one he approves), which recommends friendship to his dear England, whenever she is willing to be at peace with us. . . . In opposition, however, to Mr. Pickering, I pray God that these principles [that is, those of the Declaration] may be eternal." Jefferson to Madison, August 30, 1823, 4 Randolph's Jefferson's Writings, 375, 377.

[13] Writings of James Madison, 336.

that he did excellently well, admirably well, would be inadequate and halting praise. Let us rather say, that he so discharged the duty assigned him, that all Americans may well rejoice that the work of drawing the title-deed of their liberties devolved upon him." [14]

But while it takes nothing from the Declaration of Independence, or the just fame of its author, that it was not the promulgation of a novel creed, but the annunciation of familiar doctrine, yet, notwithstanding, this disclaimer of originality is of the first importance in one aspect. It does not isolate the Declaration of Independence from all other state-papers, and make the Declaration itself the sole source of authoritative interpretation. It leaves open the whole body of contemporary history, as, also, the literature of the times, to clear up ambiguities, or to supply omissions. This is a most essential point.

III

No one can compare the Declaration of Independence with the Virginia Bill of Rights without being struck by the remarkable similarity, both in matter, and style, of the two documents.[15]

1. The Declaration says: "All men are created equal." In the original draft: "All men are created equal and independent."

The Bill of Rights says: "All men are by nature equally free and independent." In the original draft: "All men are created equally free and independent." [16]

2. The Declaration says: "They are endowed by their Creator with certain unalienable Rights; that among these are Life, Liberty, and the pursuit of Happiness." In the original draft: "From that equal creation, they derive rights inherent and inalienable, among which are the preservation of life, and liberty, and the pursuit of happiness." In an intermediate draft: "They are endowed by their Creator with equal rights, some of which are," etc.

The Bill of Rights says: "And have certain inherent rights, of [323] which, when they enter into a state of society, they cannot, by any compact, deprive or divest their posterity; namely, the enjoy-

---

[14] Oration on Adams and Jefferson, Faneuil Hall, Boston, August 2, 1826. 1 Works, 109, 126, 127.

[15] The collation made in this section is based upon the material in 1 Randall's Life of Jefferson, and 1 Rowland's George Mason, Life, Correspondence, and Speeches.

[16] The report of the committee reads: "All men are born," etc. 6 Force's American Archives, 1537, note.

ment of life and liberty, with the means of acquiring and possessing property, and pursuing and obtaining happiness and safety." In the original draft: "And have certain inherent natural rights, of which they cannot, by any compact, deprive or divest their posterity; among which are the enjoyment of life and liberty, with the means of acquiring and possessing property, and pursuing and obtaining happiness and safety." [17]

3. The Declaration says: "To secure these rights, Governments are instituted among Men, deriving their just powers from the consent of the governed." In the original draft: "To secure these ends," etc.

The Bill of Rights says: "All power is vested in, and consequently derived from, the people; that magistrates are their trustees and servants, and at all times amenable to them." In the original draft: "All power is by God and Nature vested in," etc.[18] Again, "Nor [can men, to wit, those] having sufficient evidence of permanent, common interest with and attachment to the community, [be] bound by any law, to which they have not, in like manner [that is, by themselves, or through their representatives, freely elected, as in case of taxation], assented, for the public [in the original draft, "common"] good." [19]

4. The Declaration says: "Whenever any Form of Government becomes [in the original draft, "shall become"] destructive of these ends, it is the Right of the People to alter or to abolish it, and to institute new Government, laying its foundation on such principles, and organizing its powers in such form, as to them shall seem most likely to effect their Safety and Happiness."

The Bill of Rights says: "When [in the original draft, "whenever"] any government shall be found inadequate or contrary to these purposes, a majority of the community hath an indubitable, unalienable, and indefeasible right to reform, alter, or abolish it, in such manner as shall be judged most conducive to the public weal." [20]

5. The Bill of Rights has a clause, which the Declaration has [324] not (unless the restriction upon the character of the new government to be instituted after revolution be such): "Government is, or

[17] The report of the committee is like the original draft. 6 Force's American Archives, 1537, note.
[18] The report of the committee is like the final draft. Ib.
[19] The report of the committee reads: "any laws," and "common good." Ib.
[20] The report of the committee is like the original draft. Ib.

ought to be, instituted for the common benefit, protection, and security of the people, nation, or community. Of all the various modes and forms of government, that is best, which is capable of producing the greatest degree of happiness and safety, and is most effectually secured against the danger of mal-administration." [21] A hereditary monarchy, however, was excluded from this class: "Neither ought the offices of magistrate, legislator, or judge, to be hereditary." [22]

IV

It is a singular fact, that, in all the attacks upon the Declaration, as a copy, and not an original, greater stress has not been laid upon its manifest debt to the Virginia Bill of Rights. If there were no external evidence, the internal evidence itself would be sufficient to convince any candid mind, that there must have been some relation between these two great state-papers, and that they cannot possibly be conceived of as the products of two distinct minds, working apart, one from the other, without opportunity of communication. While similarity of thought, with difference of phrase may exist, and yet there be no necessary connection, identity of thought and phrase (to the extent, at least, that this occurs in the Declaration, and the Virginia Bill of Rights) cannot. If, therefore, there was a desire to rob Jefferson of any title of glory, why has it not been shown, as it readily could have been, that the Bill of Rights was the predecessor of the Declaration, and that the immortal part of the latter was taken from it.

It seems hard to say, unless the discovery of the real truth (as, indeed, was the fact with Adams) was not the sole object of inquiry. Perhaps, also, some investigators have been misled by the letter of Wythe to Jefferson, of July 27, 1776,[23] and that of Jefferson to Woodward, of April 3, 1825.[24] By this evidence, it appears, that Jefferson was the author, practically, of the *preamble* to the Constitution of Virginia. This *preamble*, however, must not be [325] confounded with the Virginia Bill of Rights. It consists merely of a recapitulation of grievances, similar to that included in the *body* of the Declaration of Independence, and, unlike the Bill of Rights, and

---

[21] The report of the committee is like the final draft. 6 Force's American Archives, 1537, note.
[22] The report of the committee reads: "The idea of a man being born a magistrate, a legislator, or a judge, is unnatural, and absurd." Ib.
[23] 1 Randall's Life of Jefferson, 195, note.   [24] Ib. 195.

the *preamble* to the Declaration of Independence, is not a statement of the Rights of Man.[25]

V

Jefferson was not the author of the Virginia Bill of Rights, and never made any claim to being such. On the contrary, he always frankly acknowledged that George Mason was the author. In the letter to Woodward, quoted above, he says:—

"The fact is unquestionable, that the Bill of Rights, and the Constitution of Virginia, were drawn originally by George Mason, one of our really great men, and of the first order of greatness." [26]

And he repeats the statement, in a letter to Henry Lee:—

"That George Mason was the author of the Bill of Rights, and of the constitution founded on it, the evidence of the day established fully in my mind." [27]

If further corroborative proof be needed, it may be found in the recent biography of George Mason, which deals of this matter in detail.[28]

VI

It only remains to establish the relation of Jefferson to the Virginia Bill of Rights. While, as has been said, the internal evidence is such as to leave no doubt in an unprejudiced mind, yet, perhaps, it is fair, that the physical possibility of such relation should be demonstrated. It is true, that, in 1823, in the letter to Madison, Jefferson says:—

"Whether I had gathered my ideas from reading or reflection, I do not know. I know only that I turned to neither book nor pamphlet while writing it." [29] [326]

But this was nearly fifty years after the event,—and less than three before his death,—when the particular circumstances attending composition may well have passed out of his mind, or become

---

[25] Ford, the latest editor of Jefferson, frankly admits the similarity of the *preamble* of the Declaration to the Virginia Bill of Rights: "A comparison of the former [the *preamble* of the Declaration] with the Virginia Declaration of Rights would seem to indicate the source from which Jefferson derived a most important and popular part." 1 Ford's Writings of Jefferson, 25.

[26] Jefferson to Woodward, April 23, 1825, 1 Randall's Life of Jefferson, 195.

[27] Jefferson to Henry Lee, May 8, 1825, 1 Rowland's George Mason, Life, Correspondence, and Speeches, 253.

[28] Rowland's George Mason, Life, Correspondence, and Speeches, c. vii.

[29] Jefferson to Madison, August 30, 1823, 1 Randall's Life of Jefferson, 186.

dimmed by lapse of time. One thing is certain, there are passages in the Declaration of Independence so nearly like passages in Jefferson's "Draft of a Virginia Constitution," [30] and "A Summary View of the Rights of British America," [31] that the conclusion seems inevitable, that, at the time of the drafting of the Declaration, Jefferson must have had one, or possibly both, of these documents before him. However that may be, it can easily be established, that the Virginia Bill of Rights, either in the form in which it was presented to the Virginia Convention, or that in which it was finally adopted by it, was in Philadelphia, in season to have been consulted by Jefferson. The committee to draft the Declaration of Independence was chosen [32] by the Continental Congress, June 11, 1776, and did not make its report thereto till June 28 following. The Bill of Rights was reported to the Virginia Convention, May 27, 1776, and was adopted by it, June 12, 1776. Thomas Ludwell Lee, a member of the Virginia Convention, writes from Williamsburg to Richard Henry Lee, at Philadelphia, June 1, 1776: "I enclosed you by last post a copy of our Declaration of Rights nearly as it came through Committee. It has since been reported to the Convention." [33] On the day that it was reported to the Convention, it was ordered "printed for the perusal of the members." [34] June 10, 1776, Josiah Bartlett, one of the delegates from New Hampshire, then present in Congress, writes from Philadelphia to John Langdon: "I shall enclose you a paper containing the Bill of Rights drawn up by Virginia." [35] It is evident, therefore, that the Virginia Bill of Rights was in circulation, in manuscript, or print among the members of Congress, at Philadelphia, in the first days of June, and that like the instructions to the Virginia delegates on Independence, of May 15, 1776, had attracted wide attention. Under these circumstances, it is impossible to believe, that Jefferson, a member of the delegation that introduced the Resolution of Independence, and [327] heartily in sympathy with Lee in respect of the expediency of it, should have remained ignorant of what was common knowledge among other members of Congress, if not, at large, among the public itself. And if there was no impossibility of his being familiar with Mason's draft of the bill

[30] 2 Ford's Writings of Jefferson, 7.
[31] 1 Ford's Writings of Jefferson, 421.
[32] The Journals say, "appointed," but, from a thorough examination of them, it will appear, that this word was used by Charles Thomson, the Secretary, in cases of "election."
[33] 1 Patrick Henry, Life, Correspondence and Speeches, 424.
[34] 6 Force's American Archives (4th Series), 1538.   [35] Ib. 1026, 1027.

of rights, who can doubt, after a comparison of the two papers, such as has been made here, that much of the *preamble* of the Declaration of Independence, if not in substance, in form, was taken,—and by taken, is, by no means, meant improperly taken,—but taken, —and taken as the occasion justified—from the Virginia Bill? For, as has been demonstrated, George Mason, and not Jefferson, was the author of that bill.

VII

The importance of this historical fact, if fact it is, lies in this: that the Virginia Bill of Rights is much more explicit than the Declaration of Independence, and more clearly indicates than the Declaration does the source of its origin. The Bill of Rights is plainly founded upon the "social compact" theory of government, and the terminology is the terminology of Locke, and other like writers, who have founded government upon the "social compact" basis. Indeed, the Virginia Bill of Rights uses the specific word, "compact" and, in its amended form, contains the phrase, "when they [men] enter into a state of society." Of this theory, then, George Mason and Jefferson were the modern expounders.

VIII

What, therefore, is meant by the phrases in the Declaration of Independence, "All men are created equal"? "Unalienable Rights of Life, Liberty, and the pursuit of Happiness"? "Governments derive their just powers from the consent of the governed"? and that other phrase, in the introduction to the *preamble,* not hitherto referred to: "Nature, and Nature's God"?

Are these phrases, as the Declaration asserts, (of all but the last), "self-evident truths," or are they, as Rufus Choate said, "glittering and sounding generalities"? [36] [328]

[36] "If it [the Republican Party] accomplishes its objects, and gives the government to the North, I turn my eyes from the consequences. To the fifteen States of the South that government will appear an alien government. It will appear worse. It will appear a hostile government. It will represent to their eye a vast region of States organized upon anti-slavery, flushed by triumph, cheered onward by the voices of the pulpit tribune, and press; its mission to inaugurate freedom, and put down the oligarchy; its constitution the *glittering and sounding generalities* of natural right which make up the Declaration of Independence. And then, and thus is the beginning of the end."—Rufus Choate to the Maine Whig State Central Committee, August 9, 1856, 1 Brown's Works of Rufus Choate, 212, 215.

Do they stand for the freedom of the slave? For negro suffrage? For Indian suffrage? For manhood suffrage? For woman suffrage? For universal suffrage? For a republic? For representative government? And if for these, or any of these, for these, and any of these, without limitation, or qualification? Do they apply to barbarous states, as well as to civilized states? To all sorts and conditions of men, the uneducated as well as educated, with property or without? Or did the framers of the Declaration intend a different application? And, if a different application, what application?

IX

The answer to these questions, or to many of them, must, in the nature of things, always remain more or less debatable. And yet it will not do to say, that there is no answer, and still less, to take refuge in empty rhetoric. There is much wit in the remark, apropos of the Declaration: "No intelligent man has ever misconstrued it, unless intentionally;" [37] but such an answer is hardly convincing. It may suffice for the arguments of the Confederacy, Utah polygamists, and woman suffragists,—those who have carried the doctrines of the Declaration to an absurdity, but it is not the answer which the vital importance of the question, seriously considered, fairly demands. And while perhaps, as has been intimated, no answer can be given, wholly free from dispute, yet this is far from saying that no progress is possible towards a correct solution.

X

Several things can be predicated of the Bill of Rights and the Declaration:

1. Their first care was the justification of the Colonists in the right of revolution.[38]

2. They were adopted with no intention of conferring suffrage upon the negro, and probably with none of freeing him.[39] [329]

[37] Morse's Life of Jefferson, 40.
[38] Introduction to the *preamble* of the Declaration.
[39] The portion of the Declaration relating to the slave trade was struck out, from political exigencies. Lincoln said in his speech, in Chicago, July 10, 1858: "I should like to know,—taking this old Declaration of Independence, which declares that all men are equal upon principle, and making exceptions to it,— where will it stop? If one man says it does not mean a negro, why not another say it does not mean some other man? If that Declaration is not the truth, let us get the statute book in which we find it, and tear it out." 1 Complete Works, 247, 259. He was speaking of what it should be held to mean then, rather than

3. They had no relation to woman suffrage, in fact, to the suffrage, at all, manhood, property, universal, or otherwise.⁴⁰ [330]

4. They had no relation to the Indians.⁴¹

---

of what it was held to mean in 1776, but, even thus, he took pains to guard himself later at Charleston, Ill., September 18, 1858, as follows: "I will say that I am not, nor ever have been, in favor of bringing about in any way the social and political equality of the white and black races—that I am not, nor ever have been, in favor of making voters or jurors of negroes, nor of qualifying them to hold office, nor to intermarry with white people; and I will say in addition to this that there is a physical difference between the white and black races which I believe will forever forbid the two races living together on terms of social and political equality." 1 Complete Works, 369. What he believed that the rights of the negro were, he had defined in a previous speech, at Ottawa, August 21, 1858: "I agree with Judge Douglas, he [the negro] is not my equal in many respects—certainly not in color, perhaps not in moral or intellectual endowment. But in the right to eat the bread, without the leave of anybody else, which his own hand earns, he is my equal, and the equal of Judge Douglas, and the equal of every living man." 1 Complete Works, 286, 289. Whatever the original meaning was, the Declaration left the slave as it found him. "Upon the revolution, no other change took place in North Carolina than was consequent on the transition from a colony dependent on a European king, to a free and sovereign State. Slaves remained slaves. British subjects in North Carolina became North Carolina freemen. Foreigners, until made members of the State, remained aliens. Slaves, manumitted here, became freemen, and, therefore, if born within North Carolina, are citizens of North Carolina, and all free persons born within the State are born citizens of the State." State v. Manuel, 4 Dev. & Bat. 20, quoted with approval by Judge Curtis in the Dred Scott Case. Edmund Randolph's MS. "History of Virginia" would seem to indicate, that the difficulty was smoothed over in the Virginia Convention, on the hypothesis, that slaves were property. He says: "The Declaration in the first article of the bill of rights, that all men are by nature equally free and independent, was opposed by Robert Carter Nicholas, as being the forerunner, or pretext, of civil convulsion. It was answered, perhaps, with too great an indifference to futurity, and not without inconsistency, that, with arms in our hands, asserting the general rights of man, we ought not to be too nice, and too much restricted, in the delineation of them, but that slaves, not being constituent members of our society, could never pretend to any benefit from such a maxim." Conway's Edmund Randolph, 30.

⁴⁰ "When the Federal Constitution was adopted, all the States with the exception of Rhode Island and Connecticut, had constitutions of their own. These two continued to act under their charters from the Crown. Upon an examination of those constitutions we find that in no State were all citizens permitted to vote. Each state determined for itself who should have that power." Minor v. Happersett, 21 Wall. 162, 172. The new constitutions made the following minimum stipulations as preliminary to the suffrage: New Jersey (1776), property; Pennsylvania (1776), taxes; Maryland (1776), property; North Carolina (1776), taxes; Georgia (1777), property, or mechanical trade; New York (1777), property; Massachusetts (1780), property; New Hampshire (1784), poll tax; Rhode Island (charter), Connecticut (charter), South Carolina (1776), Virginia (1776), and Delaware (1776), as before. It is interesting to note particularly, that Virginia retained her previous high property qualification.

⁴¹ Talk to the Six Nations, of July 13, 1775: "Brothers and Friends! We desire you will hear and receive what we have now told you, and that you will open a good ear, and listen to what we are now going to say. This a family quarrel

5. They did not assert, that the Colonists had a right of representation in Parliament,—that right the Colonists waived as impracticable, and did not want,—nor yet, that the Colonists desired an opportunity to interfere with imperial concerns,—they were willing to leave these entirely to a Parliament, in which they were not represented. What the Bill and Declaration did complain of, was the novel interference by the King and Parliament with the local affairs of the colonies, which had always hitherto been left solely to the Colonial legislatures, and, more particularly, of the taking of the property of the Colonists, in the shape of taxes, without their consent.

6. The Bill and Declaration were adopted by men mainly of British descent,—the equals of native-born subjects,—with the same capacity for government,—and morally entitled to the same rights. And the claims made by the Bill and Declaration, if not in terms, in fact, were made of a form of government, and state of society, that were civilized.

7. There was no *necessary* antagonism between the Declaration of Independence, and a monarchy. That is to say, it did not preach a crusade against all kingdoms. Nor does the Bill of Rights, though possibly more radical, do that.

XI

It is impossible, within the scope of the present article, to develop these different propositions at full length. And, indeed, most of them are so indisputable as to make development superfluous. The most superficial knowledge of American history is sufficient to remove all doubt as to the first four, and, possibly, even as to the fifth, sixth, and seventh. The last three, however, while [331] unquestionably not admitting of much doubt, may yet perhaps be not entirely so axiomatic as the others, and should receive, therefore, a brief word or two by way of explanation.

---

between us and old England. You Indians are not concerned in it." (The Six Nations, however, were inhabitants of New York State.) Journals of Congress, July 13, 1775. The committee consisted of five members: Philip Schuyler (N. Y.); Patrick Henry (Va.); James Duane (N. Y.); James Wilson (Penn.); and Philip Livingston (N. Y.). See also, Elk v. Wilkins, 112 U. S. 94: "The members of these tribes [Indian tribes] owed immediate allegiance to their several tribes, and were not part of the people of the United States. They were in a dependent condition, a state of pupilage, resembling that of a ward to his guardian" (p. 97).

XII

And, *first*, of proposition 5, that the Colonists made no complaint, of non-representation in Parliament, to act upon imperial affairs, but, on the contrary, rather feared, that this right might be conceded to them.

January 30, 1768, Samuel Adams wrote to Dennys Deberdt, the Massachusetts colonial agent, in London:—

"You will observe that the House still insist upon that inestimable right of nature and the Constitution of being taxed only by representatives of their own free election; which they think is infringed by the late acts for establishing a revenue in America. *It is by no means to be understood that they desire a representation in Parliament, because, by reason of local circumstances, it is impracticable, that they should be equally and fairly represented. There is nothing, therefore, the Colonies would more dread.*" [42]

The assertion is frequently reiterated.

In the Declaration of Rights and Grievances, of October 14, 1774—:

"*Resolved*, 4. That the foundation of English liberty and of all free government, is a right in the people to participate in their legislative council; *and as the English colonists are not represented, and from their local and other circumstances cannot properly be represented, in the British parliament, they are entitled to a free and exclusive power of legislation in their several provincial legislatures, where their right of representation can alone be preserved, in all cases of taxation and internal polity, subject only to the negative of their sovereign, in such manner as has been heretofore used and accustomed.*" [43]

This paragraph contains such a definite, and exact, statement of the position of the Colonists, prior to the Revolution, that it is worth quoting in full:—

"But from the necessity of the case, and a regard to the mutual interests of both countries, we cheerfully consent to the operation of such acts of the British Parliament as are *bona fide* restrained to the regulation of our external commerce, for the purpose of securing the commercial [332] advantages of the whole empire to the mother country, and the commercial benefits of its respective members; excluding every idea of taxation, inter-

[42] 1 Wells's Life and Public Services of Samuel Adams, 167, 168.
[43] Journals of Congress, October 14, 1774.

nal or external, for raising a revenue on the subjects in America without their consent." [44]

In the Address to the People of Great Britain, of October 21, 1774:—

"You have been told that we are seditious, impatient of government, and desirous of independency. Be assured that these are not facts, but calumnies. . . .

. . . . .

"Place us in the same situation that we were at the close of the last war, and our former harmony will be restored." [45]

In the Petition to the King, of October 25, 1774:—

"We wish not a diminution of the prerogative, nor do we solicit the grant of any new right in our favor. *Your royal authority over us, and our connection with Great Britain, we shall always carefully and zealously endeavor to support and maintain."* [46]

In the Second Address to the People of Great Britain, of July 8, 1775:—

"After the most valuable right of legislation was infringed; *when the powers assumed by your parliament in which we are not represented, and from our local and other circumstances cannot properly be represented, rendered our property precarious;* after being denied," etc., etc.[47]

In the Reply to Lord North's "Conciliatory Proposals," of July 31, 1775:— [333]

[44] Journals of Congress, October 14, 1774. The committee consisted of twenty-seven members, as follows: N. H., Nathaniel Folsom, John Sullivan; Mass., Samuel Adams, John Adams, Thomas Cushing; R. I., Stephen Hopkins, Samuel Ward; Conn., Eliphalet Dyer, Roger Sherman; N. Y., James Duane, John Jay; Penn., Edward Biddle, Joseph Galloway, Thomas Mifflin; N. J., John de Hart, William Livingston; Md., Robert Goldsborough, Thomas Johnson; Del., Caesar Rodney, Thomas M'Kean; Va., Patrick Henry, Richard Henry Lee, Edmund Pendleton; S. C., Thomas Lynch, John Rutledge; N. C., Joseph Hewes, William Hooper.
[45] Journals of Congress, October 21, 1774. The committee consisted of three members, as follows: Richard Henry Lee (Va.); [William] Livingston (N. J.); and John Jay (N. Y.).
[46] Journals of Congress, October 25, 1774. The committee consisted of six members, as follows: Richard Henry Lee (Va.); John Adams (Mass.); Thomas Johnson (Va.); Patrick Henry (Va.); [John] Rutledge (S. C.); and John Dickinson (Penn.).
[47] Journals of Congress, July 8, 1775. The committee consisted of three members, as follows: Richard Henry Lee (Va.); Robert R. Livingston (N. Y.); and Edmund Pendleton (Va.).

"While *parliament* pursue *their plan* of civil government within *their own* jurisdiction, *we* also hope to pursue *ours* without molestation." [48]

And in the Reply to the Royal Proclamation, August 23, 1775, of December 6, 1775:—

"We condemn, and with arms in our hands, a resource which freemen will never part with, we oppose the claim and exercise of *unconstitutional powers, to which neither the crown nor parliament were ever entitled.*" [49]

XIII

Secondly, of proposition 6, that the Colonists spoke for, and in the name of, themselves, as British subjects, the equals, in all respects, of those native-born within the kingdom.

The instances of this character are so numerous as almost to defy recapitulation. Several examples, however, will suffice.

In "A Summary View of the Rights of British America," published by order of the Virginia convention of 1774, Jefferson says:—

"To remind him [the King] that our ancestors, before their emigration to America, were the free inhabitants of the British dominions in Europe," etc.[50]

See also:—
Declaration of Rights and Grievances, of October 14, 1774:—

"*Resolved*, 2. That our ancestors, who first settled these Colonies, were at the time of the emigration from the mother Country, entitled to all the rights, liberties, and immunities of free and natural born subjects, within the realm of England.

"*Resolved*, 3. That by such emigration they by no means forfeited, surrendered, or lost any of those rights, but that they were, and their descendants now are, entitled to the exercise and enjoyment of all such of them, as their local and other circumstances enable them to exercise and enjoy." [51]

Address to the People of Great Britain, of October 21, 1774:—
[334]

[48] Journals of Congress, July 31, 1775. The committee consisted of four members, as follows: Benjamin Franklin (Penn.); Thomas Jefferson (Va.); John Adams (Mass.); and Richard Henry Lee (Va.).
[49] Journals of Congress, December 6, 1775. The committee consisted of three members, as follows: Richard Henry Lee (Va.); James Wilson (Penn.); and William Livingston (N. J.).
[50] 1 Ford's Writings of Thomas Jefferson, 421, 429.
[51] Journals of Congress, October 14, 1774.

"Know then, that we consider ourselves, and do insist, that we are and ought to be, as free as our fellow subjects in Britain, and that no power on earth has a right to take our property from us, without our consent. "That we claim all the benefits secured to the subject by the English constitution," etc.[52]

Petition to the King, of October 25, 1774:—

"The apprehension of being degraded into a state of servitude, from the pre-eminent rank of English freemen," etc.[53]

Address to the Inhabitants of Quebec, of October 26, 1774:—

"On the solid foundation of this principle, Englishmen reared up the fabric of their constitution, with such a strength, as for ages to defy time, tyranny, treachery, internal and foreign wars; and, as an illustrious author [Montesquieu] of your nation, hereafter mentioned, observes: 'They gave the people of their colonies the form of their own government, and, this government carrying prosperity along with it, they have grown great nations in the forests they were sent to inhabit.' " [54]

Declaration upon Taking Up Arms, of July 6, 1775:—

"Our forefathers, inhabitants of the island of Great Britain, left their native land, to seek on these shores a residence for civil and religious freedom. At the expense of their blood, at the hazard of their fortunes, without the least charge to the country from which they removed, by unceasing labor, and an unconquerable spirit, they effected settlements in the distant and inhospitable wilds of America, then filled with numerous warlike nations of Barbarians. Societies or governments, vested with perfect legislatures, were formed under charters from the Crown, and an harmonious intercourse was established between the colonies and the kingdom from which they derived their origin." [55]

Reply to Royal Proclamation, August 23, 1775, of December 6, 1775:—

"By the British constitution, our best inheritance, rights, as well as duties, descend upon us. We cannot violate the latter by defending the [335] former. We should act in diametrical opposition to both, if we per-

[52] Journals of Congress, October 21, 1774.
[53] Journals of Congress, October 25, 1774.
[54] Journals of Congress, October 26, 1774. The committee consisted of three members, as follows: Thomas Cushing (Mass.); Richard Henry Lee (Va.); and John Dickinson (Penn.).
[55] Journals of Congress, July 6, 1775. The committee consisted of seven members, as follows: John Rutledge (N. C.); William Livingston (N. J.); Benjamin Franklin (Penn.); John Jay (N. Y.); Thomas Johnson (Md.); John Dickinson (Penn.); Thomas Jefferson (Va.).

mitted the claims of the British parliament to be established, and the measures pursued in consequence of those claims to be carried into execution among us. Our sagacious ancestors provided mounds against the inundation of tyranny and lawless power on one side, as well as against that of faction and licentiousness on the other. On which side has the breach been made?

. . . . .

"We mean not, however, by this declaration, to occasion or to multiply punishments. Our sole view is to prevent them. In this unhappy and unnatural controversy, in which Britons fight against Britons, and the descendants of Britons, let the calamities immediately incident to a civil war suffice. We hope," etc.[56]

And so on, *ad infinitum*.

XIV

Thirdly, of proposition 7, that the Declaration of Independence was not a war upon all monarchy, constitutional or otherwise, here and elsewhere. It is not as sweeping, in this particular, as the Virginia Bill of Rights, and it would probably have surprised even the author of that, if he had been given to understand, that the Bill of Rights questioned the title of George III. to the throne of Great Britain. Even as late as December 6, 1775, the Colonists, in their Reply to the Royal Proclamation, August 23, 1775, say:—

"What allegiance is it that we forget? Allegiance to parliament? We never owed,—we never owned it. Allegiance to our king? Our words have ever avowed it, our conduct has ever been consistent with it."

The principles of the Revolution were not of such mushroom growth. As Bancroft says:—

"In the next place, the declaration, avoiding specious and vague generalities, grounds itself with anxious care upon the past, and reconciles right and fact. Of universal principles enough is repeated to prove that America chose for her own that system of politics which recognizes the rule of eternal justice: and independence is vindicated by the application of that rule to the grievous instructions, laws and acts proceeding from the King, in the exercise of his prerogative, or in concurrence with the lords and commons of Great Britain. The colonies professed to drive back innovations, and not, with roving zeal, to overturn all traditional inequalities; they were no rebels against the past, of which they knew [336] the

[56] Journals of Congress, December 6, 1775.

present to be the child; with all the glad anticipations of greatness that broke forth from the prophetic soul of the youthful nation, they took their point of departure from the world as it was. They did not declare against monarchy itself; they sought no general overthrow of all kings; no universal system of republics; nor did they cherish in their hearts a lurking hatred against princes. Till within a few years or months, loyalty to the house of Hanover had been to them another name for the love of civil and religious liberty; the British constitution, the best system that had ever been devised for the security of liberty and property by a representative government. Neither Franklin nor Washington, nor John Adams, nor Jefferson, nor Jay had ever expressed a preference for a republic.[57] The voices that rose for independence spoke also for alliances with kings. The sovereignty of George III. was renounced, not because he was a king, but because he was deemed to be a tyrant." [58]

XV

If Judge Taney was wrong upon the point of constitutional law involved in the Dred Scott case, he was, at least, right in demanding, that the principles of the Declaration be brought into conformity with the acts of those who professed them. He says:—

"The general words, above quoted ['All men,' etc.], would seem to embrace the whole human family, and if they were used in a similar instrument at this day would be so understood. But it is too clear for dispute, that the enslaved African race were not intended to be included, and formed no part of the people who framed and adopted this declaration; for if the language, as understood in that day, would embrace them, the conduct of the distinguished men who framed the declaration of independence would have been utterly and flagrantly inconsistent with the principles they asserted; and instead of the sympathy of mankind to which they so confidently appealed, they would have deserved and received universal rebuke and reprobation." [59]

The key to this problem, and other problems, before suggested, is to be found in Locke.

XVI

The Declaration, primarily, had one thing, and one thing only, in view, and that was, a justification of the separation of the Colonies

[57] Query, if text would not be more exact, with the words, "had ever," omitted?
[58] 4 Bancroft's History of the United States, 451.
[59] Dred Scott v. Sandford, 19 How. 393, 410.

from Great Britain, and incidentally, therefore, a defence of [337] the rights of revolution in respect of the then condition of the original thirteen States. To this end, the lawyers of the day, who were, for the most part, the framers of state-papers then as now, turned to Locke's essay, and other kindred writings, to establish the justice of their contention. Locke's essay, as is said by him in the preface, was written in defence of the English Revolution of 1688,[60] and he had to prove, as the Colonies had to prove, that there was no such thing as the divine right of kings, and that, when a government failed to be true to its trust, it was the right, inherent, and inalienable, of the people, "to alter or abolish it, and to institute new government." Otherwise, there could have been no justification for that series of events, which, at the close of the 17th century, resulted in the replacing of James the Second upon the throne by William, Prince of Orange. Locke accomplished his object in this way: He first demolished the patriarchal theory of government, as descending from God through Adam, defended by Sir John Filmer in an essay, called "Patriarcha, or the Natural Power of Kings;" and then proceeded to the true foundation of civil society. Like other writers of his, and the 18th centuries, he traced this to the state of Nature,[61] and asserted that, in that state, all men are "equal" and "independent." [62] These are the exact words of the original draft of the Declaration; and,

---

[60] "'Thou hast here the beginning and end of a discourse concerning government: what fate has otherwise disposed of the papers that should have filled up the middle, and were more than all the rest, it is not worth while to tell thee. These which remain I hope are sufficient to establish the throne of our great restorer, our present King William; to make good his title in the consent of the people; which being the only one of all lawful governments, he has more fully and clearly than any prince in Christendom; and to justify to the world the people of England, whose love of their just and natural rights, with their resolution to preserve them, saved the nation when it was on the very brink of slavery and ruin." Preface to the Two Treatises.

[61] "To understand political power right, and derive it from its original, we must consider what estate all men are *naturally* in." Second Treatise, § 4.

[62] "A state of *perfect freedom* to order their actions, and dispose of their possessions and persons as they think fit, within the bounds of the law of nature, without asking leave or depending upon the will of any other man. A state also of *equality* wherein all the power and jurisdiction is reciprocal, no one having more than another, there being nothing more evident than that creatures of the same species and rank, promiscuously born to all the same advantages of nature, and the use of the same faculties, should also be equal one amongst another, without subordination or subjection." Second Treatise, § 4. Again: "The state of nature has a law of nature to govern it, which obliges every one; and reason, which is that law, teaches all mankind, who will but consult it, that being all *equal* and *independent*, no one ought to harm another in his life, health, liberty, or possessions," etc. Ib. § 6.

also, of the Bill of Rights. By "equal" and "independent," Locke did not [338] mean, that every man was born of the same height, or with the same mental or physical vigor,[63] but "equal," in the case of rational beings,[64] in respect of the laws of Nature, and the primordial right to enforce these laws. Every man according to Locke, until a state of society was entered into, was entitled to enforce the laws of Nature; [65] and it was only, when society was formed, that this right of enforcement was transferred from the individual to the government.[66] [339] This result was effected by "compact," [67] from

---

[63] "Though I have said above, 'That all men by nature are equal,' I cannot be supposed to understand all sorts of equality: age or virtue may give man a just precedency: excellency of parts and merit may place others above the common level: birth may subject some, and alliance or benefits others, to pay an observance to those to whom nature, gratitude, or other respects, may have made it due; and yet all this consists with the equality which all men are in, in respect of jurisdiction or dominion one over another; which was the equality I there spoke of, as proper to the business in hand, being that equal right that every man hath to his natural freedom, without being subjected to the will or authority of any other man." Second Treatise, § 54.

[64] "The freedom then of man and liberty of acting according to his own will, is grounded on his having reason, which is able to instruct him in that law he is to govern himself by, and make him know how far he is left to the freedom of his own will. To turn him loose to an unrestrained liberty, before he has reason to guide him, is not the allowing him the privilege of his nature to be free, but to thrust him out amongst brutes and abandon him to a state as wretched, and as much beneath that of a man, as theirs. This is that which puts the authority into the parent's hands to govern the minority of their children. God hath made it their business to employ this care on their offspring, and hath placed in them suitable inclinations of tenderness and concern to temper this power, to apply it, as His wisdom designed it, to the children's good, as long as they should need to be under it." Second Treatise, § 63. And again: "Thus we are born free, as we are born rational; not that we have actually the exercise of either; age, that brings one, brings with it the other too." Second Treatise, § 61.

[65] "And that all men may be restrained from invading others' rights, and from doing hurt to one another, and the law of nature be observed, which willeth the peace and preservation of all mankind, the execution of the law of nature is, in that state, put into every man's hands, whereby every one has a right to punish the transgressors of that law to such a degree as may hinder its violation: for the law of nature would, as all other laws that concern men in this world, be in vain, if there were nobody that in the state of nature had a power to execute that law, and thereby preserve the innocent, and restrain offenders: And if any one in the state of nature may punish another for any evil he has done, every one may do so: for in that state of perfect equality, where naturally there is no superiority or jurisdiction of one over another, what any may do in prosecution of that law, every one must needs have a right to do." Second Treatise, § 7.

[66] "Whenever, therefore, any number of men are so united into one society, as to quit every one his executive power of the law of nature, and to resign it to the public, there and there only is a political or civil society. And this is done, wherever any number of men, in the state of nature, enter into society to make

which arose obligations on the part of the government, as well as the governed, to respect the chief object and end of civil society, to wit, the security of the individual in his life, liberty, and property, and that happiness that springs from the free enjoyment of these. In other words, government derived its powers directly from man, and not from God; and, of course, if government was established by consent, it could, when occasion demanded, be altered or abolished by that consent which created it. Locke does not say, that this consent is necessarily expressly given; it may be given by implication; [68] and the principle, as such, is as consistent with a [340]

---

one people, one body politic, under one supreme government; or else when any one joins himself to, and incorporates with any government already made: for hereby he authorizes the society, or, which is all one, the legislative thereof, to make laws for him, as the public good of the society shall require; to the execution whereof, his own assistance (as to his own decrees) is due: And this puts men out of a state of nature into that of a commonwealth, by setting up a judge on earth, with authority to determine all the controversies, and redress the injuries that may happen to any member of the commonwealth; which judge is the legislative or magistrate appointed by it. And wherever there are any number of men, however associated, that have no such decisive power to appeal to, there they are still in the state of nature." Second Treatise, § 89.

[67] "Men being, as has been said, by nature all *free, equal* and *independent*, no one can be put out of his estate, and subjected to the political power of another, without his own consent. The only way whereby any one divests himself of his natural liberty, and puts on the bonds of civil society, is by agreeing with other men to join and unite into a community for their comfortable, safe, and peaceable living one amongst another, in a secure enjoyment of their properties, and a greater security against any that are not of it. This any number of men may do, because it injures not the freedom of the rest; they are left, as they were, in the liberty of the state of nature. When any number of men have so consented to make one community or government, they are thereby presently incorporated, and make one body politic, wherein the majority have a right to act and conclude the rest." Second Treatise, § 95. Again: "Whosoever, therefore, out of a state of nature unite into a community, must be understood to give up all the power necessary to the ends for which they unite into society, to the majority of the community, unless they expressly agreed in any number greater than the majority. And this is done by barely agreeing to unite into one political society, which is all the compact that is, or needs be between the individuals that enter into, or make up a commonwealth. And thus that which begins and actually constitutes any political society, is nothing but the consent of any number of freemen capable of a majority, to unite and incorporate into such a society. And this is that, and that only, which did or could give beginning to any lawful government in the world." Ib. § 99.

[68] "Every man being, as has been showed, naturally free, and nothing being able to put him into subjection to any earthly power, but only his own consent; it is to be considered, what shall be understood to be a sufficient declaration of a man's consent to make him subject to the laws of any government. There is a common distinction of *an express* and *a tacit consent*, which will concern our present

monarchy, or an oligarchy, as it is with a republic.[69] The point that Locke makes, is, that kings do not have an imprescriptible right to their thrones, but that all government rests ultimately upon the will of the people, and that they, for adequate cause, when they so choose, can change it, or do away with it altogether. That is to say, there is somewhere an ultimate right of revolution.[70]

---

case. Nobody doubts but an express consent of any man, entering into any society, makes him a perfect member of that society, a subject of that government. The difficulty is, what ought to be looked upon as a tacit consent, and how far it binds,—*i.e.*, how far any one shall be looked on to have consented, and thereby submitted to any government, where he has made no expressions of it at all. And to this I say, that every man, that hath any possessions, or enjoyment of *any part of the dominions* of any government, doth thereby give his tacit consent, and is as far forth obliged to obedience to the laws of that government, during such enjoyment, as any one under it, whether this his possession be of *land, to him and his heirs for ever*, or a *lodging only for a week*; or whether it be barely *travelling freely on the highway*; and, in effect, it reaches as far as the *very being of any one within the territories* of that government." Second Treatise, § 119.

[69] "The majority having, as has been showed, upon men's first uniting into society, the whole power of the community naturally in them, may employ all that power in making laws for the community from time to time, and executing those laws by officers of their own appointing; and then the form of the government is a perfect democracy: or else may put the power of making laws into the hands of a few select men, and their heirs or successors; and then it is an oligarchy: or else into the hands of one man, and then it is a monarchy: if to him and his heirs, it is an hereditary monarchy: if to him only for life, but upon his death the power only of nominating a successor to return to them, an elective monarchy. And so accordingly of these the community may make compounded and mixed forms of government as they think good. And if the legislative power be at first given by the majority to one or more persons only for their lives, or any limited time, and then the supreme power to revert to them again; when it is so reverted, the community may dispose of it again anew into what hands they please, and so constitute a new form of government: for the form of government depending upon the placing the supreme power, which is the legislative (it being impossible to conceive that an inferior power should prescribe to a superior, or any but the supreme make laws), according as the power of making laws is placed, such is the form of the commonwealth." Second Treatise, § 132.

[70] "221. There is, therefore, secondly, another way, whereby governments are dissolved, and that is, when the legislative, or the prince, either of them, act contrary to their trust. First, the legislative acts against the trust reposed in them, when they endeavor to invade the property of the subject, and to make themselves, or any part of the community, masters, or arbitrary disposers of the lives, liberties, or fortunes of the people. 222. The reasons why men enter into society is the preservation of their property; and the end why they choose and authorize a legislative is, that there may be laws made, and rules set, as guards and fences to the properties of all the members of the society: to limit the power, and moderate the dominion, of every part and member of the society: for since it can never be supposed to be the will of the society that the legislative should have a power to destroy that which every one designs to secure by entering

This postulate it was, and this principally, wherewith the Declaration had to deal, and not the institution of government. What form that was to take, the Congress had not the authority to [341] determine, but, at most, a power of suggestion, or recommendation. The people of the several States, were to say, and they, of course, would decide, in the manner suitable to their habits and prejudices as English freemen, and in keeping with the necessities and requirements of the case as they found them. These of themselves, forbade a monarchy, or an aristocracy, but all such issues were to be of a later determination. Matters of forms of government, and systems of suffrage and representation, were not now involved. The question then and there was one purely of political dominion. Was a revolution justifiable? Even this question would not have arisen, if the Parliament and King had confined themselves to imperial affairs, and not attempted, contrary to precedent, to meddle with the internal concerns of the Colonies.

XVII

Here, then, at last, is the solution. It removes the inconsistency, which always seems so baffling, when we contrast what the fathers said with what they did. It takes nothing from the glory of the Declaration, or the fame of the great men who framed it. It leaves these intact. But it does make the Declaration what it was,—the justification of the Revolution,—the right of a people to revolt against oppression,—and yet, at the same time, furnishes no basis for the charge against the fathers of inconsistency, or self-stultification. These men were largely men of the English race, and they had the traits of character that have given that race predominance in the world. They built on facts, and proceeded one step at a time, looking before, and around as well as above them. They had no love of failure, or intangible ideals, or disorder, or confusion. All their acts bear out this judgment of them. When they gave the Declaration to the world, they gave it as the pledge of their faith, and meant by it, not the propaganda of anarchy, or the demolition of civil society,

---

into society, and for which the people submitted themselves to legislators of their own making; whenever the legislators endeavor to take away and destroy the property of the people, or to reduce them to slavery under arbitrary power, they put themselves into a state of war with the people, who are thereupon absolved from any farther obedience, and are left to the common refuge, which God hath provided for all men, against force and violence." Second Treatise, § 221, § 222.

but the foundation of government, upon the basis of law and justice, with freedom as broad and full as the dictates of prudence and sagacity suggested, or was compatible with the sovereign principle, never to be overlooked, that that government is best, which, not in purpose only, but in fact, brings the greatest good to the greatest number.[71] [342]

[71] See an interesting letter of John Adams to James Sullivan, May 26, 1776, discouraging the latter from raising the question of suffrage in Massachusetts at the time of the discussion of the form of the State Constitution. Also the Virginia Bill of Rights, cited above: "Government is, or ought to be, instituted for the common benefit, protection, and security of the people, nation, or community. Of all the various modes and forms of government that is best, which is capable of producing the greatest degree of happiness and safety, and is most effectually secured against the danger of mal-administration." And also the Declaration of Independence, which seems to hint at a like doctrine: "*To secure these Rights* [Life, Liberty, and the pursuit of Happiness], governments are instituted among men," etc. And again: "Whenever, etc., . . . it is the right of the people, etc., . . . to institute new government, laying its foundation on such principles, and organizing its powers in such form, as to them shall seem *most likely to effect their safety and happiness.*"

⳹ 15 ⳼

The Accusations

SYDNEY GEORGE FISHER

The Declaration of Independence consists roughly of two parts. The first part may be described as composed of the two or three opening paragraphs which set forth with much eloquence the right of revolution and the doctrine of political equality and other rights of men, as they were called, which have become the foundation principles of our American life. The second and much longer part is the rest of the document devoted to the twenty-eight charges against the King.

In a book published some years ago called "The True History of the American Revolution" I showed how the doctrines of political equality, self-government for naturally separated communities, and other rights of man described in the Declaration had originated in the Protestant Reformation and had been studied by the people of our revolutionary period in the works of Burlamaqui, Beccaria, Locke, Grotius, and Puffendorf. These doctrines are extremely interesting and when the Declaration is nowadays read at Fourth of July celebrations the audience listens with much [257] attention to the opening paragraphs. But when the Twenty-eight Charges against the King are reached the audience listens only out of politeness or patriotic duty. The charges seem very dull and tiresome and mean nothing much to a modern mind except that one carries away a general impression that the King must have been a horrible monster of tyranny and cruelty against an innocent child-like and loving people.

But when we know in some detail the facts and circumstances which underlie the Twenty-eight Charges they are fully as interest-

FROM "The Twenty-Eight Charges Against the King in the Declaration of Independence," *Pennsylvania Magazine of History and Biography*, XXXI (3rd Quarter, 1907), 257–263, 300–303. Due to limitations of space, only the introductory and concluding sections of Fisher's study are reprinted.

ing as the general reasoning about the rights of man and they contain a condensed history of the revolutionary movement up to the year 1776. The rebellious colonists had begun their protests some ten years before by denying the right of Parliament to inflict upon them what they called internal taxes of which the stamp tax was the notable instance; but they admitted that in all other respects Parliament had full jurisdiction over them. Parliament thereupon took them at their word, repealed the stamp tax and passed the paint, paper and glass act, which levied what were supposed to be only external taxes because they were duties on the importation of paint, paper and glass collected at the seaports instead of generally throughout the country, like the stamp tax. Parliament also about the same time suspended the power of the legislature of New York because it refused to furnish the British troops stationed in that province with salt, vinegar and beer.

These practical instances of the power of Parliament convinced the patriot party among the colonists, that they had made a great mistake in admitting that Parliament had jurisdiction over them in every respect except the one item of internal taxes. They soon saw that there was no real distinction between internal and external taxes. A duty collected at a seaport on articles of universal use like paint, paper and glass was in the end paid by the whole body of the people in the enhanced price of those articles and was just as much an internal tax as the stamp act. And, [258] moreover, what could be a greater or more imperial exercise of power than the suspension by Parliament of the functions of one of the legislatures. They, accordingly, changed their ground and in 1774 the extremists among them had taken the position that Parliament had no authority whatever in the colonies, either in matters of taxation or anything else; that they owed no allegiance whatever to Parliament and were not under its government. The moderates, were willing to allow Parliament to regulate their external commerce as part of the general commerce of the British empire provided the regulation did not take the form of taxation. Both parties however admitted that they owed allegiance to the king who had originally created the colonies and given them their charters in the days when Parliament was a very insignificant part of the English government.

The numerous acts of Parliament relating to the colonies which had been passed in the last hundred years were, they said, all without legal or constitutional authority and therefore void, although some of them, like the post office act, were undoubtedly beneficial and all of them had been accepted in America because the colonists were weak and careless of their rights, and Parliament being occupied with the task of driving the French from Canada, had not passed many acts relating to the colonies or attempted to regulate them very closely. But now that the French war was over and Parliament, the ministry and the King had announced their intention of reorganizing the colonies, bringing them into close relation and better obedience and had even begun passing acts to that effect, the colonists, or at least a very large party among them, declared that they would stand out against this increasing power of Parliament which had already assumed more jurisdiction than properly belonged to it and apparently intended to assume everything.

In a word, the American colonists were looking upon the beginning of the modern British empire, in which Parliament is supreme, and they had decided to break away [259] from it. Up to the time of the Declaration of Independence in 1776, the whole debate had been about Parliament and its powers. All the protests and indignation had been directed against Parliament; while the king had figured merely as the person or officer under whom the colonists were content to live instead of under Parliament. They were willing to acknowledge him as head of an empire in which they were semi-independent states under his protection against foreign invasion. They would render him a certain amount of allegiance and allow him any rights of vetoing their laws or other privileges which he had before the close of the French war. Their congress had sent to him two petitions to this effect worded in what was then known as "affectionate and dutiful language".

It is therefore a little surprising to find in the Declaration nothing about Parliament. The word Parliament does not occur. Everything is about the king and instead of being the gracious sovereign under whom the colonists were willing and anxious to live, he suddenly becomes a monster of tyranny and is charged with twenty-eight serious political crimes and misdemeanors.

The slightest reflection, however, shows that there was good reason for this change. The revolutionary movement had progressed. The patriot party having ejected from every colony its British governor and the British army having evacuated Boston and gone to Halifax, the country was *de facto* independent. British authority was for the time at least, extinguished; and the patriots in their congress had decided to declare formal independence and announce it to the world. But from what should they declare independence? Not from

Parliament, for they had said that they owed no allegiance whatever to that body and it had no authority over them. The only part of the British nation to which they had admitted allegiance was the King. Of him therefore, they declare their independence and give twenty-eight reasons for doing so.

One of these reasons, the 13th, was that "He has [260] combined with others to subject us to a jurisdiction foreign to our constitutions and unacknowledged by our laws giving his assent to their pretended acts of legislation." This is the only reference to Parliament and the word itself is not used. Nine other reasons follow, each one of them instancing one of the "pretended acts of legislation". These nine reasons may in one sense be considered the most important because they refer to matters which had been the principal subjects of controversy during the last ten years, namely the authority of Parliament in the colonies, and under this head might be written the whole previous history of the revolutionary movement. It is not well, perhaps, in the beginning of this essay to lay much stress on any one set of the reasons or charges; but the ten just mentioned would seem from our modern standpoint, as we look backward, to have furnished a very strong, if not the strongest ground for breaking away from the British empire, namely, that the King our last hold and only connection in the empire, had deserted us and broken his contract with us by joining with Parliament in an effort to fasten forever the jurisdiction of that body on America.

Of the remaining reasons the five from the 23rd to the 27th, are based on the ground that the King by declaring war upon us, sending out troops and war ships to stop what he called the rebellion, fighting the battles of Lexington and Bunker Hill, occupying Boston, burning with his fleets the town of Portland in Maine and the town of Norfolk in Virginia, had by those acts abdicated his government over us, declared us out of his protection and friendliness, broken, in short, his side of the allegiance or contract with us and therefore, we were at liberty to declare the contract and allegiance void and extinguished. The English, of course, said that it was very absurd to give the acts of a mother country in suppressing a rebellion as legal reasons to justify the rebellion. But it is probable, nevertheless, that these reasons carried great weight among our people and showed to them the uselessness of trying to remain in the [261] empire by relying upon the King alone who, as it now seemed, would obey the majority of Parliament and make war upon us at Parliament's demand.

Of the remaining charges the 1st to the 12th are concerned principally, with complaints about colonial laws, which the King had
vetoed and complaints of his efforts to check the rising tide of opposition to the authority of Parliament or rebellion, as he called it. The
last and 28th charge is to the effect that the patriot colonists had
petitioned the King several times in the most humble terms to ab-
stain from his objectionable course of conduct, but he would not
listen and was therefore a tyrant and unfit to be the ruler of a free
people.

Immediately after the Declaration was published in England,
John Lind, a London barrister, wrote for the British ministry a
detailed analysis of the charges and this analysis called "the Answer
to the Declaration of the Congress" was published and passed
through many editions. Thomas Hutchinson, who had been governor of Massachusetts, and was now living in England, also wrote a
pamphlet called "Strictures upon the Declaration of the Congress,"
not so complete as Lind's, but of great value in helping us to understand the situation from the English point of view. These pamphlets
have been seldom, if ever, used by historians; and with their aid and
such other information as I can gather, I shall now make a modern
analysis of the charges, and try to accomplish the very difficult task
of candidly considering both the patriot and the English side.[1]

It is important for the reader to remember that the key to the
whole situation is that our people or, to be more accurate, the patriot party among them, at the period of the Revolution, did not
want to be ruled by a government three thousand miles away, no
matter how well or beneficently [262] that government fulfilled its
task. Everything that government did in the way of control was
distasteful to them; and it is impossible to consider or decide many
of the subjects of controversy on their merits, because it was entirely
a question of point of view. From England's point of view of a great
and obedient colonial empire many of the things she did were perfectly right and justifiable and the same substantially that she does
now in her modern empire. But our patriot party totally rejected that
idea of empire and so practically everything England did was to
them entirely wrong. The great point against which they protested
namely, the complete authority of Parliament has ever since our

[1] American Archives, 5th series, vol. iii., p. 1009 note. I have obtained much
light from Mr. Herbert Friedenwald's "The Declaration of Independence" reprinted from the International Monthly for July, 1901. See also Hazelton's
"Declaration of Independence."

Revolution been accepted without question by England's colonies, and the modern constitutional text books, like those of Todd and Jenkyns refer to it again and again as the cardinal foundation principle on which all rules and regulations of the colonial relation rest. England to this day taxes without their consent, and without representation millions of people in India as well as in the crown colonies.

"The legislative supremacy of Parliament over the whole of the British dominions is complete and undoubted in law, though for constitutional or practical reasons, Parliament abstains from exercising that supreme legislative power. xxxx This doctrine is quite consistent with the very effective indirect taxing power and financial control which, as will be mentioned below is exercised in practice by the Home Government over British India and the crown colonies." (Jenkyns, "British Rule & Jurisdiction Beyond the Seas" p. 10.) [263]

· · · · ·

It may now be well to summarize the instances that have been brought to light under the twenty-eight charges and view in brief the case made out against the king. The declaration lays no particular stress on any one of the charges; but looking backward at the whole history of the subject the two charges under which can be found the strongest instances, as they now seem, for breaking off the allegiance or contract with the King, are the 17th "For imposing taxes on us without our consent" and the 22d "For suspending our own legislatures and declaring themselves invested with power to legislate for us in all cases whatsoever."

Under the first are the instances of the stamp tax, the paint, paper and glass tax, and the tea tax, about which there had been such tremendous controversy during the last twelve years. These taxes had all been repented of and repealed except the tea tax, which still stood. But repentance in the opinion of the patriots amounted to nothing, because Parliament had passed the Declaratory act as it was called, which announced as an unalterable principle of the British Constitution, that no matter what taxes might be repented of or considered bad policy for the moment and repealed, Parliament retained and always would retain the right, not only to tax the colonies, but to legislate for them "in all cases whatsoever." In proof of this Parliament had suspended the power of the legislature of New York, had [300] shown that it was omnipotent and supreme throughout the whole British empire, and that a colony and a colony legislature were mere dependencies which might have considerable privileges and indulgencies, but no positive and fixed rights as against Parliament.

It was against this great principle of Parliamentary omnipotence over the whole British empire that our ancestors rebelled; and they decided to cast off their allegiance to the King because he approved of this principle, and was sending fleets and armies to America to enforce it. All the other political offences of the King were mere trifles compared to this one, and in a sense may be said to have been put into the Declaration as mere make-weight. They might, perhaps, never have been heard of and the American communities might have remained for some years nominally within a sort of British empire, if Parliament had announced that it had no jurisdiction whatsoever in the colonies. But that was not the sort of colonial empire England wanted and it could hardly be called an empire in the usual meaning of the word.

In the matter of disallowance of colonial laws the king had vetoed acts creating paper money, acts granting divorces, acts taxing the slave trade, and acts checking the sending of convicts to America.

In instructions to governors to veto all legislative acts of imperial importance unless they contained a clause suspending their operation until the King's pleasure was known, I have found only two instances. The governors were instructed not to assent to any act establishing a lottery unless it contained the suspending clause; and the governor of North Carolina vetoed the judiciary act of 1773, because it had no suspending clause. The act was afterwards passed with the suspending clause, and the crown took no action on it. I am inclined to think there were other instances which in time, may be found.

In the disallowance of acts creating new counties because representation in the legislature was given the new [301] counties, and thus the strength of the patriot party increased, there were instances in New Hampshire, Massachusetts, New York, New Jersey and Virginia.

In the matter of calling legislatures to meet at a place other than their usual place of meeting there were instances in Massachusetts and South Carolina. In dissolving legislatures for opposing crown measures and refusing for some time to reassemble them, there were instances in Virginia, Massachusetts, and South Carolina. In the matter of naturalization, the crown had in 1773, instructed all governors to veto any naturalization act that should be passed by a colonial legislature. How many acts of this sort were vetoed has not yet been ascertained; but for the purposes of the Declaration the King's offense consisted in his instruction to all the governors to veto such acts. He had also to prevent the growth of the popular or patriot party, raised the price of wild land.

In discouraging migration which might also increase the patriot party only one instance is as yet known and that was the disallowance of a North Carolina act exempting immigrants from all taxation for four years. In obstructing the administration of justice by refusing his assent to laws establishing judiciary powers only one instance is known and that was in North Carolina. As to making colonial judges dependent on his will for the tenure of their offices, there was no question about that, for it had always been Great Britain's policy; and in attempting to deprive the colonial legislatures of the privilege and advantage of paying the salaries of the judges and securing that advantage for the crown, there was a notorious instance in Massachusetts. In erecting a "multitude of new offices and sending hither swarms of officers" he had taken part in creating four new admiralty courts and five new commissioners of customs with some forty or fifty clerks, and assistants.

As to keeping standing armies in the colonies in times of peace without the consent of the colonial legislatures [302] that had always been the British practice. As to rendering "the military independent of and superior to the civil power," there was a notorious instance in Massachusetts when General Gage was made governor and commander-in-chief for the purpose of suppressing what in England, was considered rebellion.

As to combining with Parliament to subject the colonists to that body's jurisdiction, some of the instances have already been mentioned; and there were the other instances of quartering troops in the colonies, having soldiers tried in England when accused of murdering colonists, the Fisheries act which was intended to check the rising rebellion by prohibiting the colonists from trading with or obtaining supplies from any foreign nation, the acts creating admiralty courts which tried without juries, the old act of Henry VIII. allowing colonists to be taken to England to be tried for treason, the Quebec act extending the boundaries of Canada to the Ohio, and establishing by law the Roman Catholic religion, and the act altering the charter of Massachusetts without its consent.

In waging war upon the colonies and thereby putting them out of his protection and allegiance the instances were, of course, innumerable, because several battles had been fought and two or three towns shelled and burnt. In the matter of compelling American sailors captured on the high seas to serve in British war ships the fact has never been questioned or denied. In the matter of exciting insurrections among the slaves there was a notorious instance by Lord Dunmore in Virginia and several attempts had been made to organize the Indians against the colonists. In the matter of rejection of petitions, two petitions one in 1774, the other in 1775, had been sent by the Congress to the King and both of them rejected.

Such were the instances; certainly numerous enough; and as to the weight to be given to each the previous discussion has, it is hoped, enabled the reader to judge for himself. [303]

❧ 16 ❧

Christian Wolff and the
Declaration of Independence

JULIUS GOEBEL

It is a most significant fact, hitherto overlooked, that Wolff's 'Institutiones Juris Naturæ', in Luzac's edition of 1772, which prints the Latin text opposite the French translation, was owned by Jefferson and shows a mark, presumably made by him, opposite the Latin paragraph which treats of the right of civil war: "differt a rebellione Bellum civile quo justa arma adversus *Rectorem civitatis* sumunt subditi. Licitum igitur est in omni casu, in quo Rectori civitatis resistere licet." [1] In the last part of the work numerous passages which treat of war and neutrality are underscored. While it is impossible to determine the exact year when Jefferson purchased the book his manuscript library catalogue shows that he possessed it previous to March 6, 1783.

In view of these facts it is of great interest to examine the Declaration of Independence with regard to the possible influence which Wolff's teachings might have had on Jefferson. That the conception of the inalienable rights, especially of the [80] inalienability of the right of freedom, must be traced back to Wolff has already been pointed out. Of the three rights listed by Locke: life, liberty, and property, the Declaration of Independence has only life and liberty, adding in place of property the pursuit of happiness. While the latter is not contained in Wolff's catalogue of rights, it appears among the objects for which, according to Wolff, the State has been constituted:

[1] ["Different from rebellion is Civil War, in which subjects take up just arms against the *Ruler of the state*. It is therefore permitted on every occasion when to resist he Ruler is permitted." Chr. Wolff: *Institutiones juris naturæ et gentium* (1750),] § 1233.

FROM *Jahrbuch der deutsch-amerikanischen historischen Gesellschaft von Illinois*, XVIII–XIX (1918–1919), pp. 80–83. Original title.

"unde patet, pacto hominum civitates fuisse constituendas et finem
civitatis consistere in vitæ sufficientia, abundantia eorum ad vitæ
necessitatem commoditatem et jucunditatem requiruntur ac medi-
orum felicitatis." [2] The omission of the right of property is all the
more significant, since Locke, as has been shown above, based the
entire structure of his system upon this conception. Whether Jefferson, with keen logical insight, considered the inalienability of property as debatable and irrelevant as far as the great issue was concerned, or whether he thought that the Declaration of Independence should be based upon an interpretation of the law of nature
different in some essentials from that of Locke and his follower,
Blackstone, both of whom were after all loyal Englishmen, is difficult to determine.

To justify the complete political separation from England and the
establishment of a new form of government, an exposition of the
right of resistance that could furnish the legal basis for these actions
was necessary. What Locke had to offer as a last resort in this
respect was an appeal to Heaven. Wolff, however, was far more
explicit and radical in his teachings. While he conceded to the individual only the right of passive resistance against encroachments on
his liberty, he declares that the people as a whole, by whose consent
the government exists, are entitled to disobey and give resistance
whenever their constitutional rights are infringed, for with the
breach of the social compact the people return to the original state
of nature in which each individual protects his own rights, and the
formation of a new government becomes imperative.

That this train of reasoning is at the bottom of Jefferson's arguments in support of the contention that "it is the right and [81] the
duty of the people to throw off a government designing to reduce
them under absolute despotism and to provide new guards for their
future security" is quite evident. Nor can the purpose of laying the
long list of infractions of the rights of the colonies directly at the
door of the British king, the Rector civitatis,[3] and not of the English

---

[2] ["From this it is clear that states came to be constituted by the agreement
of men, and that the end of the state consists in there being sufficiency for
life, an abundance of the things required for the needs, conveniences, and
pleasures of life and for the happiness of the average man."] *Ibid.*, § 972.

[3] The original draft of the Declaration of Independence reads "the present
majesty" which Benjamin Franklin changed into "the present King of Great
Britain."

As a matter of historical interest it may be mentioned that among "the injuries
and usurpations" with which the King of Great Britain is charged there appears
in Jefferson's original draft also the following: "He is at this time transporting

Parliament which, of course, was equally guilty of these infringe-ments, be misunderstood. Had Jefferson adhered to the fiction of the democracy of the British government and accused the Parlia-ment, his entire argumentation would have collapsed and what he wished to have considered an uprising against tyranny, justifiable by the law of nature, would have appeared as unwarrantable rebellion.

There is finally one more vital point of contact between Jefferson's Declaration and the system of Wolff. Although Locke had suc-ceeded in re-establishing the jus naturale of stoicism, his own system lacked the metaphysical foundation which the stoic doctrine pos-sessed in the principle of the universal reason, of which the jus naturale is a manifestation. Without sacrificing the rationalistic char-acter of his method or of returning to the theological explanation of the natural law of previous times, Wolff, following Leibniz, on the other hand, declared that "autor legis naturæ ipse Deus est et ad actiones suas eidem conformandas hominem obligat, sicque obligatio naturalis etiam divina est et lex naturalis divina." [4] The spirit of Deism which dictated this explanation of the origin of the law of nature would naturally appeal to Jefferson, and it is not difficult to see how it is reflected in the phrase: "That they are *endowed* by their *creator* with certain [82] inalienable rights." [5] The jus con-natum is, therefore, in the last analysis a divine law and its inalien-ability follows from its divine character.

By this allusion to the divine origin of the law of nature the doctrine of the inalienable rights of man became a message whose inspiring ring acted with irresistible force especially upon the masses. What had been slowly evolved in the quiet workshop of the German philosopher now loomed in historical reality by the estab-lishment of a democracy such as the world had not seen before. [83]

---

large armies of *Scotch and other foreign mercenaries* to complete the works of death", etc. Why the *Scotch* who were evidently classed as foreigners with the so-called "Hessians" by Jefferson, were afterwards omitted has not yet been ex-plained.

[4] ["God himself is the author of the law of nature and he obliges man to con-form his actions to it, so that natural obligation is divine, just as is natural law."] Wolff, *Institutiones*, § 41.

[5] It is most significant that in the original draft of the Declaration of Independ-ence, Jefferson intended to deduct the inalienable rights from the equality of all men: "that from that equal creation they derive in rights inherent and inalien-able."

17

The Literary Qualities

of the Declaration

CARL L. BECKER

Jefferson was chosen to draft the Declaration because he was known to possess a "masterly pen." There were perhaps other reasons, but this was the chief one. When he came to Congress in 1775, "he brought with him," says John Adams, "a reputation for literature, science, and a happy talent for composition. Writings of his were handed about remarkable for the peculiar felicity of expression." [1] *Peculiar felicity of expression*—the very words which one would perhaps choose to sum up the distinguishing characteristics of Jefferson's style.

Like many men who write with felicity, Jefferson was no orator. He rarely, if ever, made a speech. "During the whole time I sat with him in Congress," John Adams says, "I never heard him utter three sentences together"—that is, on the floor of Congress; in committees and in conversation he was, on the contrary, "prompt, frank, explicit, and [194] decisive." [2] It might seem that a man who can write effectively should be able to speak effectively. It sometimes happens. But one whose ear is sensitive to the subtler, elusive harmonies of expression, one who in imagination hears the pitch and cadence and rhythm of the thing he wishes to say before he says it, often makes a sad business of public speaking because, painfully aware of the imperfect felicity of what has been uttered, he forgets what he ought to say next. He instinctively wishes to cross out what he has

---

[1] *Works of John Adams*, II, 514.   [2] *Ibid.*, 511–514.

REPRINTED by permission of Alfred A. Knopf, Inc., from *The Declaration of Independence: A Study in the History of Political Ideas*, Vintage Edition, by Carl L. Becker. Copyright, 1922, 1942 by Carl L. Becker. Chapter V, pp. 194–223. Original title.

just said, and say it over again in a different way—and this is what he often does, to the confusion of the audience. In writing he can cross out and rewrite at leisure, as often as he likes, until the sound and the sense are perfectly suited—until the thing *composes*. The reader sees only the finished draft.

Not that Jefferson wrote with difficulty, constructing his sentences with slow and painful effort. One who, as an incident to a busy public career, wrote so much and so well, must have written with ease and rapidity. But Jefferson, as the original drafts of his papers show, revised and corrected his writings with care, seeking, yet without wearing his soul threadbare in the search, for the better word, the happier phrase, the smoother transition. His style [195] has not indeed the achieved perfection, the impeccable surface, of that of a master-craftsman like Flaubert, or Walter Pater; but neither has it the objectivity, the impersonal frigidity of writing that is perhaps too curiously and deliberately integrated, too consciously made. Having something to say, he says it, with as much art as may be, yet not solely for the art's sake, aiming rather at the ease, the simplicity, the genial urbanity of cultivated conversation. The grace and felicity of his style have a distinctly personal flavor, something Jeffersonian in the implication of the idea, or in the beat and measure of the words. Franklin had equal ease, simplicity, felicity; but no one who knows the writings of Franklin could attribute the Declaration to him. Jefferson communicated an undefinable yet distinctive quality to the Declaration which makes it his.

The Declaration is filled with these felicities of phrase which bear the stamp of Jefferson's mind and temperament: *a decent respect to the opinions of mankind; more disposed to suffer, while evils are sufferable, than to right themselves by abolishing the forms to which they are accustomed; for the sole purpose of fatiguing them into compliance with his measures; sent hither swarms of officers to harrass our people and eat out their substance; hold them as we hold the rest of* [196] *mankind, enemies in war, in peace friends.* There are some sentences in the Declaration which are more than felicitous. The closing sentence, for example, is perfection itself. Congress amended the sentence by including the phrase, "with a firm reliance upon the protection of divine Providence." It may be that Providence always welcomes the responsibilities thrust upon it in times of war and revolution; but personally, I like the sentence better as Jefferson wrote it. "And for the support of this Declaration we mutually pledge to each other our lives, our fortunes, and our sacred honor." It is true (assuming that men value life more than property, which is doubtful) that the statement violates the rhetorical rule of climax; but it was a sure sense that made Jefferson place 'lives' first and 'fortunes' second. How much weaker if he had written "our fortunes, our lives, and our sacred honor"! Or suppose him to have used the word 'property' instead of 'fortunes!' Or suppose him to have omitted 'sacred!' Consider the effect of omitting any of the words, such as the last two 'ours'—"our lives, fortunes, and sacred honor." No, the sentence can hardly be improved.

There are probably more of these Jeffersonian felicities in the Declaration than in any other writing by him of equal length. Jefferson [197] realized that, if the colonies won their independence, this would prove to be a public document of supreme importance; and the Rough Draft (which may not be the first one) bears ample evidence of his search for the right word, the right phrasing. In the opening sentence, not at all bad as it originally stood, there are four corrections. The first part of the second paragraph seems to have given him much trouble. The Rough Draft reads as follows:

self-evident
We hold these truths to be~ ~~sacred & undeniable;~~ that all men are
they are endowed by their creator with
created equal ~~& independent;~~ that~ ~~from that equal creation they derive~~
~~equal rights some of which are~~ rights; that these
~~in rights~~ inherent & inalienable~ among ~~which~~~ are ~~the preservation of~~
life, ~~&~~ liberty, & the pursuit of happiness.

When Jefferson submitted the draft to Adams the only correction which he had made was to write 'self-evident' in place of 'sacred & undeniable.' It is interesting to guess why, on a later reading, the other changes were made. I suspect that he erased '& independent' because, having introduced 'self-evident,' he did not like the sound of the two phrases both closing with 'dent.' The phrase 'they are endowed by their creator' is obviously much better than 'from that equal creation'; but this correction, as [198] he first wrote it, left an awkward wording: 'that they are endowed by their creator with equal rights some of which are inherent & inalienable among which are.' Too many 'which ares'; and besides, why suppose that some rights given by the creator were inherent and some not? Thus we get the form, which is so much stronger, as well as more agreeable to the ear: 'that they are endowed by their creator with inherent & inalienable rights.' Finally, why say 'the preservation of life'? If a

man has a right to life, the right to preserve life is manifestly included.

Again, take the close of the last paragraph but one. The Rough
Draft gives the following reading:

                & to glory   ~~must~~ tread
The road to ~~glory &~~ happiness, is open to us too; we will ~~climb,~~ it ~~in a~~
apart from them
~~separately state.~~

The phrase 'to happiness & to glory' is better than 'to glory & happiness.' Placing "glory" before "happiness" might imply that the first
aim of the colonists was glory, and that their happiness would come
as an incident to the achievement of glory. What needed to be
expressed was the idea that the colonists were defending the natural
right to happiness, and that the vindication of this inherent human
[199] right would confer glory upon them. Did Jefferson, in making
the change, reason thus? Probably not. Upon reading it over he
doubtless instinctively felt that by placing 'happiness' first and re-
peating the 'to' he would take the flatness out of a prosaic phrase. As
for the latter part of the sentence, Jefferson evidently first wrote it:
'climb it in a separate state.' Not liking the word "state," he erased
'state' and 'in a' and added '-ly' to 'separate': so that it read: 'we will
climb it separately.' But no, on second thought, that is not much
better. 'Climb it apart from them'—that would do. So apparently it
read when the Declaration was adopted, since 'climb' and not 'tread'
is the reading of all but one of the copies, including the text finally
adopted. It may be that Jefferson made the change during the
debates in Congress, and then thought better of it, or neglected to
get the change incorporated in the final text. There is another correction in the Rough Draft which does not appear in the final form
of the Declaration. "Our repeated petitions have been answered
only by repeated injury"—so the Declaration reads; but in the
Rough Draft the 'injury' has been changed to 'injuries.' This is manifestly better; and as one can hardly suppose Congress would have
preferred 'injury' to 'injuries,' it is [200] probable that the change
was made after the Declaration was adopted. Jefferson had something of the artist's love of perfection for its own sake, the writer's
habit of correcting a manuscript even after it has been published.

Apart from the peculiar felicities of phrasing, what strikes one
particularly in reading the Declaration as a whole is the absence of
declamation. Everything considered, the Declaration is brief, free of
verbiage, a model of clear, concise, and simple statement. In 1856

Rufus Choate referred to it as "that passionate and eloquent manifesto," made up of "glittering and sounding generalities of natural right." [3] Eloquent the Declaration frequently is, in virtue of a certain high seriousness with which Jefferson contrived to invest what was ostensibly a direct and simple statement of fact. Of all words in the language, 'passionate' is the one which is least applicable to Jefferson or to his writings. As to 'generalities,' the Declaration contains relatively few; and if those few are 'glittering and sounding' it is in their substance and not in their form that they are so. You may not believe

> that all men are created equal; that they are endowed by their creator with certain unalienable rights; that [201] among these are life, liberty, and the pursuit of happiness; that to secure these rights governments are instituted among men, deriving their just powers from the consent of the governed; that whenever any form of government becomes destructive of these ends, it is the right of the people to alter or to abolish it, and to institute new government, laying its foundations on such principles, and organizing its powers in such form, as to them shall seem most likely to effect their safety and happiness.

You may not believe this; but if you do believe it, as Jefferson and his contemporaries did, you would find it difficult to say it more concisely; in words more direct, simple, precise, and appropriate; with less of passionate declamation, of rhetorical magniloquence, or of verbal ornament. The second paragraph of the Declaration of Independence reminds one of Lincoln's Gettysburg Address in its unimpassioned simplicity of statement. It glitters as much, or as little, as that famous document.

Logical sequence and structural unity are not always essential to good writing; but the rambling and discursive method would scarcely be appropriate to a declaration of independence. Jefferson's declaration, read casually, seems not to possess a high degree of unity. [202] Superficially considered, it might easily strike one as the result of an uneasy marriage of convenience between an abstract philosophy of government and certain concrete political grievances. But in truth the Declaration is built up around a single idea, and its various parts are admirably chosen and skilfully disposed for the production of a particular effect. The grievances against the king occupy so much space that one is apt to think of them as the main theme. Such is not the case. The primary purpose of the Declaration

---

[3] Letter to E. W. Farley, Aug. 9, 1856; Brown, S. G., *Life of Rufus Choate*, 324, 326.

was to convince a candid world that the colonies had a moral and legal right to separate from Great Britain. This would be difficult to do, however many and serious their grievances might be, if the candid world was to suppose that the colonies were politically subordinate to the British government in the ordinary sense. It is difficult to justify rebellion against established political authority. Accordingly, the idea around which Jefferson built the Declaration was that the colonists were not rebels against established political authority, but a free people maintaining long established and imprescriptible rights against a usurping king. The effect which he wished to produce was to leave a candid world wondering why the colonies had so long submitted to the oppressions of this king.

The major premise from which this conclusion [203] is derived is that every 'people' has a natural right to make and unmake its own government; the minor premise is that the Americans are a 'people' in this sense. In establishing themselves in America, the people of the colonies exercised their natural rights to frame governments suited to their ideas and conditions; but at the same time they voluntarily retained a union with the people of Great Britain by professing allegiance to the same king. From this allegiance they might at any time have withdrawn; if they had not so withdrawn it was because of the advantages of being associated with the people of Great Britain; if they now proposed to withdraw, it was not because they now any less than formerly desired to maintain the ancient association, but because the king by repeated and deliberate actions had endeavored to usurp an absolute authority over them contrary to every natural right and to long established custom. The minor premise of the argument is easily overlooked because it is not explicitly stated in the Declaration—at least not in its final form. To have stated it explicitly would perhaps have been to bring into too glaring a light certain incongruities between the assumed premise and known historical facts. The rôle of the list of grievances against the king is to make the assumed premise emerge, [204] of its own accord as it were, from a carefully formulated but apparently straightforward statement of concrete historical events. From the point of view of structural unity, the role which the list of grievances plays in the Declaration is a subordinate one; its part is to exhibit the historical circumstances under which the colonists, as a 'free people,' had thrust upon them the high obligation of defending the imprescriptible rights of all men.

Although occupying a subordinate place in the logical structure, the list of grievances is of the highest importance in respect to the total effect which the Declaration aims to produce. From this point of view, the form and substance of these paragraphs constitute not the least masterly part of the Declaration. It is true, books upon rhetoric warn the candidate for literary honors at all hazards to avoid monotony; he ought, they say, to seek a pleasing variety by alternating long and short sentences; and while they consider it correct to develop a single idea in each paragraph, they consider it inadvisable to make more than one paragraph out of a single sentence. These are no doubt good rules, for writing in general; but Jefferson violated them all, perhaps because he was writing something in particular. Of set purpose, throughout this part of the Declaration, [205] he began each charge against the king with 'he has': 'he has refused his assent'; 'he has forbidden his governors'; 'he has refused to pass laws'; 'he has called together legislative bodies'; 'he has refused for a long time.' As if fearing that the reader might not after all notice this oft-repeated 'he has,' Jefferson made it still more conspicuous by beginning a new paragraph with each 'he has.' To perform thus is not to be 'literary' in a genteel sense; but for the particular purpose of drawing an indictment against the king it served very well indeed. Nothing could be more effective than these brief, crisp sentences, each one the bare affirmation of a malevolent act. Keep your mind on the king, Jefferson seems to say; he is the man: 'he has refused'; 'he has forbidden'; 'he has combined'; 'he has incited'; 'he has plundered'; 'he has abdicated.' I will say he has.

These hard, incisive sentences are all the more effective as an indictment of the king because of the sharp contrast between them and the paragraphs, immediately preceding and following, in which Jefferson touches upon the sad state of the colonists. In these paragraphs there is something in the carefully chosen words, something in the falling cadence of the sentences, that conveys a mournful, almost a funereal, sense of evils apprehended and long forefended but [206] now unhappily realized. Consider the phrases which give tone and pitch to the first two paragraphs: 'when in the course of human events'; 'decent respect to the opinions of mankind'; 'all experience hath shewn'; 'suffer while evils are sufferable'; 'forms to which they are accustomed'; 'patient sufferance of these colonies'; 'no solitary fact to contradict the uniform tenor of the rest.' Such phrases skilfully disposed have this result, that the opening passages of the Declaration give one the sense of fateful things impending, of hopes defeated and injuries sustained with unavailing fortitude. The

contrast in manner is accentuated by the fact that whereas the king
is represented as exclusively aggressive, the colonists are represented
as essentially submissive. In this drama the king alone acts—he
conspires, incites, plunders; the colonists have the passive part,
never lifting a hand to burn stamps or destroy tea; they suffer while
evils are sufferable. It is a high literary merit of the Declaration that
by subtle contrasts Jefferson contrives to conjure up for us a vision
of the virtuous and long-suffering colonists standing like martyrs to
receive on their defenseless heads the ceaseless blows of the tyrant's
hand.

Like many men with a sense for style, Jefferson, although much
given to polishing and [207] correcting his own manuscripts, did not
always welcome changes which others might make. Congress discussed his draft for three successive days. What uncomplimentary
remarks the members may have made is not known; but it is known
that in the end certain paragraphs were greatly changed and others
omitted altogether. These 'depredations'—so he speaks of them—
Jefferson did not enjoy: but we may easily console ourselves for his
discomfiture since it moved the humane Franklin to tell him a story.
Writing in 1818, Jefferson says:

I was sitting by Dr. Franklin, who perceived that I was not insensible to
these mutilations. 'I have made it a rule,' said he, 'whenever in my power,
to avoid becoming the draughtsman of papers to be reviewed by a public
body. I took my lesson from an incident which I will relate to you. When
I was a journeyman printer, one of my companions, an apprentice Hatter,
having served out his time, was about to open shop for himself. His first
concern was to have a handsome signboard, with a proper inscription. He
composed it in these words: 'John Thompson, Hatter, makes and sells
hats for ready money,' with a figure of a hat subjoined. But he thought he
would submit it to his friends for their amendments. The first [208] he
shewed it to thought the word 'hatter' tautologous, because followed by
the words 'makes hats' which shew he was a hatter. It was struck out.
The next observed that the word 'makes' might as well be omitted, because his customers would not care who made the hats. If good and to
their mind, they would buy, by whomsoever made. He struck it out. A
third said he thought the words 'for ready money' were useless as it was
not the custom of the place to sell on credit. Every one who purchased
expected to pay. They were parted with, and the inscription now stood
'John Thompson sells hats.' 'Sells hats' says his next friend? Why nobody
will expect you to give them away. What then is the use of that word? It
was stricken out, and 'hats' followed it, the rather, as there was one

painted on the board. So his inscription was reduced ultimately to 'John Thompson' with the figure of a hat subjoined.' [4]

Jefferson's colleagues were not so ruthless as the friends of John Thompson; and on the whole it must be said that Congress left the Declaration better than it found it. The few verbal changes that were made improved the phraseology, I am inclined to think, in every case. [209] Where Jefferson wrote: "He has erected a multitude of new offices by a self-assumed power, and sent hither swarms of officers to harrass our people and eat out their substance," Congress cut out the phrase, "by a self-assumed power." Again, Jefferson's sentence, "He has abdicated government here, withdrawing his governors, and declaring us out of his allegiance and protection," Congress changed to read, "He has abdicated government here by declaring us out of his protection and waging war against us." Is not the phraseology of Congress, in both cases, more incisive, and does it not thus add something to that very effect which Jefferson himself wished to produce?

Aside from merely verbal changes, Congress rewrote the final paragraph, cut out the greater part of the paragraph next to the last, and omitted altogether the last of Jefferson's charges against the king. The final paragraph as it stands is certainly much stronger than in its original form. The Declaration was greatly strengthened by using, for the renunciation of allegiance, the very phraseology of the resolution of July 2, by which Congress had officially decreed that independence which it was the function of the Declaration to justify. It was no doubt for this reason mainly that Congress rewrote the paragraph; but the revision had [210] in addition the merit of giving to the final paragraph, what such a paragraph especially needed, greater directness and assurance. In its final form, the Declaration closes with the air of accepting the issue with confident decision.

In cutting out the greater part of the next to the last paragraph, Congress omitted, among other things, the sentence in which Jefferson formulated, not directly indeed but by allusion, that theory of the constitutional relation of the colonies to Great Britain which is elsewhere taken for granted: "We have reminded them [our British brethren] . . . that in constituting indeed our several forms of government, we had adopted one common king; thereby laying a foundation for perpetual league and amity with them; but that submis-

[4] *Writings of Thomas Jefferson* (Ford ed.), X, 120.

sion to their parliament was no part of our constitution, nor ever in idea, if history may be credited." Perhaps the Declaration would have been strengthened by including an explicit formulation of this theory. But if the theory was to be expressly formulated at all, Jefferson was unfortunate both in the form and in the order of the statement. Unfortunate in the form, which is allusive, and in the last phrase ambiguous—"Nor ever in idea, if history may be credited." Unfortunate in the order, because, if the theory was to be expressly formulated at all, its formulation [211] should manifestly have preceded the list of charges against the king. In general, this paragraph, as originally written, leaves one with the feeling that the author, not quite aware that he is done, is beginning over again. In the form adopted, it is an admirable brief prelude to the closing paragraph.

The last of Jefferson's charges against the king was what John Adams called the "vehement philippic against negro slavery." [5]

He has waged cruel war against human nature itself, violating its most sacred rights of life and liberty in the persons of a distant people who never offended him, captivating and carrying them into slavery in another hemisphere, or to incur miserable death in their transportation thither. This piratical warfare, the opprobrium of *infidel* powers, is the warfare of the *Christian* king of Great Britain. Determined to keep open a market where MEN should be bought and sold, he has prostituted his negative for suppressing every legislative attempt to prohibit or to restrain this execrable commerce; and that this assemblage of horrors might want no fact of distinguished die, he is now exciting these very people to rise in arms among us, and to purchase that liberty [212] of which *he* deprived them, by murdering the people upon whom *he* also obtruded them; thus paying off former crimes committed against the *liberties* of one people, with crimes which he urges them to commit against the *lives* of another.

Congress omitted this passage altogether. I am glad it did. One does not expect a declaration of independence to represent historical events with the objectivity and exactitude of a scientific treatise; but here the discrepancy between the fact and the representation is too flagrant. Especially, in view of the subsequent history of the slave trade, and of slavery itself, without which there would have been no slave trade, these charges against the king lose whatever plausibility, slight enough at best, they may have had at the time. But I have quoted this passage in full once more, not on account of its sub-

[5] *Works of John Adams,* II, 514.

stance but on account of its form, which is interesting, and peculiarly significant in its bearing upon Jefferson's qualities and limitations as a writer. John Adams thought it one of the best parts of the
Declaration. It is possible that Jefferson thought so too. He evidently
gave much attention to the wording of it. But to me, even assuming
the charges against the king to be true, it is the part of the [213]
Declaration in which Jefferson conspicuously failed to achieve literary excellence.

The reason is, I think, that in this passage Jefferson attempted
something which he was temperamentally unfitted to achieve. The
passage was to have been the climax of the charges against the king;
on its own showing of facts it imputes to him the most inhuman acts,
the basest motives; its purpose, one supposes, is to stir the reader's
emotions, to make him feel a righteous indignation at the king's acts,
a profound contempt for the man and his motives. Well, the passage
is clear, precise, carefully balanced. It employs the most tremendous words—"murder," "piratical warfare," "prostituted," "miserable
death." But in spite of every effort, the passage somehow leaves us
cold; it remains, like all of Jefferson's writing, calm and quiescent; it
lacks warmth, it fails to lift us out of our equanimity. There is in it
even (something rare indeed in Jefferson's writings) a sense of labored effort, of deliberate striving for an effect that does not come.

This curious effect, or lack of effect, is partly due to the fact that
the king's base actions are presented to us in abstract terms. We are
not permitted to see George III. George III does not repeal a statute
of South Carolina in order that Sambo may be sold at the port [214]
of Charleston. No, the Christian king wages "cruel war against
human nature," he prostitutes "his negative for the suppression of
every legislative attempt to prohibit or to restrain this execrable
commerce." We have never a glimpse of poor dumb negroes gasping
for breath in the foul hold of a transport ship, or driven with whips
like cattle to labor in a fetid rice swamp; what we see is human
nature, and the "violation of its most sacred rights in the persons of
a distant people." The thin vision of things in the abstract rarely
reaches the sympathies. Few things are less moving than to gaze
upon the concept of miserable death, and it is possible to contemplate "an assemblage of horrors that wants no fact of distinguished
die" without much righteous indignation.

Yet the real reason lies deeper. It is of course quite possible to
invest a generalized statement with an emotional quality. Consider
the famous passage from Lincoln's second Inaugural:

Fondly do we hope—fervently do we pray—that this mighty scourge of war may speedily pass away. Yet, if God wills that it continue until all the wealth piled by the bondsman's two hundred and fifty years of unrequited toil shall be sunk, and until every drop of blood drawn with the lash shall be paid by another drawn by the sword, [215] as was said three thousand years ago, so still it must be said, "the judgments of the Lord are true and righteous altogether."

Compare this with Jefferson's

And that this assemblage of horrors might want no fact of distinguished die, he is now exciting these very people to rise in arms against us, and to purchase that liberty of which *he* deprived them, by murdering the people upon whom *he* also obtruded them; thus paying off former crimes committed against the *liberties* of one people, with crimes which he urges them to commit against the *lives* of another.

Making every allowance for difference in subject and in occasion, these passages differ as light differs from darkness. There is a quality of deep feeling about the first, an indefinable something which is profoundly moving; and this something, which informs and enriches much of Lincoln's writing, is rarely, almost never present in the writing of Jefferson.

This something, which Jefferson lacked but which Lincoln possessed in full measure, may perhaps for want of a better term be called a profoundly emotional apprehension of experience. One might say that Jefferson felt with the [216] mind, as some people think with the heart. He had enthusiasm, but it was enthusiasm engendered by an irrepressible intellectual curiosity. He was ardent, but his ardors were cool, giving forth light without heat. One never feels with Jefferson, as one does with Washington, that his restraint is the effect of a powerful will persistently holding down a profoundly passionate nature. One has every confidence that Jefferson will never lose control of himself, will never give way to purifying rage, relieving his overwrought feelings by an outburst of divine swearing. All his ideas and sentiments seem of easy birth, flowing felicitously from an alert and expeditious brain rather than slowly and painfully welling up from the obscure depths of his nature. "I looked for gravity," says Maclay, giving his first impressions of Jefferson, "but a laxity of manner seemed shed about him. He spoke almost without ceasing; but even his discourse partook of his personal demeanor. It was loose and rambling; and yet he scattered information wherever he went, and some even brilliant sentiments sparkled from him."

Jefferson's writing is much like that—a ceaseless flow, sparkling, often brilliant, a kind of easy improvisation. There are in his writings few of those ominous overtones charged with emotion, and implying more than is expressed. [217] Sometimes, indeed, by virtue of a certain facility, a certain complacent optimism, by virtue of saying disputed things in such a pleasant way, his words imply even less than they mean. When, for example, Jefferson says "the tree of liberty must be refreshed from time to time with the blood of patriots and tyrants," so far from making us shudder, he contrives to throw about this unlovely picture a kind of arcadian charm. You will hardly think of Jefferson, with lifted hand and vibrant voice, in the heat of emotion striking off the tremendous sentence, "Give me liberty or give me death!" I can imagine him saying, "Manly spirit bids us choose to die freemen rather than to live slaves." The words would scarcely lift us out of our seats, however we might applaud the orator for his peculiar felicity of expression.

Felicity of expression—certainly Jefferson had that; but one wonders whether he did not perhaps have too much of it. This sustained felicity gives one at times a certain feeling of insecurity, as of resting one's weight on something fragile. Jefferson's placidity, the complacent optimism of his sentiments and ideas, carry him at times perilously near the fatuous. One would like more evidence that the iron had some time or other entered his soul, more evidence of his having profoundly reflected upon the [218] enigma of existence, of having more deeply felt its tragic import, of having won his convictions and his optimisms and his felicities at the expense of some painful travail of the spirit. What saved Jefferson from futility was of course his clear, alert intelligence, his insatiable curiosity, his rarely failing candor, his loyalty to ideas, his humane sympathies. Yet we feel that his convictions, his sympathies, his ideas are essentially of the intellect, somehow curiously abstracted from reality, a consciously woven drapery laid over the surface of a nature essentially aristocratic, essentially fastidious, instinctively shrinking from close contact with men and things as they are.

Not without reason was Jefferson most at home in Paris. By the qualities of his mind and temperament he really belonged to the philosophical school, to the Encyclopaedists, those generous souls who loved mankind by virtue of not knowing too much about men, who worshipped reason with unreasoning faith, who made a religion of Nature while cultivating a studied aversion for 'enthusiasm,' and strong religious emotion. Like them, Jefferson, in his earlier years especially, impresses one as being a radical by profession. We often feel that he defends certain practices and ideas, that he denounces certain customs or [219] institutions, not so much from independent reflection or deep-seated conviction on the particular matter in hand as because in general these are the things that a philosopher and a man of virtue ought naturally to defend or denounce. It belonged to the eighteenth-century philosopher, as a matter of course, to apostrophize Nature, to defend Liberty, to denounce Tyranny, perchance to shed tears at the thought of a virtuous action. It was always in character for him to feel the degradation of Human Nature when confronted with the idea of Negro Slavery.

This academic accent, as of ideas and sentiments belonging to a system, of ideas uncriticized and sentiments no more than conventionally felt, is what gives a labored and perfunctory effect to Jefferson's famous 'philippic against Negro salvery.' Adams described it better than he knew. It is indeed a philippic; it is indeed vehement; but it is not moving. It is such a piece as would be expected of a *philosopher* on such an occasion. We remain calm in reading it because Jefferson, one cannot but think, remained calm in writing it. For want of phrases charged with deep feeling, he resorts to italics, vainly endeavoring to stir the reader by capitalizing and underlining the words that need to be stressed—a futile device, which [220] serves only to accentuate the sense of artifice and effort, and, in the case of 'the *Christian* king of Great Britain,' introduces the wholly incongruous note of snarling sarcasm, reminding us for all the world of Shylock's 'these be the *Christian* husbands.' Jefferson apprehended the injustice of slavery; but one is inclined to ask how deeply he felt it.

It may be said that Jefferson touches the emotions as little in other parts of the Declaration as in the philippic on slavery. That is in great measure true; but in the other parts of the Declaration, which have to do for the most part with an exposition of the constitutional rights of the colonies, or with a categorical statement of the king's violations of these rights, the appeal is more properly to the mind than to the heart; and it was in appealing to the reader's mind, of course, that Jefferson was at his best. Taking the Declaration as a whole, this is indeed its conspicuous quality: it states clearly, reasons lucidly, exposes felicitously; its high virtue is in this, that it makes a strong bid for the reader's assent. But it was beyond the power of Jefferson to impregnate the Declaration with qualities that would give to the reader's assent the moving force of profound conviction.

With all its precision, its concise rapidity, its clarity, its subtle [221] implications and engaging felicities, one misses a certain unsophisticated directness, a certain sense of impregnable solidity and massive strength, a certain effect of passion restrained and deep convictions held in reserve, which would have given to it that accent of perfect sincerity and that emotional content which belong to the grand manner.

The Declaration has not the grand manner—that passion under control which lifts prose to the level of true poetry. Yet it has, what is the next best thing, a quality which saves it from falling to the prosaic. It has elevation. I have said that Franklin had, equally with Jefferson, clarity, simplicity, precision, felicity. If Franklin had written the Declaration it would have had all of these qualities; but Franklin would have communicated to it something homely and intimate and confidential, some smell of homespun, some air of the tavern or the print shop. Franklin could not, I think, have written this sentence:

When in the course of human events it becomes necessary for one people to dissolve the political bands which have connected them with another, and to assume among the powers of the earth the separate and equal station to which the laws of nature and of nature's god entitle them, [222] a decent respect to the opinions of mankind requires that they should declare the causes which impel them to the separation.

Or this one:

Prudence indeed will dictate that governments long established should not be changed for light and transient causes; and accordingly all experience hath shewn that mankind are more disposed to suffer, while evils are sufferable, than to right themselves by abolishing the forms to which they are accustomed.

Or this:

And for the support of this declaration we mutually pledge to each other our lives, our fortunes, and our sacred honor.

These sentences may not be quite in the grand manner; but they have a high seriousness, a kind of lofty pathos which at least lift the Declaration to the level of a great occasion. These qualities Jefferson was able to communicate to his writing by virtue of possessing a nature exquisitely sensitive, and a mind finely tempered; they illustrate, in its subtler forms, what John Adams called his 'peculiar felicity of expression.' [223]

ᑫᑫ 18 ᑫᑫ

The American Argument

OTTO VOSSLER

And in the Declaration of Independence [1] Jefferson advocated the same "defensive" conception of the Revolution and the same legalistic ideology that like other Americans he had always persisted in. To be sure, the general, traditional view is that in this document the Virginian proclaimed with philosophic—indeed prophetic—spirit the fundamental ideas of American democracy, ideas that later on were to have conquered and transformed France and the world. Now, how does this interpretation stand up?

The plan of the Declaration is that of a legal document: first a preamble, then citation of laws, next establishment of evidence with detailed enumeration of the particular acts by which the accused has infringed upon the law, and finally, the pronouncement of judgment. The same holds for the language. The concluding passage as it read in Jefferson's draft before it was altered by Congress serves as the best example of the strict legalistic style: [2]

We therefore the representatives of the United States in General Congress assembled in the name and by the authority of the good people of these states, reject and renounce all allegiance and subjection to the Kings of Great Britain and all others who may hereafter claim by, [79] through, or under them; we utterly dissolve all political connection which may heretofore have subsisted between us and the people or parliament of Great Britain, and finally we do assert and declare these colonies to be

---

[1] On the Declaration of Independence *cf.* John H. Hazelton, *The Declaration of Independence* (N. Y.: 1906); Carl Becker, *The Declaration of Independence: A Study in the History of Political Ideas* (N. Y.: 1922); Friedenwald, *The Declaration of Independence: An Interpretation and an Analysis.* The text is reproduced below, p. 188.

[2] *Cf.* Hazelton for the different texts of the Declaration of Independence.

TRANSLATED by the editor from *Die amerikanischen Revolutionsideale in ihrem Verhältnis zu den Europäischen: Untersucht an Thomas Jefferson, Beiheft 17 der Historischen Zeitschrift* (Munich & Berlin: Verlag von R. Oldenbourg, 1929), pp. 79–86, by permission of the author and publisher.

free and independant and that as free and independant states, they have
full power to levy war, conclude peace, contract alliances, establish commerce, and to do all other acts and things which independant states may of
right do. . . .

The crucial phrases that were meant to settle the fate of a continent,
in the circumstantial and halting diction of a diligent notary! This is
all the more significant since Jefferson demonstrated in other places
in the Declaration of Independence that he had command, when he
wished, of a classical style of loftier expression. The traditional legalistic style at the crucial point, precisely there where the legal
bond with England is broken, was thus chosen quite intentionally
and is part of the very nature of the Declaration.

With a proper respect Jefferson turned to the public opinion of
the world, not with a boisterous shout "To everyone!" and not to
summon mankind to the revolt—quite the contrary, he wants to
justify the Americans before it, to clear them of blame for the rebellion, and to give them a proper place among nations. Through the
entire document runs the effort to absolve the former Colonies from
any revolutionary intent or revolutionary offense. Fully two-thirds
of the text is devoted to the demonstration that England has infringed
upon the Constitution, that England is the aggressor and England
the "revolutionary." Despite the enumerated instances of shocking
encroachment, the Colonies have suffered patiently [3] and borne the
evil as long as it was bearable; [4] they have at each new step of the
oppression petitioned in the most subservient manner; [5] they have
addressed themselves to their brethren in England and with repeated warning called attention to the endeavors of their Parliament
to erect an illegal dominion over America; [6] they have reminded
them that such a claim [80] is unconstitutional; [7] they have appealed
to their justice and magnanimity and conjured them by the ties of
their common race to reject these usurpations.[8] Their patience, their

---

[3] "Patient sufferance."   [4] "Suffer while evils are sufferable."

[5] "In every new stage of these oppressions we have petitioned for redress in
the most humble terms."

[6] "Nor have we been wanting in attentions to our British brethren. We have
warned them from time to time of the attempts by their legislature to extend
an unwarrantable jurisdiction over these our states."

[7] "We have reminded them of the circumstances of our emigration and settlement here, no one of which could warrant so strange a pretension: . . . that submission to their parliament was no part of our constitution nor ever in idea, if
history be credited." (Draft.)

[8] "We have appealed to their native justice and magnanimity as well as to the
ties of our common kindred, to disavow these usurpations."

entreaties, their restraint were in vain. The English people want the separation [9] and the King himself has abdicated rule over America.[10] If now finally the Colonies declare their independence, they act under constraint in righteous self-defense. This was emphasized throughout the whole document and four times explicitly articulated.[11] The separation from the mother country was not therefore joyfully proclaimed as the longed for, gloriously contested, prize of victory, but accepted with submission as bitter necessity. "We must therefore acquiesce in the necessity which denounces our eternal separation." How a revolutionary act could be represented and vindicated in a less revolutionary manner is hard to imagine.[12]

One notices further, that Jefferson acts as if America renounced only the King, who had already abdicated anyway. The sovereignty of the English Parliament, however, about which in reality the entire dispute hinged, he mentions only incidentally and presents as if Parliament never had any say in America and as if renunication of Parliament were just a small formality he executed merely out of legalistic conscientiousness. With these remarkable turns of expression he underplayed America's truly revolutionary act and showed only the relatively insignificant break with the King, who in this manner could also be made responsible for all the sins of Parliament, his deposition, then, [81] appearing all the more merited. The aim of this presentation is clear: the revolutionary "guilt" of America and the revolutionary character of the Declaration of Independence are to be reduced to a minimum, that of the enemy amassed and heightened.

One will object that not the *entire* Declaration of Independence but only the first half of the second paragraph proclaims the redeeming, fundamental credo that a new era has opened. But this would mean, in other words, that while taking the greatest pains to convincingly demonstrate the non-aggressive conduct of the colonists, and while highly enraged over the innovations and constitu-

---

[9] "Be it so, since they [these unfeeling British brethren] will have it."

[10] "He has abdicated government here."

[11] "It becomes necessary to dissolve . . ."; "it is their right, their duty to throw off . . ."; "necessity which constrains them to . . ."; "We must . . . acquiesce in the necessity which denounces our eternal separation."

[12] It is conceivable that consideration of the French government, whose aid was to be purchased by the revolt, had a moderating influence upon the composition of the Declaration. That, however, does not allow of proof. Consideration of the "legal mind" and of the still hesitant mood, in many cases, of the Americans themselves seems much more obvious to me.

tional violations of the English, Jefferson was suddenly going to propagate without firm grounds an upsetting, highly revolutionary theory that stands in crass contradiction to all the rest of the Declaration and that plainly refutes the repeated appeal to inevitable necessity. Such a flaw in logic in the birth certificate of the United States would surely be much too noticeable.

The following is part of the well-known passage:

> We hold these truths to be self-evident, that all men are created equal, that they are endowed by their creator with inherent and inalienable rights, that among these are life, liberty, and the pursuit of happiness; that to secure these rights governments are instituted among men deriving their just powers from the consent of the governed; that whenever any form of government becomes destructive of these ends, it is the right of the people to alter or to abolish it, and to institute new government, laying its foundation on such principles and organizing its powers in such form as to them shall seem most likely to effect their happiness. Prudence indeed will dictate that governments long established should not be changed for light and transient causes . . . .

It has been debated whether these "self-evident" ideas are new and original or not and from what source they spring.[13] To such questions Jefferson himself gave the best answer:

> Not to find new principles, or new arguments, never before thought of, not merely to say things which had never been said before; but to place before mankind the common sense of the subject, in terms so plain and firm as to command their assent . . . . Neither aiming at originality of principles or sentiments, nor yet copied from any particular and previous writing, it was intended to be an expression of the [82] American mind. . . . All its authority rests then on the harmonizing sentiments of the day, whether expressed in conversation, in letters, printed essays or the elementary books of public right, as Aristotle, Cicero, Locke, Sidney etc.[14]

By appeal to the "harmonizing sentiments of the day" Jefferson already intimated the answer to other more fruitful questions about the *purport* of the propositions. In 1688 and in 1789 nearly the same words were used as in 1776, and each time they meant something different: in England supremacy of a Parliament of the privileged

---

[13] *Cf.* Alfred O'Rahilly, "The Sources of English and American Democracy," in *Studies* (June 1919).

[14] Memorial Edition [of *The Writings of Thomas Jefferson*, ed. Lipscomb & Bergh], XVI, p. 117.

over the Crown; in France supremacy of the Third Estate over all the privileged; in America national independence. Who today expounds the propositions of Jefferson in terms of popular sovereignty, universal equal suffrage, republic, etc.,[15] unintentionally reads into them—influenced by the experience of the French Revolution and later developments—a sense that they did not at all have in 1776. If one goes so far as to conceive of the theory of the Declaration of Independence in terms of domestic policy, one must do so in the spirit of the times, according to the "harmonizing sentiments of the day"; and the times quite clearly conceived of the theory in the Lockean sense as the foundation of English rights and liberties or simply as these fundamental English rights and liberties themselves. For the quarrel of the preceding twelve years had indeed been over these, and the "American mind" had again and again based its rights on the same Lockean ideas that Jefferson now repeated.

Moreover, there are clearly enough concrete examples amplified upon in the Declaration of Independence itself of what is to be understood by "inalienable rights." The inalienable rights are stated; the King has violated these rights; "facts" will prove this. But what did the King, "as a matter of fact," thus violate? Besides the most universal and most elementary precepts of humanity and duty, nothing less than "the free system of English laws." [16]

This concrete, retrospective meaning of rights was, however, quite forgotten and gave way to something new. When, for example, the Democratic Party admitted the principles of the [83] Declaration of Independence into their program,[17] they surely no longer thought

[15] As the slavery issue advanced to the foreground of American history, the Abolitionists employed with predilection Jefferson's propositions as an attack upon slavery.

[16] The phrase is from the Declaration of Independence itself.

[17] From the *Platforms* of the Democratic Party of 1836, 1840, 1852, 1856, and 1884: "Resolved, that the liberal Principles embodied by Jefferson in the Declaration of Independence, and sanctioned in the Constitution, which makes ours a land of liberty and the asylum of the oppressed of every nation, have ever been cardinal principles in the Democratic faith."

From the *Platforms* of the Republican Party of 1856, 1860, and 1868: "Resolved . . . That the maintenance of the principles promulgated in the Declaration of Independence and embodied in the Federal Constitution is essential to the preservation of our republican institutions."

The *Principles of the Declaration* are further included in the following *Party Platforms:* Liberty Abolitionist Party (Anti-slavery), 1843; Free Soil, 1852; Prohibition, 1872; United Labor, 1888; Socialist Labor, 1896. *Cf. The National Conventions and Platforms of All Political Parties, 1789–1904,* edited by T. Hudson McKee (Baltimore: 1904). A comparison of these party programs shows quite clearly how the *Principles* have undergone an incessant change of meaning. In

of the English fundamental rights; but they wanted plainly to make
a profession in a republic and in democracy. It no doubt did not
occur to them here that the admitted principles had served in justification of a dynasty and even in their times still supported the throne
of a sovereign for whom they had little sympathy. The Party forgot
too that in these principles there is no word of a republic or of
democracy.

That Jefferson meant the old fundamental English rights and not
the revolutionary rights of man in the sense of 1789 is further attested by the absence of various thoughts that are properly connected with proclamation of these revolutionary ideas, and that nowadays, corresponding to the altered meaning and interpretation of the
Principles, can be heard regularly in the Fourth of July orations. In
the Declaration of Independence itself, however, there is nothing said
about democracy or a republic, nothing about national unity, and
nothing of the great future of the continent. The whole program for
the future, apart from the proclamation of independence, limited
itself to the meager remark: "We must endeavour to forget our
former love for them [our British brethren] . . . . the road to happiness and glory is open to us too, we will climb it apart from them."
[84] There completely lacks a consciousness of being the most progressive, most free, most fortunate nation in the world and the
leader of mankind, of acting in its name and determining its destiny
down to the latest generations. There lacks a summons to the nations to the common struggle against tyrants; there lacks war in the
palaces, peace in the cottages; there lacks the promise or the vision
of a new and happier time; there lacks the ideals of progress and
virtue, of enlightenment, of the reconciliation of peoples, and of
cosmopolitanism. There is nothing said of the realm of reason and
justice which will have no lords and no servants; there is no offer of
an asylum of liberty and peace to the oppressed of all nations.

Such ideas were only connected with Jefferson's propositions at a
later time, and this shift of meaning is mirrored clearly in the shift of
emphasis in the Declaration of Independence. There is no doubt
that the tone of the long list of royal offenses was to be displaced in
the course of time in favor of the theoretical passage. In a collection of

---

the *Acts* of admission into the Union for Nebraska, Nevada (1864), Colorado
(1874), North Dakota, South Dakota, Montana, Washington (1889), and Utah
(1896), we find the stipulation that the constitutions of these states must not be
in conflict with the Federal Constitution or the Principles of the Declaration of
Independence.

contemporary American judgments on the Declaration of Independence,[18] there is not one found which even mentioned the classical propositions. Two Loyalists, Hutchinson [19] and Lind,[20] reject minutely and point by point the rebuke of constitutional violations in their replies—the theory of the Declaration of Independence they both dispose of with a couple of brief remarks.[21] The famous propositions, then, did not make a special impression in America on either the friends or enemies of independence, and they were capable of rousing neither hope nor fear. The propositions first acquired their new twist and powerfully intensified meaning by interpretation in the sense of the ideology of the French Revolution, beginning in Europe and then in America.

Of most significance, however, is Jefferson's own early conception. When in 1782 he wrote the *Notes on Virginia,* he was eager to take pains in showing America from its best side. In an exhaustive controversy with Buffon, he upheld the zoological [85] superiority of his homeland, extolled its beauty, its abundance, its climate, the intelligence of the natives and colonists, etc. When (under Query XIII) he came to speak of the separation from the mother country, he again analyzed exactly the historical development of the constitutional conditions between England and Virginia or America; broached, just as in the Declaration of Independence, a list of English infringements; then continued in the following manner:

No alternative was presented but resistance or unconditional submission. Between these could be no hesitation. They closed in the appeal to arms. They declared themselves independent states. They confederated into one great republic . . . . In each state separately a new form of government was established. Of ours [Virginia] particularly the following are the outlines.[22]

And then he let follow a critique of the Virginia Constitution from a democratic standpoint. Here then Jefferson left unused the most favorable opportunity imaginable to insert a song of praise to Politics and above all to the political beliefs of the United States, something of the sort as was enthusiastically received in Europe of that

[18] Hazelton, *op. cit.,* Ch. x, pp. 220–239, "The Effect of the Declaration and what was thought of it."

[19] Thomas Hutchinson, *Strictures upon the Declaration of the Congress in Philadelphia: In a Letter to a Noble Lord* (London: 1776).

[20] John Lind, *An Answer to the Declaration of Congress* (London: 1776).

[21] Compare with this the opposite behavior of Burke who fought precisely against the spirit and theory of the French Revolution.

[22] *Notes* [*The Writings of Thomas Jefferson,* ed. P. L. Ford], III, p. 221.

day. But instead of extolling the "American Ideals" alongside the American mountains, rivers, plants, animals, and men, or at least bringing into prominence the human significance of independence, he again raised the legal questions. Of the ideas in the Declaration of Independence he reiterated the accusation, the self-defense, and the proclaiming of independence. These he judged essential. *That* part of the document, however, that today before all others or alone is fixed in the memory of Americans, the "Principles of the Declaration," their author himself kept back at that time, as not worthy of a single mention. [86]

⚜ 19 ⚜

The Moral Faith of
the Declaration

JOHN DEWEY

The text which follows * quotes at some length what Jefferson had
to say about the sources of the ideas he expressed in the Declaration
of Independence. I do not believe his remarks are intended, in their
denial of indebtedness to this and to that writer, to set up a claim
for originality. On the contrary, I believe his statement is to be taken
literally that his purpose was simply to be "an expression of the
American mind in words so firm and plain as to command assent."
There was nothing that was novel in the idea that "governments
derive their just powers from the consent of the governed," nor did
it find its origin in Locke's writings—"nearly perfect" as were the
latter in Jefferson's opinion. Even the right of the people "to alter or
abolish" a government when it became destructive of the inherent
moral rights of the governed had behind it a tradition that long
antedated the writings of even Locke.

There was, nevertheless, something distinctive, something original,
in the Declaration. It was not, however, in ideas at least as old as
Aristotle and Cicero, the civil law as expounded by Pufendorf and
others, and the political philosophy of the Fathers of the Church.
What was new and significant was that these ideas were now set
forth as an expression of the "American mind" that the American
will was prepared to *act* upon. Jefferson was as profoundly convinced of the novelty of the *action* as a practical "experiment"—

* Jefferson's statements reprinted in *The Living Thoughts of Thomas Jefferson*
following Dewey's essay.—Ed.

FROM *John Dewey Presents The Living Thoughts of Thomas Jefferson*, copyright 1940 by David McKay Company, Inc., pp. 15–16, 23–25. Reprinted by
permission of David McKay Company, Inc. Also reprinted as a "Premier Book"
in "The Living Thoughts Series," Fawcett Publications.

favorite word of his in connection with the institution of [15] self-government—as he was of the orthodox character of the ideas as mere theory. The novelty of the practical attempt was, indeed, only set out in higher relief by the lack of novelty in underlying principles.

Jefferson used the language of the time in his assertion of "natural rights" upon which governments are based and which they must observe if they are to have legitimate authority. What is not now so plain is that the word *moral* can be substituted for the word *natural* whenever Jefferson used the latter in connection with law and rights, not only without changing his meaning but making it clearer to a modern reader. Not only does he say: "I am convinced man has no natural right in opposition to his social duties," and that "man was destined for society," but also that "questions of natural right are triable by their conformity with the moral sense and reason of man." In his letter to his French friend de Nemours, Jefferson develops his moral and political philosophy at some length by making a distinction "between the structure of the government and the moral principles" on which its administration is based. It is here that he says, "We of the United States are constitutionally and conscien tiously democrats," and then goes on to give the statement a moral interpretation. Man is created with a want for society and with the powers to satisfy that want in concurrence with others. When he has procured that satisfaction by institution of a society, the latter is a product which man has a right to regulate "jointly with all those who have concurred in its procurement." "There exists a right independent of force" and "Justice is the fundamental law of society." [16]

• • • • •

As was suggested earlier, the essentially moral nature of Jefferson's political philosophy is concealed from us at the present time because of the change that has taken place in the language in which moral ideas are expressed. The "self-evident truths" about the equality of all men by creation and the existence of "inherent and inalienable rights," [1] appear today to have a legal rather than a moral meaning; and in addition, the intellectual basis of the legal theory of natural law and natural rights has been undermined by historical and philosophical criticism. In Jefferson's own mind, the words had

---

[1] "Certain" was substituted for "inherent" by the Congress. The first manuscript draft, later changed by Jefferson himself, read that "all men are created equal and independent; that from that equal creation they derive rights."

a definitely ethical import, intimately and vitally connected with his view of God and Nature. The latter connection comes out more clearly if possible in the Preamble, in which he refers to the necessity of the American people taking the "separate and equal station to which the laws of nature and of nature's God entitle them."

These phrases were not rhetorical flourishes nor were they accommodated for reasons of expediency to what Jefferson thought would be popular with the people of the country. Jefferson was a sincere theist. Although his rejection of supernaturalism and of the authority of churches and their creeds caused him to be denounced as an atheist, he was convinced, beyond any peradventure, on *natural* and rational grounds of the existence of a divine righteous Creator who manifested his purposes in the structure of the world, [23] especially in that of society and the human conscience. The natural equality of all human beings was not psychological nor legal. It was intrinsically moral, as a consequence of the equal *moral* relation all human beings sustain to their Creator;—equality of moral claims and of moral responsibilities. Positive law—or municipal law, as Jefferson termed it—and political institutions thus have both a moral foundation and a moral criterion or measure.

The word "faith" is thus applied advisedly to the attitude of Jefferson toward the people's will, and its right to control political institutions and policies. The faith had a genuinely religious quality. The forms of government and law, even of the Constitution, might and should change. But the inherent and inalienable rights of man were unchangeable, because they express the will of the righteous creator of man embodied in the very structure of society and conscience. Jefferson was not an "individualist" in the sense of the British laissez-faire liberal school. Individual human beings receive the right of self-government "with their being from the hand of nature." As an eighteenth century deist and believer in natural religion, Jefferson connected Nature and Nature's God inseparably in his thought. He writes that he has "no fear but that the result of our experiment will be that men may be trusted to govern themselves without a master. Could the contrary of this be proved, I should conclude either that there is no God, or that he is a malevolent being." These words are to be taken literally not rhetorically, if one wishes to understand Jefferson's democratic faith. He even engages in construction of the following syllogism. "Man was created for social intercourse; but social intercourse cannot be maintained without a sense of justice; then man must have been created with a sense of justice." The connection of justice—or equity—with equality of rights and duties [24] was a commonplace of the moral tradition of Christendom. Jefferson took the tradition seriously. The statements of Jefferson about the origin of the Declaration of Independence, statements already quoted, are confirmed in what he wrote shortly before his death. "We had no occasion to search into musty records, to hunt up royal parchments, or to investigate the laws and institutions of a semi-barbarous ancestry. We appealed to those of nature, and found them engraved on our hearts."

Other days bring other words and other opinions behind words that are used. The terms in which Jefferson expressed his belief in the moral criterion for judging all political arrangements and his belief that republican institutions are the only ones that are morally legitimate are not now current. It is doubtful, however, whether defense of democracy against the attacks to which it is subjected does not depend upon taking once more the position Jefferson took about its moral basis and purpose, even though we have to find another set of words in which to formulate the moral ideal served by democracy. A renewal of faith in common human nature, in its potentialities in general and in its power in particular to respond to reason and truth, is a surer bulwark against totalitarianism than is demonstration of material success or devout worship of special legal and political forms. [25]

20

The Philosophy of
the Declaration

RALPH BARTON PERRY

The American Revolution was a successful rebellion against the constituted authority. It was not a crusade undertaken in behalf of a creed formulated in advance, but a summary effect of interests and of mental dispositions, compounded among themselves and facilitated by the circumstances of time and place. Nevertheless, since the revolution assumed the form of a deliberate enterprise, calling for unanimity, prolonged effort, and sacrifice, it was necessary to invoke 'reasons.' There was need of an approving conscience, an assenting judgment, and a confirmation by the disinterested opinion of mankind. There was need for these because they are elements of strength and bonds of effective union. The rebellious colonists, then, took certain 'grounds': first, a legal ground; and then, in the last resort, a philosophical ground.

The first attempt of the colonists to justify their resistance to authority looked to the existing body of law.[1] This attempt proceeded from more specific to more general grounds. It was first argued that the imperial authority was justified in imposing external taxes and trade regulations, but not direct internal taxes, such as the stamp tax. This distinction broke down, partly because it was difficult to draw the line, and partly because if it were drawn, it became increasingly clear that the colonists did not propose to submit to *any* kind of taxation. The famous slogan "No taxation without represen-

[1] Carl Becker, *The Declaration of Independence: A Study in the History of Political Ideas,* Harcourt, Brace (now Alfred A. Knopf), 1922, Chap. III. By permission of the author.

REPRINTED by permission of the Publisher, The Vanguard Press, New York, from *Puritanism and Democracy* by Ralph Barton Perry. Copyright, 1944, by Ralph Barton Perry. Pp. 123–130.

tation" took the broader ground that Parliament's prerogative of taxation was based on its representative character: the colonists sent no member to Parliament, and their interests, being remote, had no effective spokesman in that body. But even this ground was too narrow, since it was limited to the power of taxation. Hence the next step was to insist that as constituents of the British Empire the colonists owed allegiance not to Parliament, but only to the King. This claim has been supported by recent authorities, on the precedent of Ireland; [2] and was in line with the subsequent development of the British Empire. But it afforded no justification of the defiance of the King, and when it became evident that the colonists did not propose to obey British authority at all, this, like the other and narrower legal arguments, lost its force. [123]

There was, finally, the appeal from the British imperial constitution to 'natural law,' or 'the fundamental rights of Englishmen.' This would have been a legal justification had it been submitted to duly constituted judicial authorities. But the colonists did not propose to submit to British judges any more than to Parliament or the King. They proposed to make up their minds for themselves as to the 'justice' of their cause. The issue was to be submitted to the arbitrament of reason, and that authority spoke within their own breasts. At this point their justification became extra-legal—a justification of illegality in terms of the philosophical principles on which law itself is based. A political philosophy, says Leslie Stephen, is usually "the offspring of a recent, or the symptom of an approaching, revolution." [3] It arises when the habit of obedience is broken: when men have, in effect, suspended their allegiance until their interests and intellectual faculties shall have been satisfied.

On July 2, 1776, the Continental Congress, on the motion of Richard Henry Lee, adopted the following resolution: "That these United Colonies are, and of right ought to be, free and independent States, that they are absolved from all allegiance to the British Crown, and that all political connection between them and the State of Great Britain is, and ought to be, totally dissolved." [4] The resolve and the act were unmistakably and uncompromisingly illegal. The

---

[2] *Cf.* C. H. McIlwain, *The American Revolution: A Constitutional Interpretation*, Macmillan, 1923.

[3] *History of English Thought in the Eighteenth Century*, 2 vols., London, 1902, Vol. II, p. 131.

[4] Carl Becker, *Op. cit.*, p. 3.

Declaration of Independence, which was adopted two days later, was a philosophical creed designed to justify the action of men who had taken the law into their own hands. It was at one and the same time a justification of rebellion and a statement of those common principles on which was to be founded a new state. It is as though men should say: "This is what government and law are for. Judged by this standard, the existing authority has forfeited its claim to obedience. This is at the same time the ground on which to erect a new authority which shall in the future be obeyed as commending itself to our reason and conscience." History affords few parallel instances of a state thus abruptly created, and consciously [124] dedicated to a body of ideas whose acceptance constitutes its underlying bond of agreement.

This American democratic creed, designed to justify the past and chart the future, began as follows:

When in the Course of human events, it becomes necessary for one people to dissolve the political bands, which have connected them with another, and to assume among the powers of the earth, the separate and equal station to which the Laws of Nature and of Nature's God entitle them, a decent respect to the opinions of mankind requires that they should declare the causes which impel them to the separation.—We hold them, a decent respect to the opinions of mankind requires that they are endowed by their Creator with certain unalienable Rights, that among these are Life, Liberty and the pursuit of Happiness.—That to secure these rights, Governments are instituted among Men, deriving their just powers from the consent of the governed,—That whenever any Form of Government becomes destructive of these ends, it is the Right of the People to alter or to abolish it, and to institute new Government, laying its foundation on such principles and organizing its powers in such form, as to them shall seem most likely to effect their Safety and Happiness.[5]

Not the least extraordinary feature of this remarkable document is the compactness and simplicity of statement with which a complete system of philosophy is embraced within a few brief paragraphs. It contains a political philosophy, setting forth the reasons that justify the authority of the state and define the fundamental rights which underlie the positive law; an ethics, which sets up the aggregate happiness of individuals as the supreme end; and a theistic and creationist doctrine of the origins of nature and man.

The Declaration of Independence was composed by Thomas

[5] The Declaration of Independence as it reads in the parchment copy, as quoted by Carl Becker, *Op. cit.*, pp. 185–86.

Jefferson. It owes much to his intellect as well as to his pen, for he was no phrasemaker, ghost-writer, or unconscious plagiarist. But in this document he was giving the imprint of his genius to the current wisdom of the age. To quote Jefferson himself:

With respect to our rights, and the acts of the British government contravening those rights, there was but one opinion on this side of the water. All American whigs thought alike on these subjects. When forced, therefore, to resort to arms for redress, an appeal to the tribunal of the world was deemed proper for our justification. This was the object of the Declaration of [125] Independence. Not to find out new principles, or new arguments, never before thought of, not merely to say things which had never been said before; but to place before mankind the common sense of the subject, in terms so plain and firm as to command their assent, and to justify ourselves in the independent stand we are compelled to take. Neither aiming at originality of principle or sentiment, nor yet copied from any particular and previous writing, it was intended to be an expression of the American mind, and to give to that expression the proper tone and spirit called for by the occasion. All its authority rests then on the harmonizing sentiments of the day, whether expressed in conversation, in letters, printed essays, or in the elementary books of public right, as Aristotle, Cicero, Locke, Sidney, &c.[6]

The question of Jefferson's sources is one on which authorities disagree. The earlier view that he was inspired by Rousseau has long since been abandoned. Rousseau's *Social Contract* was not published until 1762, and the essential ingredients of the thought of the Declaration were current in America before that time. There is no clear evidence, furthermore, that Jefferson had read Rousseau. A recent authority attaches importance to the fact that Jefferson had read and summarized the tracts of Lord Kames, the Scottish jurist, and traces Jefferson's political thinking to Anglo-Saxon history and jurisprudence: the Jeffersonian democracy "was born under the sign of Hengist and Horsa, not of the Goddess of Reason."[7] But to attribute the Declaration of Independence to any single source, whether French or English, is to miss its historical significance altogether. If special importance be attributed to the influence of Locke, this is not because of the fact that Jefferson is known to have been familiar with Locke's writings, or because of close parallels

[6] Letter of May 8, 1825, to Henry Lee, from *The Writings of Thomas Jefferson*, ed. by P. L. Ford, 10 vols., 1892–99, Vol. X, p. 343, courtesy of G. P. Putnam's Sons.
[7] Gilbert Chinard, *Thomas Jefferson, the Apostle of Americanism*, Little, Brown, 1929, p. 87.

between the text of the Declaration and that of Locke's *Second Treatise of Civil Government;* but because Locke was the greatest and most representative exponent of the thought of the Enlightenment —which, arising in England in the seventeenth century, gave a distinctive character to the mind of Europe and America in the century that followed.

The political ideas of the Declaration, while explained in the language and the temper of the Enlightenment, were in full accord with the principles embodied in the earliest colonial charters. For one hundred and fifty years the American mind had been prepared for their reception. The charter of Maryland (1632) provided that Lord Baltimore [126] and his heirs should make laws "consonant to Reason" and "Agreeable to the Laws, Statutes, Customs and Rights of . . . England." [8] Similar provisions were contained in the Fundamental Orders of Connecticut (1639), in the Massachusetts Body of Liberties (1641), and in William Penn's Frame of Government of Pennsylvania (1682). In the First Continental Congress John Adams was insistent that the colonies should "recur to the law of nature, as well as to the British constitution, and our American charters and grants," because he foresaw a necessity of avoiding any implied acceptance of existing authority.[9] But whether they were termed "natural," as became usual after 1760; or were referred to as "fundamental" or "ancient," or "customary," as "the laws of God," or as "the rights of Englishmen," [10] in any case there were recognized basic principles which might be invoked against the powers of any human government, and which found their sanction in reason, conscience, and piety.

The Declaration of Independence was an ex post facto justification of the American Revolution, as Locke's *Treatises of Civil Government* were an ex post facto justification of the English Revolution of 1688. Both wordings were avowedly apologetic. The Declaration of Independence was animated by "a decent respect to the opinions of mankind." Locke's *Treatises* were written

to establish the throne of our great restorer, our present king William; to make good his title, in the consent of the people . . . and to justify to

[8] *Select Charters . . . of American History, 1606–1775,* pp. 56–57.

[9] Notes on the debates in the First Continental Congress as summarized later in his Autobiography, John Adams [*The Works,* ed. by C. F. Adams, 10 vols., Little, Brown, 1850–56], Vol. II, p. 374.

[10] *Cf.* Benjamin F. Wright, Jr., *American Interpretations of Natural Law,* Harvard University Press, 1931, Chaps. II–IV.

the world the people of England, whose love of their just and natural rights, with their resolution to preserve them, saved the nation when it was on the very brink of slavery and ruin.[11]

Jefferson, like Locke, gathered and reaffirmed the reasons. This does not imply that these reasons were first in the mind of the revolutionary party, in advance of any other condition or interest; and that they were then executed by purposeful action. They were the reasons by which [127] the revolution was justified to its proponents, to its opponents, and to neutral observers. They constituted the defense of the revolution against the scruples of its own agents; they were designed to enlist the support of adherents in the enemy's camp; and to win the approval of the world and of posterity. Through this rationalization it was hoped that the revolution might be put on higher ground than sordid or partisan interest. But because it was a rationalization, the Declaration of Independence was not insulated from the stream of historical events. It expressed, and in turn affected, the minds of men. It was, in short, a *cause*—not the initial cause, not the only cause, not the sufficient cause, but, for all one can know to the contrary, a *necessary* cause. It occurred in response to a felt need, as the condition of a full and enduring concert of action.

That the Declaration of Independence should have been a social cause, reinforcing the effects of interest, habit, and passion, does not imply that its doctrines were not true. Whether they were or were not true in the sense in which political, moral, or religious doctrines can be true, is for philosophers to determine. In any case, they were intended as true, and taken as true. They expressed and were designed to invoke the 'enlightenment' of their age; and by the same token they lend themselves either to reaffirmation, or to correction, in terms of the more advanced enlightenment of later times.

The author of the best book on the Declaration of Independence, a book distinguished by its wit as well as by its penetration, delivers himself of the following judgment on the subject: "To ask whether the natural rights philosophy of the Declaration of Independence is true or false is essentially a meaningless question." As though in defense of his pronouncement, Professor Becker proceeds to show that the philosophy of the Declaration, like similar philosophies professed under similar conditions, is appealed to "in justification of actions which the community condemns as immoral or criminal." Revolutionists formulate the sort of philosophy which brings their

[11] *Works*, 10 vols., London, 1812, Vol. V, p. 209.

action, despite its conflict with established law and custom, "into harmony with a rightly ordered universe, and enables them to think of themselves as having chosen the nobler part." They invoke a "higher law," which may be a law of God, or of conscience, or of nature. Such a law, says the author, when [128] it provides "emotional inspiration," is 'true' to them whom it so fortifies; but, we are allowed to infer, not *really* true (or false) at all.[12]

This argument employs the method unhappily characteristic of the newer school of critical historians. It rests upon an unformulated philosophy of truth, which is itself assumed to be true. If the terms 'laws of nature,' 'God,' 'self-evident,' 'rights,' 'equality,' 'just,' and 'happiness,' meant anything to the Americans of 1776, then the propositions containing these terms were of necessity either true or false; and if we can recover the meanings, we can detect the truth or falsehood. That they *did* mean something can be proved only by setting forth their meanings—which I shall hope to do, ably assisted by the critical historians themselves.

The belittlement of the doctrines of the Declaration of Independence takes other forms. Thus Alvin Johnson has recently written:

American democracy has proved itself an irrepressible force for the reason that it is not a matter of philosophical definition or legal status but a complex of impulses more or less trained and of experience more or less substantial deep in the heart of the individual democrat. Three centuries of life almost wholly civil in character, within an environment rich enough to offer opportunity for independence to most men, represent the chief conditioning circumstances for the development of this peculiar and tenacious plant, the American democratic spirit.[13]

This judgment is true in what it affirms, and false in what it denies. It is false to deny that American democracy is "a matter of philosophical definition or legal status"—peculiarly false. No polity in human history has owed so much to philosophy and jurisprudence. To hold to this indisputable historical fact is quite consistent with an ample recognition of the debt which American democracy owes to its environment and experience.

It was inevitable that historians of today should rewrite the history of the American Revolution in terms of 'propaganda' and the 'ruling class':

The work of the propagandists has spoken for itself; by their fruits we have known them. Without their work independence would not have

---

[12] *Op. cit.*, pp. 277–79.
[13] "The Substance of American Democracy," in Max Ascoli and Fritz Lehmann, *Political and Economic Democracy*, Norton, 1937, pp. 323–24.

been declared in 1776 nor recognized in 1783. . . . The provincial
ruling class, threatened in its position, used legal agencies of government
and already [129] established social institutions to undermine and ultimately to overthrow the British control. Through propaganda they spread
the alarm to all classes. The propagandists identified the interests of the
provincial ruling with national interests and created a war psychosis. It
was the propagandists who made inchoate feelings articulate opinion and
provided the compulsive ideals which led to concrete action. . . . Nationalism was not the cause of the revolution, nor was it democratic in its origin, but the work of the revolutionary propagandists aided in developing
the feeling of nationalism and in stimulating the ideals of a new democracy.[14]

This account adds nothing and subtracts nothing. Leaders, statesmen, philosophers, men of influence, and founding fathers remain
the same when they are called "the provincial ruling class"; and
persuasion, argument, or emotional appeal is not changed in character when it is called "propaganda." It remains as necessary as ever to
acknowledge, define, interpret, and explain "the feeling of nationalism" and "the ideals of a new democracy."

The Declaration of Independence contains the essential ideas of
American democracy, and has remained its creed and standard
throughout the years of its subsequent development. "For the first
time in the history of the world," says Professor Corwin, "the principles of revolution are made the basis of settled political institutions."[15] These principles have been challenged by individual
thinkers, and even, as in the epoch of the Civil War, by sections or
classes; but they have invariably been invoked in times of crisis or of
patriotic fervor as constituting the moral bond of American nationality. The later history of the ideas of the Declaration concerns us only
so far as may be necessary to establish their permanence and perva-
siveness. They were promptly embodied, if they had not been anticipated, in the constitutions of the several states. Their public reading on successive anniversaries has solemnized the national memory
and aspiration. They have proved broad enough to embrace partisan
differences and cycles of political change. [130]

[14] Philip Davidson, *Propaganda and the American Revolution, 1763–1783,*
University of North Carolina Press, 1941, p. 410.
[15] Edward S. Corwin, "The 'Higher Law' Background of American Constitutional Law," *Harvard Law Review,* Vol. XLII (1929), p. 403. By permission
of the publisher and the author.

Jefferson, Copyist

JOSEPH LEWIS

*Additional Evidence that Negates the Claim
that Thomas Jefferson was the Author of
The Declaration of Independence*

Where truth is involved and once established, there suddenly appear innumerable supporting facts—as if they all had tongues, which, in a unison of voices, rush forward to offer their testimony in support of the truth.

This is nowhere more apparent than in the Declaration itself. Therein will be found previously hidden facts, which, in view of the foregoing evidence, now stand out boldly, revealing Thomas Paine as its author.

It is as if "(truth) though it have no tongue, will speak with most miraculous organ." [1]

Although the evidence already produced in the preceding pages of this book is sufficient to prove that Thomas Paine was the author of The Declaration of Independence, the evidence to follow in this chapter alone is sufficient proof that Thomas Jefferson *could not* have written that immortal document.

No stronger argument can be produced than that Jefferson, while writing The Declaration of Independence, did not create the words and express the thoughts of that document because he was guilty of making [273] mistakes that could be made only by someone *copying* the text.

This is revealed by a close examination of Jefferson's so-called Rough Draft of the Declaration. In it are found certain tell-tale

[1] *Hamlet,* 2–2–622.

REPRINTED FROM *Thomas Paine, Author of the Declaration of Independence* (New York: Freethought Press Assn., 1947), pp. 273–276, by permission of the author and publisher.

instances which preclude the possibility that Jefferson could be the original author of the text. The original author could not be guilty of such errors, and such mistakes could be made only by one *unfamiliar* with the text. It is those errors of the copyist, so glaringly exposed in the Declaration, which negate Jefferson as its author.

It is not my purpose in this study to detail the many changes, substitutions and additions made in the original Declaration by members of either the committee or of Congress, nor to point out how these changes greatly undermined both the sense and composition of the original text. However, I must take this opportunity to point out one or two grievous errors which occurred in changing the text of the original draft.

Who was responsible, I do not know, although the corrections seem to be in Jefferson's handwriting.

If he did not make them himself, then he was influenced, in one case particularly, by a pious, overzealous religionist.

"ENDOWED BY CREATOR"

The original declaration reads that "all men are created equal and independent; that from that equal creation they derive rights, etc."

This statement is *unequivocal*. It is a political truism. *We are all born equal*—politically. From both a social [274] and philosophical point of view, the statement is incontrovertible.

Now the statement in the Declaration was *changed* to read: "All men are created equal, they are endowed by their creator with certain (inherent and) inalienable rights . . ."

This is not true!

We are not *endowed* with these rights. Political and social rights are *acquired*. We are equal because we are born on an equal station, and from *that* equal creation we possess political rights equal to others—and for no other reason are they "inherent and unalienable."

If we were "endowed by our Creator" with inherent and inalienable rights, then there could never have been slavery or serfdom or, for that matter, any form of social or political inequality. We are "endowed" with certain *physical* characteristics, such as our eyes and ears, our hands and feet; some are "endowed" with an unusual face, glowing hair, great strength, a beautiful voice, or other physical traits which could not be acquired, and which would be theirs, whether they were members of society or were living on a lonely desert island.

These "endowments" are absolute.

They are not subject to abridgment or abrogation. But the rights, which are ours as a matter of social and political equality, can and have often been taken from us despite the fact that they are "inherent and unalienable." This, then, was the purpose of the Declaration: to reaffirm and to reestablish these rights, because we were deprived of them by a false government. [275] He who was responsible for this change was either ignorant of the real meaning of the original text in the Declaration or did it deliberately for some pious reason, for which, in either case, he deserves severe condemnation.

On Jefferson's Rough Draft, the word "certain" was inserted between "inherent and unalienable," and in the final draft was substituted for the word "inherent." This was done purposely as a further limitation upon our basic and inherent rights, which was in direct contradiction to the original statement in the Declaration.

To show that the original text in the Declaration reflected Paine's sentiments I need only quote these expressions from *Common Sense*. They are identical in thought with the phrase in the Declaration, "Mankind being originally equals in the order of creation, the equality could only be destroyed by some subsequent circumstances." [2]

And again, "As the exalting one man so greatly above the rest cannot be justified on the *equal rights of nature*. . . ." [3]

Speaking of the origin of government, Paine said, "In this first parliament *every* man by *natural* right will have a seat." [4]

Not only is the original statement in the Declaration identical with these fundamental rights, which Paine so eloquently expressed, but nowhere in the writings of Jefferson are such sentiments to be found. [276]

[2] [*The Writings of Thomas Paine*,] Putnam Edition, Vol. 1, p. 75.
[3] *Ibid.*, p. 76.   [4] *Ibid.*, p. 70.

How to Read the

Declaration of Independence

HAROLD ZYSKIND

Although my topic is the "Declaration of Independence," I shall not attempt a complete interpretation of it. Mr. Maclean, who follows me, will present an analysis which strikingly exemplifies a wider range of interpretive ability possessed by a mature reader. My remarks are intended to illustrate ways by which a student may be introduced to certain of the more mature problems involved in reading.

The student of whom I am thinking would be one, for example, who regards the Declaration as self-evident on its face. He is acquainted with the noble deeds the Declaration has inspired in our history. As he reads the document, he experiences the birth of his nation. He knows the tyranny of George III. He can recite the self-evident principles. He has faith that all men are created equal because the Declaration says the proposition's truth is self-evident. My purpose will be to take this student from where he is and illustrate procedures by which he may be introduced to the broader horizons made visible by an interpretation of such propositions.

The initial step, of course, is to make him feel a genuine need for interpretation. This need may be shown by suggesting doubts about the *meaning* of the Declaration's propositions. Their truth may be self-evident, but their meaning is not. Obviously, all men are *not* created equal in all respects. The differences among them in physical and mental capabilities are countless. In what respect, then, does

REPRINTED FROM *Promoting Growth Toward Maturity in Interpreting What Is Read*, ed. William S. Gray, *Supplementary Educational Monographs*, Vol. XIII, No. 74 (November, 1951), pp. 7–12, by permission of The University of Chicago Press. Copyright 1951 by The University of Chicago. This paper was read before the Annual Conference on Reading.

the Declaration mean that they are created without differences? In opportunity? In the eyes of the law? In obligation to society? They may be equal—but equal in what? Jefferson does not say. How can the truth be self-evident until its meaning is known?

Or take the idea that the just powers of government are derived from the consent of the governed. Suppose I do not consent to paying my income tax. I am one of the governed; I do not give consent. Does the Declaration mean that in this case the government has no just power to force me to obey the law? Perhaps Jefferson meant that the just powers of government are derived from the consent of the majority of the governed? Then why does he not state this vital qualification? The point is that he states no qualification. Then how can we be certain what he meant? [7]

Meaning in Origin

These illustrative questions are sufficient to indicate that either the Declaration's general propositions are unclear in meaning or the meaning must be sought in interpretation. The propositions do not sufficiently explain themselves. How can the search proceed? One method would be to look for the origin of the ideas. For example, the fact is well known that Jefferson took many of his ideas from Locke's *Of Civil Government* (second essay). Locke, unlike the Declaration, fortunately does discuss his principles at length. Hence we may be able to find in his essay the desired meanings.

By pursuing this inquiry, we find that the just powers of government are conceived as deriving not merely from the consent of the majority but fundamentally from the consent of every citizen who is governed. This is not inconsistent, as I had supposed, with the government's having the just power to force me to pay my tax. I must think of my relations with the Constitution. I enjoy rights and protections under it; I live under it; I give my consent to it. In giving *this* consent, I thereby automatically consent in advance to the government's power to compel me or any other man to obey any constitutional law.

Locke similarly discusses what he calls the natural equality of man. It is a special idea involving the political relation between men in a state of nature. Consider two men as outside the province of government. The stronger would have the power but not the right to enslave the weaker one. The weaker man would be unequal in strength but equal in his right not to be enslaved, that is, in his right to have sole jurisdiction over his person and property. With respect to that right, both men are created without difference, and this is what is meant by equality.

Redirecting the Interpretation

Having made this beginning, we could proceed to read in Locke more detailed meanings of the statements in question. But how do we know that Jefferson interprets Locke's meaning as we do? How do we account for the places where Jefferson in the Declaration seems deliberately to alter Locke's phraseology (Jefferson omits the vital term *property*)? And even if we could discover from such outside sources what Jefferson believed, how do we know that the signers of the Declaration meant what Jefferson meant? The signers of the document, after all, appointed Jefferson as their public ghost writer to present their ideas. What he wrote was first revised slightly in committee, and then the entire Congress went to work on that draft, altering words, rewriting sentences, striking out whole sections. Jefferson's task was not primarily to elaborate his own philosophy of government but to describe the principles shared by the entire Congress—and in so far as they were to win the approval of mankind, the ideas had to be shared by mankind.

From this point of view, we can see the danger of going too far with our inquiry into Locke or other sources of Jefferson's ideas. The further we should go in that direction, the more precise would be the meanings ascribed to the statements in the Declaration. The genius of the Declaration may lie precisely in the fact that precise meanings are not given to the general propositions. The congressmen of 1776 differed in their political views as widely as do the congressmen of 1951. [8] How precise should one be today in preparing a document on the principles of government to be accepted by Senator Douglas, Senator Taft, and some ninety other senators? And yet would it not be valuable if all of them could today agree unanimously on an emergency course of action, as in 1776?

If the Declaration had given precise meanings to its self-evident truths, it could not possibly have been a statement of shared principles and conceivably might not have been signed. But because different meanings can be read into the principles, two men so far apart in political philosophy as Thomas Jefferson and John Adams were both able to sign it in complete good faith and hence to join together in one of the most significant actions in history. For the same reason, in part, each age can and does reinterpret the Declaration so that it becomes a living expression of a modern creed rather than an idiom of the eighteenth century.

Literary Context

We seem now almost to have reversed ourselves. Having observed that the meaning of two propositions was not self-evident, we first employed an interpretive method which was leading us toward continually more precise conceptions of the meaning of the two statements in question. Then, when we dropped this line of inquiry and tried another, we were led toward the interpretation that almost any possible meaning is valid. The two methods of inquiry are not necessarily opposed. The statements in question are not sitting alone on a blackboard. They have, rather, many dimensions, many horizons beyond themselves. They have an origin, a beginning in someone's mind, and they have effects, consequences in the minds of the signers and other readers of all ages. In this case, when we tied the statements to one of their origins, that is, to Locke, we found a philosophic system; hence, the meaning of the propositions tended to be clear and precise. But when we tied the statements to their relation with intended readers, we found the statements to be essentially rhetorical.

Neither interpretation should be denied outright because the statements have both dimensions: obviously, they were produced out of political principles and, in turn, they were intended to produce mighty effects in history. The moral, so to speak, is to bear both points of view in mind. But to avoid merely vacillating between them, a third kind of control is needed. The statements have still another dimension: they have significant relationships with each other and with the other statements in the single documents of which they are the parts.

For the final illustration, therefore, let us turn to the context in which the statements appear. The self-evident truths are not presented as a mere list of isolated propositions; they are organically related with each other. Initially we are given the attributes with which men are created and endowed—men are equal and have certain natural rights. Then we move into the way governments are set up among men. And, finally, we conclude with the way governments which have been set up may be altered or abolished and then replaced with a new government. The series thus forms a sweeping cyclical history of the rise and fall of governments—beginning with men as they are naturally, that is, prior to their entry into government; moving then to consider these naturally endowed [9] men forming a government; and finally moving to a revolution from that government to another.

To penetrate further into the connections among these organic stages, let us begin with the final one. One truth alleged in this third stage is that governments may be destroyed or abolished when they become destructive of certain ends. On what grounds besides self-evidence is this true? We find a ground in the second stage: governments were originally instituted to secure, not destroy, these ends or rights. Such is the purpose of government, and clearly a government not fulfilling its purpose should be altered. But on what grounds besides self-evidence can we say that the purpose of government should be to secure certain rights? For the answer we must look to the first stage: these natural rights are assumed to be unalienable. If unalienable, they ought by definition to be secured. Thus, we see that a truth of the final stage finds its justification in a proposition of the preceding one, which in turn rests, as upon a first premise, on a proposition of the first stage.

Or take another truth about revolutions. The people are alleged to be the group which has the right to revolt and set up a new government as they see fit. What gives the people this right? For the answer we go to the second stage: governments originally derived their just power from the consent of the people. Since a government exists by the will of the people, the will of the people is sufficient to abolish it. If, in turn, we ask why governments should come into existence only with the will of the people, we should expect now to find the original premise in the first stage. All men are created equal. This proposition, taken as premise for the consent of the governed, clearly means in agreement with Locke that every man has a natural right to decide his own destiny. Running through this logical chain from the equality of man to the consent of the governed to the right of revolution is essentially *one* meaning. Whether one speaks of the way men are created, of the way they form governments, or of the way they depose governments, the one basic standard is that each man or people has the right to control its own destiny. Here, you notice, we have a meaning general and flexible enough to appeal to many philosophies and yet definite enough to serve as a genuine guide in broad political action; and, moreover, this is the meaning suggested by the Declaration itself.

But there remains a genuine problem of this standard's meaning. You remember that we also observed another standard running parallel through all stages of the hypothetical historic process. This other basic standard is not concerned with where the control lies but with the end or purpose for which the control is used: governments are instituted for the *purpose* of securing certain rights, governments may be abolished when they are destructive of these *ends,* and new governments are set up to achieve the ends of safety and happiness. To summarize, this chain of truths rests on the standard that what serves the best interests of the people is justified. The other chain of truths rests on the standard that what the people want or consent to is justified.

When we juxtapose these two standards, a problem of meaning emerges. Suppose the people give their consent to a government which is, in fact, like Hitler's regime, working against the best interests of the people. It would appear that on the Declaration's standard of the [10] consent of the governed, there should be no revolution. But on the Declaration's standard of the ends or interests to be served by government, there should be revolution. Or suppose that there is a government with absolute power having no reference to the will of the people but, like Plato's ideal state, ruling in the truly best interests of the people. It would appear that, on the Declaration's standard as to where the ultimate control or power lies, this ideal state should never come into existence. But on the Declaration's standard of the end or purpose served by government, this ideal state would appear most deserving of eternal existence.

When the two standards come into conflict, as in the examples just given, which of the two does the Declaration mean for us to prefer? To consider this question, let us turn to the still wider literary context—to the bill of particulars which lists the king's misdeeds. The list begins by citing the king's *misuse* of his just power. He has vetoed wholesome laws. His right to veto is not here questioned. Apparently, there was popular consent to that constitutional power. It is the use of the power for a bad end which is condemned. In the succeeding facts we see the king employing his power more and more unjustly. By the time we reach line 66, a significant change has occurred. The king has combined with others, that is, with Parliament, for certain actions. Parliament did not, in any sense, have powers derived from the consent of the people. Neither the people's laws nor their constitutions gave consent to Parliament's jurisdiction. Thus, in combining with Parliament, the king's abuse of just power has become extended into the use of unjust power. After a list of unauthorized actions under this head, the facts then take on a still darker hue. Beginning with the sentence, "He has abdicated government here," the king's resort to force is described. Where force is employed against a whole people, there can be no consent. Force of this kind implies lack of consent. The king tries to destroy the colonists; he has abdicated government.

Let us look now at the relation between these facts and the meaning of the Declaration's principles. We had left the student with the notion that the principles employed two standards which hypothetically could conflict, namely, the standard of what is for the people's best interests versus the standard of what the people want or consent to. Now, we see these same two standards running parallel through the list of the king's misdeeds. On one hand, the facts begin by telling of the king's misuse of powers derived from the consent of the people and build up climactically to the point where the king is using force and aggression, thus operating without any reference to the consent of the people. These same facts also grow more and more terrible from the standpoint of the people's best interests—the list of misdeeds culminates in the destruction of the people's property and lives. In other words, the people's interests suffer in proportion as the people's consent is ignored. According to the facts, then, the two standards we had been examining do not conflict but necessarily merge—they go hand in hand.

In so far as the Declaration's facts exemplify its principles, this conviction in the harmony between the two standards constitutes a basic meaning of the "Declaration's self-evident truths." The conviction is simple but profound, for we often tend to take one of the standards by itself or to regard the two as antagonistic. [11] When we justify a policy on the grounds that the people want it, we use only the standard of consent. When we justify the institution of a policy only on the grounds that it is what the people ought to have, we use only the standard of end or interest. The Declaration's point in this regard is that what the people ought to have cannot be determined without reference to what they want; and, conversely, we do not have a genuine democracy unless the people are reasonable enough to consent only to that which serves the interests and ends for which governments are instituted among men. This meaning of the Declaration is discoverable by interpretation; and this interpreted meaning is sufficiently profound and universal, I believe, to illustrate the good grounds America has for continually renewing its faith in the creed of the Declaration. [12]

ᘓᕽ 23 ᔈᔊ

A Marxist Interpretation

HERBERT APTHEKER

The Declaration of Independence

In June 1776 a 33-year-old Virginian, working in a room rented from a bricklayer, wrote—in the words of Moses Coit Taylor—a "passionate chant of human freedom" whose influence has been as momentous as that of any other single human creation.

He made no claim to originality; on the contrary he strove to present the "common sense of the matter"; to convey, as he said, the "American mind"; to put into a brief declaration the essential facts driving the colonists to separation, and the theory of government which, to those colonists, was so universally held as to appear "self-evident."

The members of the Congress for whom it was drafted recognized it as a masterly work; their changes were few and purely verbal, with two exceptions. Jefferson's original version contained a long denunciation of the people of Great Britain because they had not opposed their own government with sufficient vigor and had not pressed forward their support of the colonists' battle so as to force an alteration in policy. This change would appear to have been wise, for pro-American sympathy in Great Britain had been and was to continue to be very widespread (the facts will be brought forward in subsequent pages). As it is, the Declaration does contain a rather bitter, and excessive, condemnation [100] of "our British brethren" who, it incorrectly declares, "have been deaf to the voice of justice and of consanguinity."

The second major Congressional revision of Jefferson's docu

REPRINTED FROM *The American Revolution, 1763–1783*, Part II of *A History of the American People* (New York: International Publishers, 1960), Chapter VII, pp. 100–110, by permission of International Publishers Co., Inc.

ment [1] resulted in the excision of a long passage—more than 150 words—dealing with slavery and the slave trade. This passage appeared as the final, climactic, item in the listing of abominations brought upon the colonies by George III, justifying resistance to his forcible efforts to retain them. In this passage Jefferson excoriated the King for vetoing repeated colonial efforts to curtail or to ban the African slave trade and denounced not only the trade but the system of production which it served. Due to the heated objections of the delegates from slaveholding Georgia and South Carolina and the somewhat less intense objections from several delegates from Massachusetts, Connecticut, and Rhode Island, where slave-trading had been an important business, this entire passage was excised. In the Declaration not a word is found of the slave trade, and slavery appears obliquely and very briefly in an attack on the King for having "excited domestic insurrections amongst us." [2]

Most of the Declaration, as adopted, consists of an enumeration of the "repeated injuries and usurpations, all having in direct object the establishment of an absolute Tyranny over these states," the details of which have been presented in earlier pages. Its philosophic, and immortal, pronouncements consist of less than 300 words.

The Americans in their manifesto of revolution begin by declaring that "a decent respect to the opinion of mankind requires that they should declare the causes which impel" them to their momentous step. This itself is new and reflects the essence of the Declaration's political philosophy—the sovereignty of the people. Believing in this sovereignty and staking their lives on an attempt to establish it, they naturally are impelled to explain their cause and their motivation to the peoples of the world. If the people's will is to be supreme, then their good will is omnipotent.

Then comes the enunciation of that cause. It consists of three basic ideas: (1) human beings—essentially equal in attributes, needs, obligations and desires—possess basic rights to life, liberty and the pursuit of happiness; (2) to obtain these rights men [101]

[1] Strictly speaking the document was submitted by the Committee appointed to write it; but Jefferson was its author. The Committee members made very few changes—John Adams' were most numerous, and even his were altogether minor.

[2] This had reference mainly to Lord Dunmore's proclamation in Virginia, issued Nov. 7, 1775, offering freedom to all *male* slaves of *rebels* reaching his troops. Plots among slaves—with charges of British inspiration—were reported from Massachusetts and Georgia in 1774, and from New York, South Carolina, Virginia, and—most serious—North Carolina, in 1775.

create governments; (3) governments destructive of these rights are tyrannical; such governments may be, and indeed, should be, altered or abolished by the people who then have the right and the duty to create the kind of government which "to them shall seem most likely to effect their safety and Happiness."

These ideas were of international origin. Directly, in terms of the 18th century Americans who approved them, they were derived from the humanist and libertarian arguments of ancient Greece and Rome. They were derived from the whole magnificent Age of Reason with its titans who struggled against dogma and authoritarianism—Bacon, Grotius, Vesalius, Copernicus, Spinoza. More immediately the sources were the writings of the Irish revolutionist, Charles Lucas, the Italian economist, Beccaria, the Swiss philosopher, Vattel, and his compatriot, Burlamaqui, the German jurist, Pufendorf, from the Frenchmen, Montesquieu, Voltaire, Diderot, from the Englishmen, Milton, Sidney, Harrington, Priestley, and Locke, particularly, and from the Americans, Roger Williams, Jonathan Mayhew and John Wise.

All of these were products, as they were voices, of the central fact in human history—the struggle against oppression, and the dynamic, ever-advancing nature of that struggle. The international sources of the Declaration in no way, of course, contradict its national essence. It remains American, or better, therefore, it is American.

I

The political theory of the Declaration is intensely democratic and profoundly revolutionary. When Copernicus discarded the medieval concept of the qualitative inferiority of the earth's movements as compared with those of heavenly bodies, he helped revolutionize astronomy. So Jefferson's pronouncement signalized the revolutionizing of political science by discarding the medieval concept of the qualitative inferiority of earthly life as compared with heavenly bliss.

Life on earth, Jefferson held, was not supposed to be a vale of tears and suffering. The meaning of life was not unending pain to be endured meekly in order to get into heaven; and man's [102] travail was not his cross to be borne because of original sin—because man was naturally evil. Moreover, governments were not the secular arm of the Lord, as priests were not his ecclesiastical arm.

No; this entire elaborate machine for the justification and perpetuation of the hierarchical, non-dynamic, burdensome feudal order is denied. Men are good, not evil; men are capable of governing themselves well; governments are man-made; the purpose of life is its ennoblement here on earth. The "freedom and happiness of man," Jefferson wrote to Kosciusko in 1810, must be the objects of political organization and, indeed, "the end of all science, of all human endeavor."

Hierarchy is, then, rejected and with it aristocracy and monarchy and the divine right of ruler or rulers. Equality of man replaces it and therefore sovereignty lies with these equals, and it is their will which is divine, if anything is; at any rate, it is their will which must be decisive where government seeks their welfare. And this is dynamic, not static. The (then new) idea of progress permeates the whole argument, for with man good, with government well provided, surely then, as Jefferson later said, his "mind is perfectible to a degree of which we cannot form any conception," and they speak falsely who insist "that it is not probable that anything better will be discovered than what was known to our fathers."

If to the above is added its logical corollary—that government must rest on "the consent of the governed," as the Declaration says —then the right of revolution is indubitable. It is a right not to be lightly exercised, as the Declaration also declares, but, nevertheless, an inalienable right, which exists so long as government exists. It was later asserted that the right of revolution ceases where a democratic republic exists, for the people cannot rebel against themselves. This misses the point: the people must consent to being governed; if enough of them do not and if the grievances are sufficiently serious, the right of revolution is theirs. The Declaration of Independence admits of no exceptions to the right of revolution; it only warns against hastiness and adventurism.

Where governments oppress, where they stifle and are engines [103] of exploitation, where they do not serve to further happiness (and clearly the majority of the people living under such governments are the authority as to whether or not they so act), they have then become tyrannical and acquiescence in tyranny is treason to man.

Certain rights are fundamental, in the Declaration's view. These are the people's "unalienable rights," expressed in that magnificent phrase, crashing through the corridors of history—"arousing men to burst the chains," as Jefferson himself wrote in his last letter—"Life, Liberty and the Pursuit of Happiness."

It is the idea of man's right to the pursuit of happiness which is the heart of the document's revolutionary enunciation and one which, by its magnificent, timeless generalization makes the document meaningful and stirring for all time.

That Jefferson chose this expression rather than the more usual Whig-Lockeian one of "life, liberty and property" was deliberate and reflects the advanced position of Jefferson personally and of the revolutionary coalition which adopted it. True it is, as Ralph Barton Perry stated in his *Puritanism and Democracy* (1944) that: "Property as an inalienable right is not to be identified with any particular institution of property, such as the private ownership of capital, or the unlimited accumulation of wealth, or the right of inheritance, or the law of contract."

Also, in order not to exaggerate the significance of Jefferson's change of the Lockeian phrase, it is important to note that Locke viewed property in a sense much broader than mere material possession. Typically, in his *Two Treatises on Government*, Locke wrote that "every man has a property in his own person"[3] and also referred to "that property which men have in their persons as well as goods." Howard Mumford Jones, in his study of *The Pursuit of Happiness* (1953), aptly summarizes Locke's idea: "Property is what belongs to a man as a man, not merely his physical possessions but also that extension of intangible values—life, freedom, one's stake in society."

It is also to be noted that when Jefferson stated he had tried to say nothing novel in the Declaration, but rather to offer in summary fashion the generally accepted view of things to most Americans, he did not mean to exclude the idea of the pursuit [104] of happiness. Indeed this idea, expressed in identical language, recurs in Locke himself and appears in the writings of such influential contemporaries of Jefferson as Oliver Goldsmith, Joseph Priestley and Adam Smith.

Nevertheless, Jefferson's choice of words to omit and words to include is indicative of the intensely democratic content of the American Revolution, especially at its high point. Jefferson did conceive of liberty, as had the Levellers in the 17th century, in the sense of freedom of speech and press and person, and of the pursuit of

---

[3] Locke's idea was used by him explicitly in an anti-slavery sense; that is, the effort to enslave or the fact of enslavement, was declared by Locke to be a "state of war." It is interesting to note that, on Lockeian thinking, later Abolitionists justified militant resistance to slavery. John Brown, for example, insisted the slaves were "prisoners of war."

happiness, as more elemental, more profound than property rights.

Relevant, too, is it that Jefferson—while, of course, in no way conceiving of, let alone favoring, Socialism, but, on the contrary, assuming private ownership of means of production—was very sensitive to the concentration of property-holding and felt it to be the central threat to democratic rights. He saw "enormous inequality" of property ownership, especially in land, as the cause of "so much misery to the bulk of mankind" that he insisted, in 1785, that "legislators cannot invent too many devices for subdividing property."

Basic to the Declaration also, of course, is its affirmation of a nation's right to self-determination. This clearly is the meaning of the first sentence in the Declaration, affirming the right of "one people to dissolve the political bands which have connected them with another, and to assume among the powers of the earth, the separate and equal station to which the Laws of Nature and of Nature's God entitle them." This right is also derived from popular sovereignty, but it is simultaneously expressive of another central force in modern history—the sense of nationality.

The revolutionary content of the Declaration refutes Louis Hartz's insistence that in their Revolution, "the Americans refused to join in the great Enlightenment enterprise of shattering the Christian concept of sin, replacing it with an unlimited humanism, and then emerging with an earthly paradise as glittering as the heavenly one that had been destroyed."

On the contrary, the Declaration of Independence is the greatest political expression of "the great Enlightenment," is expressive of an "unlimited humanism," and does reflect the idea of [105] discarding pie in the sky for milk and honey here on earth. On the committee drafting it was Benjamin Franklin, personifying, with Voltaire, the Enlightenment, and convinced that "It is impossible to imagine the height to which may be carried, in a thousand years, the power of man over matter." Franklin was sure of progress, of man's developing mastery, not only over nature but over himself and so expressed regrets that he had been "born so soon."

John Adams, also of the drafting committee, saw man's capabilities as unlimited, and especially in his younger years, was certain of his steady progress. Man, he wrote, "by the exercise of his reason" could and would accomplish "the most astonishing designs." He would make mountains of valleys and valleys of mountains, he would "rend the rocks and level the proudest trees," he would solve the mysteries of the heavens and of the infinitely small, so that even that which "escapes the observation of our naked sight" would still be comprehended and mastered.

Jefferson himself, typical of the American revolutionary feeling, saw that effort as the light and inspiration of all mankind. His sense of a universal humanism and of the creation of a social order throughout the world fully worthy of human beings runs through his life and works, as it pervades the bold and confident language of his Declaration. Characteristic is his letter to John Dickinson, March 6, 1801:

A just and solid republican government maintained here will be a standing monument and example for the aim and imitation of the people of other countries; and I join with you in the hope and belief that they will see from our example that a free government is of all others the most energetic; that the enquiry which has been excited among the mass of mankind by our revolution and its consequences, will ameliorate the condition of man over a great portion of the globe. What a satisfaction have we in the contemplation of the benevolent effects of our efforts, compared with those of the leaders of the other side, who have discountenanced all advances in science as dangerous innovations, have endeavored to render philosophy and republicanism terms of reproach, to persuade us that man cannot be governed but by the rod &c. I shall have the happiness of dying in the contrary hope.

It is necessary to notice, also, the widespread idea, as repeated by Boorstin in his already cited *Genius of American Politics,* that [106] the colonists "were fighting not so much to establish new rights as to preserve old ones" and that actually it was "Parliament that had been revolutionary, by exercising a power for which there was no warrant in English constitutional precedent."

But such an exercise of power can also be counter-revolutionary, rather than revolutionary. Which it is, depends upon who exercises it and for what purposes. It is true that the colonists had insisted that they were seeking "the rights of Englishmen," but insisting upon this in the face of rulers who declare that colonists do not have such rights is revolutionary, though the rights themselves may not be new. Moreover, insisting upon the exercise of old rights under new conditions may also be revolutionary. It is exactly because the colonists discovered that under the new conditions they would not be granted the rights of Englishmen—and would be forbidden them by force and violence—that they came to see that to have the rights of Englishmen they had to cease being Englishmen. Contemporaries made this quite explicit. Thus, as early as September 6, 1769, one finds this sentence in a leading article in the *Georgia Gazette:* "If we are no longer to be allowed the rights of Britons, we MUST be Americans." They had to become what in fact they were—Americans; for this purpose they adopted their Declaration of Independence, indeed a revolutionary act.

II

The limitations of the Declaration of Independence are the limitations of the century and the class which produced it. The Declaration presents the State in an idealist fashion; it sees man in an abstract manner, not men and women in a class society, with the state as a reflection and a bulwark of the dominant class.

The revolutionary bourgeoisie sees the state, which it is capturing and remolding, as an object in itself, standing above classes, or as some sort of an arbiter between conflicting classes within society. While its insistence that men create the state for their own purposes is a leap beyond the feudal concept, it is perhaps an even greater distance short of the historical-materialist class concept of the state. [107]

This supra-class view limits, too, the Declaration's theory of equality, for while that theory is revolutionary *vis-à-vis* feudal hierarchical notions, it is largely illusory in terms of the material base of bourgeois society, in terms of property and class relationship, in terms of effective power—considerations of vital importance for a full understanding of equality.

The relationship between property ownership and inequality was, of course, axiomatic to the Revolutionary Fathers. Said Alexander Hamilton, for example (in the 79th number of *The Federalist*): "In the general course of human nature, *a power over a man's subsistence amounts to a power over his will*" (italics in original). But they generally saw the State in abstracted political terms and so expressed a theory of equality, which while of the highest consequence in the whole democratic struggle of mankind, was itself largely confined to the political and even there, in practice, was highly partial.

As a result, property limitations on the political power of adult white males are not per se condemned in the Declaration and existed in the rebellious colonies while their delegates signed the document. Other limitations, as religious tests for the enjoyment of political power, were viewed by many as not incongruous or inconsistent.

As the disabilities become even more complete, the incongruity becomes less apparent to the Declaration's signers. Thus, the full, if temporary, disability of the several hundred thousand indentured servants was quite compatible, to the signers, with the Declaration.

Especially striking is the fact that while the Declaration spoke of equality, liberty, and the pursuit of happiness, 600,000 American slaves—slaves for life, who transmitted their status to all offspring, through the maternal line—were held to labor under the lash. It is indeed one of the most painful and yet most revealing facts in American history that the author of the Declaration of Independence was himself a slave-owner.

This central failing of the Declaration, and of the American Revolution, reflects the organic connection between the rise of capitalism and the ideology and practice of racism, as elaborated [108] in *The Colonial Era*. It is certainly racism which helps account for the revolutionists going into battle with the slogan, "Liberty or Death" on their banners, and over half a million slaves on their fields.

That which Frederick Engels wrote, in *Anti-Duehring*, of the American Constitution is pertinent also to the Declaration: "It is significant of the specifically bourgeois character of these human rights that the American Constitution, the first to recognize the rights of man, in the same breath confirmed the slavery of the colored races in America."

Also reflective of the limitations of the Declaration is the fact that when it said, "All men are created equal," it did not mean all men and women; had this been offered for ratification the document would not have been signed. This limitation did not go unremarked at the time, for both in England and in the colonies there were rudimentary stirrings of what, in three generations, was to become a major social movement.

Thus it is that John Adams' wife, Abigail, wrote him: "I cannot say that I think you are very generous to the ladies; for, whilst you are proclaiming peace and good-will to men, emancipating all nations, you insist upon retaining an absolute power over wives." Somewhat later, in 1778, this splendid woman declared: "I regret the trifling, narrow, contracted education of the females of my own country." Rare were the men in America who agreed, but there were some. Among others, James Wilson and William White, both of Pennsylvania, criticized the subordination of women and denied their mental inferiority by 1768.

Women were frequently outstanding in support of the Revolution and this, too, made more pointed Mrs. Adams' comments. Thus, in the colonies, Mercy Otis Warren—sister of James Otis and wife of General James Warren, slain at Bunker Hill—began publishing material in support of the American cause by 1773, and consistently threw her support to the Left wing of the revolutionary movement. In England, one of the staunchest supporters of the Revolutionists —beginning in the 1760's—was Catherine Sawbridge Macaulay, author of an eight-volume *History of England*. She wrote pamphlets and articles in defense of the [109] American struggle during the Revolution, too, and corresponded or conferred with Benjamin Franklin, Ezra Stiles, George Washington, James Otis, Josiah Quincy and other leading rebels.

Even earlier, in fact, in the work of Mary Astell and Daniel Defoe in England, there were protests against the social and political subordination of women, and during the Revolution itself Yale men were debating: "Whether Women ought to be admitted into the Magistracy and Government of Empires and Republics."

Thus, the ignoring of women in the Declaration, drawing comment from Abigail Adams, must be pointed to as a limitation, not only in the clear view of hindsight, but also in the view of some of the more advanced contemporaries.

But, of course, it is not the limitations of the Declaration of Independence which define its historic impact. Those limitations, of time and place and class, are omissions; the actual words of the document, having universality and humanity, remain fresh and inspiring.

Elie Halévy aptly wrote that for the radicals of its day the Declaration represented "to a large extent the cause of the whole of humanity"; "it seemed to foreshadow the fulfillment of the Biblical prophecies, the coming reign of reason and virtue in which the Gospel of Peace should be better understood and should be glorified."

For generations, as Merle Curti has pointed out, the Declaration was abhorred as seditious by the earth's rulers; its distribution or possession in many places was a capital crime. Professors in Italy, France, Denmark, Austria, and Prussia, well into the 19th century, were fired, and even imprisoned, for insisting on teaching their students its challenging ideas.

Butt of cynics, yet scourge of tyrants, the birth certificate of the American Republic stands today as Lincoln said in 1859—when a slave-holding class jeered at it as pernicious and false—"a rebuke and a stumbling block to the very harbingers of reappearing tyranny and oppression." [110]

The Declaration of
Independence and
Eighteenth-Century Logic

WILBUR SAMUEL HOWELL

I

"When forced, therefore, to resort to arms for redress," wrote Thomas Jefferson in explaining what his most famous work was designed to do, "an appeal to the tribunal of the world was deemed proper for our justification. This was the object of the Declaration of Independence. Not to find out new principles, or new arguments, never before thought of, not merely to say things which had never been said before; but to place before mankind the common sense of the subject, in terms so plain and firm as to command their assent, and to justify ourselves in the independent stand we are compelled to take. Neither aiming at originality of principle or sentiment, nor yet copied from any particular and previous writing, it was intended to be an expression of the American mind, and to give to that expression the proper tone and spirit called for by the occasion. All its authority rests then on the harmonizing sentiments of the day, whether expressed in conversation, in letters, printed essays, or in the elementary books of public right, as Aristotle, Cicero, Locke, Sidney, &c." [1]

[1] Letter to Henry Lee, May 8, 1825. See Paul Leicester Ford, ed., *The Writings of Thomas Jefferson* (New York and London, 1892–99), X, 343.

REPRINTED FROM *William and Mary Quarterly*, 3rd Ser., XVIII (October, 1961), 463–484, by permission of Wilbur Samuel Howell, Professor of Rhetoric and Oratory, Princeton University. Original title.

These serene and judicious words have been on occasion invoked not only to prove Jefferson's own full awareness that the Declaration of Independence made use of familiar ideas but also to provide the opportunity to assert that the greatness of that document lies in its being a true and living reflection of what the men of its time accepted and believed. Thus Carl Becker, as he prepares to examine the antecedents of Jefferson's philosophy of natural rights, quotes part of the passage just cited to give weight to his own belief that Jefferson was right in drawing upon familiar [463] sentiments and that "nothing could have been more futile than an attempt to justify a revolution on principles which no one had ever heard of before." [2] Thus also, having taken note of similarities between the Declaration and certain treatises by John Locke and James Wilson, Julian P. Boyd has this to say in justifying Jefferson's use of sources: "But even if Jefferson had 'copied from any particular and previous writing,' even if he had used an identifiable model—and his colleagues in Congress would have agreed as to the excellence of Locke—the most that would be proved by this is that he had failed to be original in an enterprise where originality would have been fatal. The greatness of his achievement, aside from the fact that he created one of the outstanding literary documents of the world and of all time, was that he identified its sublime purpose with the roots of liberal traditions that spread back to England, to Scotland, to Geneva, to Holland, to Germany, to Rome, and to Athens." [3]

For the student of eighteenth-century logic and rhetoric, Jefferson's statement of the object of the Declaration and of its conscious concern for accepted ideas is interesting in still another direction. So far as Jefferson intended the Declaration to appeal to the tribunal of the world, to command the assent of mankind, to justify the rebellion of the colonies against the British Crown, and to express the American mind in the proper tone and spirit called for by the occasion, he intended it to achieve logical and persuasive goals. Thus the question arises whether it conforms in these respects, as it so obviously does in political philosophy and liberal outlook, to the best traditions of its time—whether in so vital a matter as its actual capacity to influence men, to appeal to their reason, and to induce

---

[2] Carl Becker, *The Declaration of Independence: A Study in the History of Political Ideas* (New York, 1940), 24–25.

[3] Julian P. Boyd, *The Declaration of Independence: The Evolution of the Text as Shown in Facsimiles of Various Drafts by Its Author, Thomas Jefferson* (Princeton, 1945), 5.

them to support the extreme alternative of civil disobedience and mutiny, it can be shown to follow the accepted persuasive principles of the eighteenth century and to rest consciously upon them rather than upon an uncalculated, an accidental, or perhaps even an original persuasive design.

The answer to this question is outlined in the following article. I shall attempt in it to show that an unmistakable parallelism exists between the argumentative structure of the Declaration and the theory of argumentative structure set forth in the most significant of the logics and rhetorics of [464] Jefferson's time. In fact, I shall point to a particular logic that can be shown to have influenced the Declaration, and I shall explain how that influence made itself felt and under what auspices it reached Jefferson. This sort of analysis will indicate that, although all the authority of the Declaration rests, as Jefferson said, "on the harmonizing sentiments of the day," its ideas were given added persuasive power by their adherence to the best contemporary standards of mathematical and scientific demonstration and to what the best contemporary thinkers expected of proof before it could claim to convince the reason. This sort of analysis will also indicate the direction to be followed in supplementing Carl Becker's adroit critical appraisal of the literary qualities of the Declaration.[4] For the literary standards of Jefferson's era are stated more exactly in eighteenth-century logic and rhetoric than in the similar works of our time, and yet those logics and rhetorics are now so far forgotten or disparaged as unhappily to have lost their opportunity to teach us what we cannot afford to do without if we would fully understand the literature of their time.

II

The chief logical treatises in England during the seventeen hundreds consciously followed the great *Port-Royal Logic* of the preceding century in dividing their subject into four parts, namely, perception, judgment, reasoning, and method, which were conceived as operations of the mind.[5] [465] The theory of perception involved

---

[4] Becker, *Declaration*, 194–223.

[5] In addition to *The Port-Royal Logic*, which was published at London in a total of 10 editions in French, Latin, and English between 1664 and 1717, the major logical works in England during the late 17th and most of the 18th centuries were the following (listed after each title are dates indicating editions that I have thus far been able to locate in surviving copies): John Wallis, *Institutio Logicae* (1687, 1702, 1715, 1729, 1763); Henry Aldrich, *Artis Logicae Com-*

not only the traditional doctrine of the logical term but also the emerging theories of sensations and images, later to be taken over by psychology. Judgment, the second part of logic, dealt with such matters as thoughts, ideas, statements, and intuitions, all of which amounted to a theory of terms connected into logical propositions. Reasoning in logic meant the combination of terms and propositions into syllogistic or inductive structures, and this part of logical theory blended traditional Aristotelian doctrine with insights from the philosophy of Francis Bacon, René Descartes, and Locke. As for the fourth part of eighteenth-century logic, it continued the practice, made popular by Peter Ramus in the sixteenth century, of insisting upon *dispositio* or method as a main division of logical theory; but it followed the reform of later logicians in giving method an investigative as well as a presentational aspect.[6]

Investigative arrangement in eighteenth-century English logic was called the analytic method, after the terminology endorsed by the Port-Royalists. This consisted in going from the known to the unknown over the route that an investigator would follow in proceeding from observed facts to a theory explaining them. It involved in the first instance the making of original discoveries in experimental science or in scholarship, and not unnaturally it was given such subordinate names as the method of inquiry, of invention, of discovery, and of resolution. The analytic method could of course be fol-

---

pendium (1691, 1692, 1696, 1704, 1723, 1750 [in English], 1771, 1793) (There were many 19th-century editions); Jean Pierre de Crousaz, *A New Treatise of the Art of Thinking. . . . Written in French. . . . Done into English* (1724); Isaac Watts, *Logick* (1725, 1726, 1729, 1733, 1736, 1740, 1745, 1751, 1763, 1779, 1786, 1789, 1792, 1793, 1797) (There were several 19th-century editions); William Duncan, *The Elements of Logick*, in Robert Dodsley's *The Preceptor* (1748, 1754, 1758, 1763, 1769, 1775, 1783, 1793), and as a separate work (1748, 1752, 1759, 1764, 1770, 1776, 1787, 1790, 1792) (There were several 19th-century editions).

Of these, Aldrich failed to adhere to the fourfold organization here described. He repudiated the Port-Royalists as innovators and went back himself to a conservative Aristotelianism. For his attack on the Port-Royalists, see the abridged (not the full) text of his *Artis Logicae Compendium* (Oxford, 1961), sig. G4ʳ–H2ʳ. But he did nevertheless treat method, even if he decided not to make it a formal division of logic. Wallis's *Institutio Logicae* treats perception, judgment, and reasoning, and places method as a subdivision of the latter topic.

For a discussion of *The Port-Royal Logic* as an offshoot of Descartes's *Discours de la Méthode* and a reform of the logic of Peter Ramus, see my *Logic and Rhetoric in England, 1500–1700* (Princeton, 1956), 342–363.

[6] Howell, *Logic and Rhetoric*, 146–172, 282–317. For the antecedents of Ramus's theory of method, see Walter J. Ong, S.J., *Ramus Method, and the Decay of Dialogue* (Cambridge, Mass., 1958), 225–269; see also Neal W. Gilbert, *Renaissance Concepts of Method* (New York, 1960), 3–128.

lowed in acquainting someone else with a discovery after it had been made, and thus it had a presentational as well as an investigative aspect. But it owed its fundamental character to its use in research, whether employed for that purpose or for the business of teaching.

The reverse of the analytic method in eighteenth-century logic was called the synthetic method, and this was properly the instrument of instruction, exposition, communication, and proof. It too moved from the known to the unknown. But it did so over the route traveled by the teacher in giving his students knowledge to replace their ignorance rather [466] than over the route of an investigator seeking to replace his own ignorance by knowledge. Thus the teacher would begin his demonstration by citing the established truths upon which his conclusion would later be made to depend, and he would proceed to connect that conclusion with the established truths by showing that a fundamental aspect of the latter was also a fundamental aspect of the former. The logicians called this procedure, not only the synthetic method, but also the method of doctrine, of instruction, and of composition. Like the analytic method, it too had a double function. It could be used for discovering new knowledge in certain fields, notably in mathematics; and it could be used for the presentation of the knowledge thus discovered. But in its fundamental character it was the method of instruction, communication, and conviction in respect to truths already known.

III

The discipline of rhetoric had traditionally dealt with *dispositio* or arrangement of discourse, along with the other rhetorical subjects of invention, style, memory, and delivery. Rhetorical *dispositio* was, however, a fully developed theory of the classical form of an oration; and this form, as described in the rhetorical writings of Cicero, and in various modified or extended ways by later rhetoricians, had consisted of six major parts—the exordium, the narration, the division, the proof, the refutation, and the conclusion. Within these six terms the theory of oratorical structure was comprised during the classical Roman era, the Middle Ages, the Renaissance, and the seventeenth century.

One obvious thing about the eighteenth century in England is that these six terms were no longer supreme in the theory of oratorical arrangement. Only John Ward among the major eighteenth-century rhetoricians used them in the manner advocated by Cicero and Quintilian.[7] His later contemporaries—George Campbell, Joseph Priestley, and Hugh Blair—recognized in varying degrees that the analytic and synthetic methods of the new logic were having a strong influence upon the dispositional theory of rhetoric and were threatening to crowd out the elaborate six-part oratorical structure of the past.

Campbell's great work, *The Philosophy of Rhetoric*, begun in 1750 [8] and first published in 1776, gives no place at all to the traditional six parts [467] of the classical oration. In fact, it discusses only analysis and synthesis as terms for the theory of argumentative form. These two terms appear in the course of Campbell's treatment of subject matter and sense in discourse, where he associates rhetoric with logic and thus analyzes not only intuitive evidence and deductive evidence, as the bases of conviction, but also the methods by which argument is put together.[9] Campbell does not present analysis and synthesis as a fully developed formula for oratorical structure, but in the absence of such a formula, his use of these two terms indicates that his sympathies lie with the logical rather than the rhetorical antecedents of the doctrine of *dispositio:*

In moral reasoning we proceed by analysis, and ascend from particulars to universals; in syllogizing we proceed by synthesis, and descend from universals to particulars. The analytic is the only method which we can follow, in the acquisition of natural knowledge, or of whatever regards actual existences; the synthetic is more properly the method that ought to be pursued in the application of knowledge already acquired. It is for this reason it has been called the didactic method, as being the shortest way of communicating the principles of a science.[10]

If Campbell seems here to be advocating that rhetoric throw out its traditional theory of the six-part classical oration and substitute for it the logical theory of method, the same thing can be said of Priestley's *Course of Lectures on Oratory and Criticism.* These lectures, by the way, have the distinction of being a great scientist's contribution to a subject little cultivated in its theoretical aspects by the scientific community. And when Priestley comes to speak of rhetorical arrangement, his lectures also have the distinction of offering to oratory the logical as opposed to the rhetorical theory of *dispositio,* and of calling that theory "method," after its name in

[7] John Ward, *A System of Oratory* (London, 1759), Lectures 12–18.
[8] See George Campbell, *The Philosophy of Rhetoric* (London, 1776), I, iii.
[9] *Ibid.*, I, 95–166.   [10] *Ibid.*, I, 165–166.

200 WILBUR SAMUEL HOWELL

logic. "Logicians," says Priestley, "speak of two kinds of method in argumentative discourses, the *analytic* and the *synthetic;* and the distribution is complete and accurate. For, in all science, we either proceed from particular observations to more general conclusions, which is *analysis;* or, beginning with more general and comprehensive propositions, we descend to the particular propositions which are contained in them, which is *synthesis.*"[11] Priestley goes on to emphasize that the [468] analytic method is obligatory as the method of investigation but optional as a method of communicating truth to others, whereas the synthetic method is generally more convenient in explaining a science.[12] Speaking of the analogy between geometry and oratory in respect to the synthetic method, he observes:

> Every proposition is, by geometricians, demonstrated either from *axioms,* that is, self-evident truths; or such as have been elsewhere demonstrated from those which are self-evident.
> In like manner, whatever we propose to demonstrate, the last appeal lies to *self-evident truths;* in moral subjects, to consciousness, or internal feelings; and in matters or revelation, to the plain sense of scripture: and it is very expedient and adviseable, in discourses upon important subjects of any kind, after the manner of geometricians, to premise these self-evident truths, beyond which no appeal can be admitted.[13]

Priestley's *Lectures* were not published until 1777, but he began to deliver them in 1762, when he was tutor in languages and belles-lettres in the academy at Warrington.[14] Three years before, in 1759, Hugh Blair, the last great British rhetorician of the eighteenth century, inaugurated at the University of Edinburgh his famous lectures on rhetoric and belles-lettres, which eventually were published in 1783.[15] As part of his subject Blair treated the theory of *dispositio.* Like John Ward in his earlier Gresham College lectures on rhetoric, which had been collected and published in the year in which Blair started his lectures at Edinburgh, Blair treated *dispositio* with the traditional parts of the classical oration in mind; and thus he speaks of the introduction, the proposition, the division, the narration, the argument, the pathetic part, and the conclusion.[16] But when it comes to argument or proof, says Blair, "two different methods may

---

[11] Joseph Priestley, *A Course of Lectures on Oratory and Criticism* (London, 1777), 42. Italics are Priestley's.
[12] *Ibid.,* 42–43.   [13] *Ibid.,* 46.   [14] *Ibid.,* i.
[15] Robert Morell Schmitz, *Hugh Blair* (New York, 1948), 62, 142. See also Hugh Blair, *Lectures on Rhetoric and Belles Lettres* (Dublin, 1783), I, iii.
[16] Blair, *Lectures,* II, 359–416.

be used by Orators in the conduct of their reasoning; the terms of art for which are, the Analytic, and the Synthetic method." [17] Blair's explanation of these terms is brief and does not add to what has already been observed. But it might be added that he regards the analytic method as less suitable to popular speaking than is the synthetic. The latter consists in laying [469] down the point to be proved, and making one argument after another bear upon it, "till the hearers be fully convinced." [18]

IV

William Duncan, who was commissioned professor of natural philosophy at Marischal College in Aberdeen in 1752,[19] deserves a special place in the present discussion. His *Elements of Logick*, first published at London in 1748, and reprinted many times during the next half-century,[20] is the dominant logical treatise of its time and place. Moreover, although its contribution to the development of George Campbell's *Philosophy of Rhetoric*, itself a work of considerable stature, has never been worked out in detail, a mere reading of the two books will convince anyone that Campbell owes an important debt to Duncan. In this connection we might remind ourselves that both men graduated from Marischal College, Duncan in 1735 and Campbell in 1738, and that, during the last year of Duncan's term of service as member of the Marischal College faculty, Campbell was appointed the college principal.[21] No such ties link Duncan and Priestley; and yet it seems obvious that the latter's account of method in rhetoric owes its philosophical groundwork to the former's *Logick*—a point that probably has not been noticed since the eighteenth century.

But Duncan's *Logick* has much stronger claims than these to our present attention. It originally appeared as the first treatise of the second volume of Robert Dodsley's *The Preceptor*, a meritorious compilation in which, as its title page declares, "The First Principles of Polite Learning Are laid down In a Way most suitable for trying the Genius, and advancing the Instruction of Youth." Special prestige was given this collection by virtue of its containing a preface by

---

[17] *Ibid.*, II, 392. [18] *Ibid.*, II, 393–394.
[19] Peter John Anderson, *Fasti Academiae Mariscallanae Aberdonensis* (Aberdeen, 1889–98), II, 45.
[20] For details, see above, n. 5.
[21] Anderson, *Fasti Academiae Mariscallanae*, II, 29–30, 45, 308, 310.

Dr. Samuel Johnson.[22] Of profound interest to us, however, is that
Thomas Jefferson's library contained the second volume of Dodsley's
Preceptor and thus also Duncan's *Logick*, although the latter fact
has hitherto not been noticed.[23] Nor has it been [470] noticed that
Jefferson must certainly have studied the *Logick* when he was en-
rolled at William and Mary between 1760 and 1762. Not only does
the Declaration of Independence conform to the structure recommended by Duncan for works that seek to achieve a maximum
degree of conviction and certainty, but also it contains an important
verbal echo of the *Logick*, as I shall show later. Moreover, William
Small, Jefferson's highly respected teacher at William and Mary,
who, as Jefferson himself later testified, "probably fixed the destinies
of my life," [24] had graduated from Marischal College in 1755,[25] and
thus had been a student under William Duncan. To be sure, Small
came to William and Mary to teach natural philosophy, which was
of course Duncan's own subject at Marischal College. But shortly
after his arrival at his academic post in Virginia, he was given the
temporary assignment of teaching moral philosophy as well as natural philosophy, the former being at that time limited by the statutes
of the college to "Rhetorick, Logick, and Ethicks," whereas the latter
was made up of "Physicks, Metaphysicks, and Mathematicks." [26]

[22] See *Boswell's Life of Johnson* (London, 1927), I, 129; also *The Works of
Samuel Johnson* (Troy, New York, 1903), XII, 154–175.

[23] E. Millicent Sowerby, *Catalogue of the Library of Thomas Jefferson* (Washington, 1952–59), I, 507.

Miss Sowerby does not describe the contents of the second volume of *The
Preceptor*, nor does she seek to identify the edition which Jefferson held. It can
be established, however, Jefferson owned a fifth or a later edition. The first and
second editions were printed for R. Dodsley; the third and fourth, for R. and J.
Dodsley; and the fifth, sixth, seventh, and eighth, for J. Dodsley. Since the edition in Jefferson's possession contained this last designation, it must have borne
the date of 1769, 1775, 1783, or 1793. Thus Jefferson's copy was not the one
that he would have used at William and Mary. His college copy may have been
lost, and the copy in his library could have been purchased later to replace it.

[24] Herbert L. Ganter, "William Small, Jefferson's Beloved Teacher," *William
and Mary Quarterly*, 3rd Ser., IV (1947), 505. See also Dumas Malone, *Jefferson
and His Time*, I, *Jefferson the Virginian* (Boston, 1948), 49–61.

[25] Anderson, *Fasti Academiae Mariscallanae*, 323.

[26] *The Charter, Transfer and Statutes, of the College of William and Mary, in
Virginia: In Latin and English* (Williamsburg, 1758), 135. Cited below as *The
Charter and Statutes*.

Small attended his first faculty meeting at William and Mary on Oct. 18, 1758.
At that time the Reverend Jacob Rowe, M.A., was professor of moral philosophy,
having occupied that post since the preceding June 14. Rowe was expelled from
his professorship on Aug. 14, 1760, and his permanent successor, the Reverend
Richard Graham, M.A., was not elected until June 12, 1761. Thus Small's term
as temporary professor of moral philosophy dated from the late summer of 1760

Small was evidently not a man to take a temporary assignment lightly. He made [471] such substantial changes at once in the teaching of ethics and rhetoric at William and Mary as to cause Jefferson to say later that "he was the first who ever gave in that college regular lectures in Ethics, Rhetoric & Belles lettres." [27] There would have been every reason for Small to have given the study of logic a new direction, too. For one thing, the statutes of the college left it "to the President and Masters, by the Advice of the Chancellor," to feel no compulsion to follow "*Aristotle*'s Logick and Physicks, which reigned so long alone in the Schools," but "to teach what Systems of Logick, Physicks, Ethicks, and Mathematicks, they think fit. . . ." [28] For another thing, and this is crucial, we may be sure that Small, when forced by circumstances to add logic, rhetoric, and ethics to his teachings at William and Mary during Jefferson's first college year, would naturally remember the famous *Logick* that his own master had published in 1748, and would naturally recommend that work to young Jefferson, his daily companion and close friend.[29] Thus if the Declaration of Independence carries out the directions laid down by Duncan for discourse that would compel the assent of mankind, and if its cadences, in an outstanding instance, match one of Duncan's most important logical terms, there is every reason to believe that the influence of Duncan's *Logick* upon Jefferson is involved, and that his admired teacher, William Small, is the key figure in the transmission of that influence.[30] Indeed, there is every

---

to the middle of the following June, and coincided with the last seven months of Jefferson's first college year and the opening three months of his second. Small served on the faculty of William and Mary until 1764. For the dates given here concerning him, Rowe, and Graham, see *William and Mary College Quarterly* 1st Ser., III (1894–95), 60–62, 130–132; XIV (1905–6), 75–76; XXIV (1915–16), 221–222.

[27] Ganter, "William Small," 505, quoting Jefferson's autobiography.

[28] *The Charter and Statutes*, 133.

[29] Ganter, "William Small," 505. Ganter quotes Jefferson's autobiography as follows on Small's relations with him: "He, most happily for me, became soon attached to me & made me his daily companion when not engaged in the school; and from his conversation I got my first views of the expansion of science & of the system of things in which we are placed."

[30] Duncan's *Logick* can be established on other grounds as part of the curriculum at William and Mary during the 18th century. In letters of Nov. 4 and Dec. 9, 1799, from J. Shelton Watson to his brother David, the former being an undergraduate of that era at the Virginia college, the *Logick* is unfavorably mentioned as one of Shelton's current academic assignments. See "Letters from William and Mary College, 1798–1801 . . . ," *Virginia Magazine of History and Biography*, XXIX (1921), 145–146, 148–149.

There is also some evidence of the general circulation of the *Logick* in 18th-century Virginia. For example, it is listed among 344 books that were being of-reason to suspect that, if Small fixed the destinies of [472] Jefferson's life, William Duncan helped to fix the destinies of the Declaration of Independence.

Like all the progressive logics in England during the eighteenth century, Duncan's is arranged according to the four basic operations of the mind in discovering and ordering knowledge.[31] Thus Duncan successively treats perception, judgment, reasoning, and method. His basic thesis is that knowledge has three branches, each with a corresponding form of judgment and way of reasoning. These three branches, arranged in order of descent from absolute certainty to the lowest of the acceptable degrees of probability, are science, natural philosophy, and history. Perhaps the following quotation will best represent his basic view of them all:

In *Scientifical* Knowledge, which regards wholly the abstract Ideas of the Mind, and those Relations and Connections they have one with another; our Judgments are grounded on *Intuition,* and the Manner of Reasoning is by *Demonstration.* In *Natural* Knowledge, respecting Objects that exist without us, their Powers, Properties and mutual Operations; we judge on the Foundation of *Experience,* and reason by *Induction* and *Analogy.* Lastly, in *Historical* Knowledge, which is chiefly conversant about past Facts and Transactions; *Testimony* is the Ground of Judgment, and the Way of Reasoning is by *Criticism* and *probable Conjecture.*[32]

So far as my present argument is concerned, the terms which have most importance in this statement are intuition, demonstration, and science. To Duncan, intuition is the immediate recognition that the ideas in a proposition are in fact related as the proposition declares them to be. "Thus, *that the Whole is greater than any of it's Parts,*" he observes, "is an intuitive Judgment, nothing more being required to convince us of it's Truth, than an Attention to the Ideas of *Whole*

---

fered for sale in the printing office and bookshop of Dixon and Hunter in Williamsburg in 1775. See *Wm. and Mary College Qtly.* 1st Ser., XV (1906–7), 109. For another example, it was one of the volumes in the library of John Parke Custis of Fairfax County, according to an inventory made in 1782. See "The Library of John Parke Custis, Esq., of Fairfax County, Virginia," *Tyler's Quarterly Historical and Genealogical Magazine,* IX (1927–28), 101. Custis briefly attended King's College, now Columbia, in 1773.

The first American edition of the *Logick* was published at Philadelphia, Aug. 10, 1792, from the press of Mathew Carey. There is a copy in the Huntington Library, San Marino, Calif.

[31] All my references are to Duncan's *Logick* as it appears in [Robert Dodsley], *The Preceptor* (London, 1748), II. For Duncan's mention of the four operations of the mind, see that volume, pages 3–6.

[32] *Ibid.,* 180. Italics and punctuation are Duncan's here and below.

and *Part.*"[33] Demonstration means syllogistic reasoning, as distinguished from induction and analogy; and it is the process by which intuitive judgments, as recognized [473] truths in their own right, are made to yield derivative propositions that are themselves absolutely certain. Science is that which comes into being as a result of demonstration: "For whatever is deduced from our intuitive Perceptions, by a clear and connected Series of Proofs, is said to be demonstrated, and produces absolute Certainty in the Mind. Hence the Knowledge obtained in this manner, is what we properly term *Science*; because in every Step of the Procedure, it carries it's own Evidence along with it, and leaves no room for Doubt or Hesitation."[34]

Somewhat later Duncan clarifies still further the relation between the certainty produced by intuition and that produced by demonstration; and he identifies the intuitive judgment by calling it the "self-evident proposition or perception," this term being one that is repeated over and over again in the course of the *Logick.* Here are Duncan's own words:

> When any Proposition is offered to the View of the Mind, if the Terms in which it is expressed are understood; upon comparing the Ideas together, the Agreement or Disagreement asserted is either immediately perceived, or found to lie beyond the present Reach of the Understanding. In the first Case the Proposition is said to be *self-evident,* and admits not of any Proof, because a bare Attention to the Ideas themselves, produces full Conviction and Certainty; nor is it possible to call in any thing more evident, by way of Confirmation. But where the Connection or Repugnance comes not so readily under the Inspection of the Mind, there we must have Recourse to Reasoning; and if by a clear Series of Proofs we can make out the Truth proposed, insomuch that Self-evidence shall accompany every Step of the Procedure, we are then able to demonstrate what we assert, and the Proposition itself is said to be *demonstrable.* . . .
>
> From what has been said it appears, that Reasoning is employed only about demonstrable Propositions, and that our intuitive and self-evident Perceptions, are the ultimate Foundation on which it rests.[35]

Mathematics offers to Duncan the purest example of science, the best illustration of first principles and self-evident truths, and the happiest models for demonstrations that produce absolute certainty. In fact, long before he explains the analytic and synthetic methods

[33] *Ibid.,* 79.   [34] *Ibid.,* 80.   [35] *Ibid.,* 96–97.

of logic, he outlines the steps by which the mathematicians arrive at truth: "First then it is to be observed, that they have been very careful in ascertaining their Ideas, and fixing the Signification of their Terms. For this Purpose they begin [474] with *Definitions.* . . ." [36] "When they have taken this first Step, . . . their next Care is, to lay down some self-evident Truths, which may serve as a Foundation for their future Reasonings." [37] To the mathematician, self-evident truths are known as axioms and postulates, the former being self-evident speculative, the latter self-evident practical propositions, whereas demonstrable propositions are correspondingly known as theorems and problems. Having laid down his self-evident truths, the mathematician as his next step invokes corollaries, which are propositions flowing so immediately from the self-evident or demonstrated truths as to require no separate proof of their own. And finally, the mathematician uses scholia, which are independently annexed to definitions, propositions, or corollaries, and serve the same purpose as annotations upon a classical text. "In a System of Knowledge so uniform and well connected," writes Duncan, "no wonder if we meet with Certainty; and if those Clouds and Darknesses, that deface other Parts of human Science, and bring Discredit even upon Reason itself, are here scattered and disappear." [38]

As if fascinated by self-evident truths more than by anything else in logic, Duncan adds that they cannot be detected by external marks or characteristics. Nothing in them more striking than their self-evidence can be used to identify them. With a touch of poetic fervor, he declares: "Intuitive Judgments need no other distinguishing Marks, than that Brightness which surrounds them; in like manner as Light discovers itself by its own Presence, and the Splendor it universally diffuses." [39]

The immediate authority behind Duncan's regard for mathematical method is John Locke. This fact is plainly established when Duncan discusses reasoning as the third part of logic. Speaking of the studies that will help the beginner to master the art of reasoning, he mentions that for such a purpose no science is better than mathematics:

Not that we look upon it as necessary, (*to use the Words of the great Mr.* Locke) that all Men should be deep Mathematicians, but that, having got the Way of Reasoning which that Study necessarily brings the Mind to, they may be able to transfer it to other Parts of Knowledge, as they

---

[36] *Ibid.*, 98.   [37] *Ibid.*, 99.   [38] *Ibid.*, 102.   [39] *Ibid.*, 103.

shall have Occasion. For in all sorts of Reasoning, every single Argument should be managed as a Mathematical Demonstration, the Connection and Dependence of Ideas should be followed, till the Mind is brought to the Source on which it bottoms, and can trace the Coherence through the whole Train of Proofs. . . . Nothing does this better than Mathematicks, [475] which therefore I think should be taught all those, who have the Time and Opportunity, not so much to make them Mathematicians, as to make them reasonable Creatures. . . .[40]

One other aspect of Duncan's treatment of reasoning should be given attention at this time to emphasize his conception of demonstration or proof and its origin in self-evident truths and syllogistic order. After his discussion of the forms, figures, and moods of the syllogism, during which he refers his readers to *The Port-Royal Logic*,[41] he speaks briefly of induction, and then devotes a chapter to the standards that must be met in proving a proposition. His doctrine is not original, but his emphasis and wording give it a special attractiveness:

When a Proposition is thus by means of Syllogisms, collected from others more evident and known, it is said to be *proved;* so that we may in the general define *the Proof of a Proposition,* to be a Syllogism, or Series of Syllogisms, collecting that Proposition from known and evident Truths. But more particularly, if the Syllogisms of which the Proof consists, admit of no Premisses but Definitions, self-evident Truths, and Propositions already established, then is the Argument so constituted called a *Demonstration;* whereby it appears, that Demonstrations are ultimately founded on Definitions, and self-evident Propositions.[42]

As for the standards finally to be met in achieving certainty in a demonstration, Duncan finds them in the rules governing syllogisms of the first figure. "For since all the Syllogisms that enter the Demonstration," he remarks, "are reducible to Syllogisms of some one of the four Figures, and since the Syllogisms of all the other Figures are farther reducible to Syllogisms of the First Figure, it is evident, that the whole Demonstration may be resolved into a Series of these last Syllogisms."[43] The universal principles of certainty in all syllogisms of the first figure, the great laws of deductive reasoning, the

[40] *Ibid.,* 121–122. The whole quotation from Locke occupies 33 lines of Duncan's text. Duncan credits it to Locke's essay, "Of the Conduct of the Understanding." For the first 11 lines of the quotation, see *Posthumous Works of Mr. John Locke* (London, 1706), 30–31; for the rest, *ibid.,* 26–27. Duncan's quotation is not entirely faithful to Locke's original text, but he does not change Locke's meaning in any real sense.
[41] *The Preceptor,* II, 124.   [42] *Ibid.,* 134–135.   [43] *Ibid.,* 135.

self-evident truths of logic itself, are what the logicians call the *Dictum de omni* and the *Dictum de nullo,* respectively defined by Duncan as follows: *"Whatever may be affirmed universally of any Idea, may be affirmed of every or any Number of Particulars* [476] *comprehended under that Idea,"* and, *"Whatever may be denied universally of any idea, may be in like Manner denied, of every or any Number of it's Individuals."* [44]

Duncan's discussion of method as the fourth part of logic constitutes an important statement of the accepted distinction between the analytic and the synthetic methods. He recognizes the two established methods of arranging and communicating thought, he gives each its conventional terminology,[45] and he makes a contribution of his own to the theory of synthetic method by urging that it be called the method of science, "not only as in the Use of it we arrive at *Science* and Certainty, but because it is in Fact the Method, in which all those Parts of human Knowledge, that properly bear the Name of *Sciences,* are and ought to be delivered." [46]

Above all, he emphasizes the essential identity between the method used by mathematicians and that required in any other field where abstract ideas of the mind are involved. The last words of the *Logick* lay stress upon this important fact, so central to his whole design:

It is true the Method here laid down, hath hitherto been observed strictly, only among Mathematicians; and is therefore by many thought, to be peculiar to Number and Magnitude. But it appears evidently from what we have said above, that it may be equally applied in all such other Parts of Knowledge, as regard the abstract Ideas of the Mind, and the Relations subsisting between them. And since wherever it is applied, it necessarily begets *Science* and *Certainty,* we have hence chosen to denominate it the *Method of Science,* the better to intimate its true Nature and Extent.[47]

V

Even if we did not know that Thomas Jefferson owned a copy of Duncan's *Logick,* and that his beloved teacher, William Small, who taught him rhetoric, logic, and ethics during his first year at William and Mary, had been a disciple of William Duncan at Marischal College, and would have been certain to transport to Virginia his own master's logical as well as scientific teachings—even if we were not sure of these facts, we would nevertheles suspect, upon examin-

[44] *Ibid.,* 137. [45] *Ibid.,* 148–149. [46] *Ibid.,* 149. [47] *Ibid.,* 192.

ing Duncan's *Logick* in relation to the Declaration of Independence, that the former influenced the latter. The nature of that influence must now be briefly examined.

As the Declaration is usually printed, its second paragraph begins with the famous words, "We hold these truths to be self-evident, that all men [477] are created equal, that they are endowed by their Creator with certain unalienable Rights, that among these are Life, Liberty and the pursuit of Happiness." [48] It is difficult to believe that the word "self-evident" appears at this point in the Declaration by mere chance. Jefferson is here laying down the major premise of the syllogism that constitutes the whole demonstrative strategy of the Declaration, and is here thinking in terms of the need to make that syllogism command the assent of mankind. It was Duncan who repeatedly insisted, as we have seen, that for a syllogistic argument to achieve certainty, to compel assent, to reach the highest status in philosophy, it must be founded upon a self-evident major premise, that is to say, upon a proposition that would be equivalent to axioms and postulates in mathematics, and that would convince any reasonable man of its truth if he merely gave his attention to the ideas making it up. In other words, "self-evident" as it appears in Duncan's *Logick* has a precise technical meaning and is used in a stable, precisely defined context. As it appears in the Declaration, does it not have the same technical meaning, and the same exact context, except that it is being used in an operational as distinguished from a doctrinal sense? A parallelism of this sort could of course be attributed to accident, and perhaps it should be. But a reader of Duncan's *Logick* is strongly inclined to feel otherwise.

Again, it does not seem to be merely the result of accident that the Declaration turns out in fact to be a perfect example of the method of science as described so convincingly by Duncan. To be sure, this method, under its older rubric, synthesis, was a fixed part of eighteenth-century logical doctrine, and there are descriptions of it in *The Port-Royal Logic*, in Crousaz's *Art of Thinking*, and in four

[48] In Jefferson's original draft, this passage begins thus: "We hold these truths to be sacred & undeniable; that all men are created equal & independant. . . ." See Boyd, *Declaration*, 19. The words "sacred & undeniable" were crossed out later, and "self-evident" was written above them. Mr. Boyd feels that this correction, as written upon Jefferson's original draft, is in Jefferson's own handwriting and therefore originated with him (*ibid.*, 22, 24). Becker, *Declaration*, 142, 198, thought that the correction is in Franklin's handwriting or that it comes from Adams. This seems to me to be a case in which the physical evidence cited by Mr. Boyd to link Jefferson with the correction is squarely corroborated by all the evidence linking Jefferson with Duncan's *Logick*.

of the seven logical treatises that were in Jefferson's library and could have been read by him before 1776.[49] But of all the logics that flourished in England during the first [478] two-thirds of the eighteenth century, only Duncan's can be said to elevate the theory of method into a vital role in the philosophy of knowledge and in the strategy of scientific proof. Thus it would appeal above all to a mature writer or speaker seeking a persuasive formula more compelling and more fateful than any that would be merely prescribed in college exercises in composition.

If we may consider that the beginning words of Jefferson's immortal document have the effect of a logical definition, so far as they bring his present purposes into relation with a specific series of disruptive events, on the one hand, and with a generalized "respect to the opinions of mankind," on the other, then it is obvious that the Declaration as a whole fits Duncan's recommended plan for demonstrative proof. For after that opening, almost as if he were following Duncan's own prescription, Jefferson undertakes next "to lay down some self-evident Truths,"[50] which will serve as the foundation of his future reasonings; and he then proceeds syllogistically, so as to meet the requirements for a necessarily valid conclusion, while

---

[49] Sowerby, Catalogue, V, 13–15, lists eight logics in Jefferson's library, as follows: Abraham Fraunce's The Lawiers Logike (London, 1558); Aristotle's Logica, in . . . Opervum Aristotelis . . . noua Editio, Graece et Latiné [ed. J. Pacius] ([Lyon], 1597); Richard Crakanthorp's Logicae Libri Quinque, 4th ed. (Oxford, 1677); Wallis's Institutio Logicae (Oxford, 1702); Aldrich's Artis Logicae Compendium (Oxford, 1723); Watts's Logick, 8th ed. (London, 1745); Étienne Bonnot de Condillac's Logica (Madrid, 1794); Joseph Neef's The Logic of Condillac (Philadelphia, 1809). To this list must be added Duncan's Logick as printed in the second volume of The Preceptor.

Of these nine logics, Aristotle's Logica does not deal with what was later called the synthetic method, although his Topica, as one of his logical writings, provides the basis for the later division of dialectic into invention and dispositio; Crakanthorp's Logicae Libri Quinque does not recognize method as a part of logic, and thus remains thoroughly traditional in an age that was intent upon reforming the dialectical system of Ramus; Fraunce's Lawiers Logike treats method in the manner of a devout Ramist, and thus does not include refinements introduced by Crakanthorp's contemporaries; Condillac's Logica and Neef's The Logic of Condillac were published too late to have influenced Jefferson in writing the Declaration; but the remaining four (Wallis, Aldrich, Watts, and Duncan) discuss the synthetic and the analytic methods in some detail.

There were other logics in Jefferson's library in volumes not devoted exclusively to that subject. For example, John Brightland's Logic accompanied his Grammar and other works in a volume held by Jefferson. See Sowerby, Catalogue, V, 116. But such elementary treatises as that do not require attention in this study.

[50] The source of this quotation is given above in n. 37. For the quotation immediately following, see Duncan's Logick in The Preceptor, II, 102.

corollaries flow "naturally and of themselves," and particulars needed to illustrate the subject and to complete the reader's information are thrown in as scholia.

The argument of the Declaration falls naturally into the form of a [479] categorical syllogism of the first figure. One attempt to reconstruct the propositions making up this syllogism will inevitably differ from another, as the critics' interests shift from politics to logic. Although Carl Becker's reconstruction is lucid and graceful, he states the syllogism from the point of view of its political implications,[51] and thus he does not reproduce the contours of Jefferson's own logical structure. In contrast, I should like to propose that we visualize Jefferson's argument in the following terms:[52]

Major Premise: All governments denying that men are created equal and that mankind therefore have inalienable rights to life, liberty, and the pursuit of happiness, may be altered or abolished at the hands of the people, from whose consent alone can governments derive their just powers.

Minor Premise: The history of his present majesty is a history of unremitting injuries and usurpations having in direct object the establishment of an absolute tyranny over the American states.

Conclusion: All allegiance and subjection of these states to the kings of Great Britain and all others who may hereafter claim by, through, or under them, are therefore rejected, renounced, dissolved, and broken off.

The corollaries stated in the course of framing these propositions flow "naturally and of themselves," as Duncan says they should;[53] and their effect is to create the positive counterpart of the main syllogism, or to reinforce its conclusion. For example, a corollary of

[51] Becker, *Declaration*, 203–204.
[52] In framing this syllogism I have worked, not from the accepted official text of the Declaration, but from Jefferson's own original draft before it was revised by Adams and Franklin, by the Committee of Five appointed to draw the document up, or by Congress itself in the process of giving it final form. I could not have done so with any confidence, however, if it had not been for Mr. Boyd's excellent study of the evolution of the text of the Declaration, to which I have earlier referred, and to which I now pay grateful tribute. For a reconstruction of Jefferson's original draft, see Boyd, *Declaration*, 19–21.
[53] See above, n. 50.

the right of the people to destroy a tyrannous government is their right "to institute new government, laying it's foundation on such principles & organising it's powers in such form, as to them shall seem most likely to effect their safety & [480] happiness." [54] Thus it is later possible for Jefferson to declare, as a corollary of his conclusion, that the colonies are "free and independant states, and that as free & independant states they shall hereafter have full power to levy war, conclude peace, contract alliances, establish commerce, & to do all other acts and things which independant states may of right do." [55] For another example, a prudent people asserting their right to destroy a tyrannous government acknowledge as a corollary their duty to be patient under trivial and temporary political evils; thus governments abrogating the fundamental rights of the governed have to acknowledge in turn that such an action frees their people from the obligations of patient sufferance and places upon them the duty to revolt. Jefferson memorably develops these corollaries as follows: "Prudence indeed will dictate that governments long established should not be changed for light & transient causes: and accordingly all experience hath shewn that mankind are more disposed to suffer while evils are sufferable, than to right themselves by abolishing the forms to which they are accustomed. But when a long train of abuses & usurpations, begun at a distinguished period, & pursuing invariably the same object, evinces a design to subject them to arbitrary power, it is their right, it is their duty, to throw off such government & to provide new guards for their future security." [56]

As for scholia, they appear in the Declaration, not as marginal glosses or footnotes, to be sure, but as if they were otherwise intended to conform to Duncan's requirement that they should illustrate the subject and complete the reader's information in the manner of annotations upon a classical text.[57] One such annotation occurs when, after commenting upon the native reluctance of mankind to revolt against oppression, Jefferson calls attention to the situation facing the American people: "Such has been the patient sufferance of these colonies; & such is now the necessity which constrains them to expunge their former systems of government." [58] Another annotation occurs after the minor premise has been stated: "To prove this, let facts be submitted to a candid world, for the truth of which we

---

[54] Boyd, *Declaration*, 19.   [55] *Ibid.*, 21.   [56] *Ibid.*, 19.
[57] See Duncan's *Logick* in *The Preceptor*, II, 101–102.
[58] Boyd, *Declaration*, 19.

pledge a faith yet unsullied by falsehood." [59] Indeed, the list of eighteen specific injuries and usurpations alleged against the King as proof of the [481] minor premise is a series of annotations upon Jefferson's text to complete the information of the reader. And his later notations concerning the cold reception of the petitions and remonstrances that the colonies had addressed to the King have precisely the same character and function.

VI

Those who approach the Declaration in the belief that the principles of rhetoric are timeless and unchanging, and that the Declaration, or any other major persuasive work of any period or place, should of course conform to those unchanging principles, or else be judged inartistic, are at once confronted by a paradox. For the Declaration is obviously persuasive in purpose and effect; but it does not conform to what would have been called in its own time the principles of traditional rhetorical theory. For example, it does not follow the prescriptions so fully described in John Ward's early eighteenth-century lectures at Gresham College on the classical rhetorical system of Aristotle, Cicero, and Quintilian. Ward emphasizes persuasion, not pre-eminently conviction, as the end of oratory; he makes probability, not certainty, the orator's normal attainable goal; he stresses appeals to passion and interest, not alone the appeal to reason, as the orator's means; he points to the enthymeme and the example rather than to the syllogism as the usual types of oratorical argument; he discusses the topics of proof rather than the axioms of politics and morality and the facts of contemporary life as the source of oratorical materials; he recommends the classical form of the oration rather than the form of mathematical demonstration as the proper structure of persuasive discourse; and he prefers appropriate amplification and ornament to the short dry way of logic as the accepted standard of oratorical style. According to these principles, which Jefferson could have read in his own copy of Ward,[60] the Declaration seems antirhetorical. Yet it stands as one of the most persuasive and influential discourses of the modern world. How then do we explain this apparent contradiction?

The answer is, of course, that rhetoric is not fixed and changeless.

[59] *Ibid.*
[60] See Ward, *Oratory,* Lectures 2–4, 10–19. See also Sowerby, *Catalogue,* V, 17.

It changes as the culture around it does. Thus the Declaration is an expression, not of traditional eighteenth-century rhetoric, as expounded by Ward, but of a newly emerging rhetoric that was influenced by Locke and by Duncan and that would be fully expressed later in the century by Priestley [482] and above all by Campbell. This new rhetoric was created out of new attitudes towards science, towards knowledge, towards reason, and towards man. There is hence no real strangeness involved in finding that the Declaration is not only in accord with the principles of Duncan's *Logick* but is also by that very fact a better specimen of effective rhetoric than it would have been if Jefferson had written it with the formulas of John Ward in mind. It delivered its ideas by the method of science to a generation which greatly respected scientific standards of thought and expression. In a century which revered John Locke, it followed Locke's dictum that "in all sorts of Reasoning, every single Argument should be managed as a Mathematical Demonstration, the Connection and Dependence of Ideas should be followed, till the Mind is brought to the Source on which it bottoms, and can trace the Coherence through the whole Train of Proofs." It employed the forms of philosophical address at a time when such forms were believed equal to the tasks of persuasion and appropriate as the means of expressing the doctrine of human rights. According to Jefferson's own intention, as expressed in the quotation with which this paper opened, it sought "to place before mankind the common sense of the subject, in terms so plain and firm as to command their assent, and to justify ourselves in the independent stand we are compelled to take." If anyone says that a discourse written to conform to these requirements is not a good example of rhetoric, he is saying in effect that rhetoric is the art of ignoring the sources of effectiveness in literary composition, and is the art of producing something beneath the status of good literature.

Jefferson's preference for a logical rhetoric as distinguished from a rhetoric of probability and ornamentation is rooted no more deeply in his devotion to the ideals of the Enlightenment than in his abiding admiration for the classics of Greek and Roman antiquity. One good expression of that admiration is found in his letter to Joseph Priestley on January 27, 1800; another, in his letter of July 1, 1814, to the Reverend Jason Chamberlayne; and still another, in his letter to David Harding on April 20, 1824.[61] As president of the Jefferson

[61] For the letter to Priestley, see Ford, ed., *Writings of Jefferson*, VII, 413–416. The letters to Chamberlayne and Harding are as yet unpublished, but they

Debating Society of Hingham, [483] Harding had written to notify
Jefferson that the Society was being given his name. Jefferson's reply
reads in part as follows:

The object of the institution is laudable, and in a republican nation
whose citizens are to be led by reason and persuasion and not by force,
the art of reasoning becomes of first importance. In this line antiquity has
left us the finest models for imitation, and he who studies and imitates
them most nearly will nearest approach the perfection of the art. Among
these I should consider the speeches of Livy, Sallust and Tacitus as pre-
eminent specimens of logic, taste, and that sententious brevity which
using not a word to spare, leaves not a moment for inattention to the
hearer. Amplification is the vice of modern oratory. It is an insult to an
assembly of reasonable men, disgusting and revolting instead of per-
suading.

These sentiments indicate that Jefferson saw no contradiction between logic, taste, and brevity, on the one hand, and perfection in
the art of persuasion, on the other. That such a contradiction seems
inherent in the culture of twentieth-century America is a sign, not
that wisdom has increased since Jefferson's day, but that superficial-
ity and confusion have come upon us. [484]

---

will appear in due course in a future volume of Mr. Boyd's great work, *The Papers of Thomas Jefferson* (Princeton, 1950—). Mr. Boyd kindly furnished me
with the complete text of the letter to Harding, and my excerpt comes from that
source. A shorter excerpt and a brief quotation from the letter to Chamberlayne
are printed in Sowerby, *Catalogue*, V, 13.

The Lost Meaning of
"The Pursuit of Happiness"

ARTHUR M. SCHLESINGER

Probably no historical expression is more familiar to Americans than "the pursuit of happiness," immortalized by the preamble of the Declaration of Independence. Yet it has puzzled many that life and liberty should be pronounced by the great document as "unalienable rights" of "all men" but not happiness—only the pursuit of it. It is worth asking, however, what Jefferson and his associates on the drafting committee really meant by the famous phrase. Able scholars have repeatedly examined the meaning of the text as a whole, but none has given attention to this particular wording.[1]

What, then, was the import of the term "pursuit" in the minds of the framers of the Declaration? Did it signify merely the pursuing or seeking of happiness, as is conventionally assumed, or was it used in a different sense, as when we today refer to the pursuit of law or the pursuit of medicine? According to the *New English Dictionary* it has borne both meanings since at least the sixteenth century.[2] Obviously

---

[1] Among the more notable book-length studies are Carl Becker, *The Declaration of Independence, a Study in the History of Political Ideas* (New York, 1922); Julian P. Boyd, *The Declaration of Independence: The Evolution of the Text as Shown in Facsimiles of Various Drafts by Its Author* (Washington, 1943); Edward Dumbauld, *The Declaration of Independence and What It Means Today* (Norman, Okla., 1950); Herbert Friedenwald, *The Declaration of Independence, an Interpretation and an Analysis* (New York, 1904); and John H. Hazelton, *The Declaration of Independence, Its History . . .* (New York, 1906). Howard Mumford Jones, *The Pursuit of Happiness* (Cambridge, Mass., 1953), deals with the meaning of the word "happiness," especially as later interpreted, but not with that of "pursuit," which alone concerns the present essay.

[2] The alternative definitions there given are: "The action of pursuing, chasing, or following, with intent to overtake and catch . . . ," and "The action of fol-

FROM *William and Mary Quarterly*, 3rd Ser., XXI (July, 1964), 325–327, copyrighted by the author and reprinted by his permission. Original title.

the distinction is a vital one, for, if the common supposition is mistaken, it follows that the historic manifesto proclaimed the *practicing* rather than the *quest* of happiness as a basic right equally with life and liberty. For evidence of this [325] usage contemporary with the Anglo-American dispute the *New English Dictionary* cites a letter of Edmund Burke in 1774 in which he wrote, "Your constitution of mind is such, that you must have a pursuit." [3]

In this sense of the actual practicing—and in no other, so far as I have found—the concept also appeared in patriot writings during the controversy. Thus James Otis in *The Rights of the British Colonies Asserted and Proved* (Boston, 1764) affirmed that the duty of government is "above all things to provide for the security, the quiet, and happy enjoyment of life, liberty, and property." [4] More categorically, Josiah Quincy, Jr., in his *Observations on the Act of Parliament Commonly Called the Boston Port-Bill* (Boston, 1774) avowed that the proper object of civil society is "the greatest happiness of the greatest number," [5] and James Wilson in his *Considerations on the Nature and Extent of the Legislative Authority of the British Parliament* (Philadelphia, 1774) asserted that "the happiness of the society is the *first* law of every government." [6] Likewise John Adams in his *Thoughts on Government* (Philadelphia, 1776) declared that "the happiness of society is the end of government." [7] In short, none of these spokesmen of the American cause thought of happiness as something a people were entitled simply to strive for but as something that was theirs by natural right.

As though to make this conception unquestionably clear, the revolutionary Virginia Convention's memorable Declaration of Rights on June 12, 1776, particularized it as the "pursuing and obtaining" of happiness.[8] The language was that of George Mason, Jefferson's

---

lowing or engaging in something, as a profession, business, recreation, etc. . . ."
James A. H. Murray, ed., *A New English Dictionary on Historical Principles* (Oxford, Eng., 1888–1925), VII, 1636.
[3] *Ibid.*
[4] James Otis, *Some Political Writings*, in Charles F. Mullett, ed., *University of Missouri Studies*, IV (Columbia, Mo., 1929), 309.
[5] Josiah Quincy, *Memoir of the Life of Josiah Quincy, Junior, of Massachusetts, 1774–1775*, 2d ed. (Boston, 1874), 323.
[6] Bird Wilson, ed., *The Works of the Honourable James Wilson* . . . (Philadelphia, 1804), III, 206.
[7] Charles Francis Adams, ed., *The Works of John Adams* . . . (Boston, 1850–56), IV, 193.
[8] Helen Hill, *George Mason, Constitutionalist* (Cambridge, Mass., 1938), 136.
This wording may have seemed the more necessary because John Locke, whose

long-time friend whom he described in his autobiography as "a man of the first order of wisdom among those who acted on the theatre of the [326] Revolution." [9] It is unlikely that in drawing up the Declaration of Independence shortly afterward for the Continental Congress he did not take Mason's phrasing into account.

Why he determined upon his own more concise rendering we do not know, but doubtless he deemed the added words sheer excess baggage. As John Adams, one of his colleagues on the drafting committee, said, Jefferson was noted for "a happy talent of composition" and "peculiar felicity of expression." [10] In any case the latter part of the sentence containing his formulation stated explicitly that it is a government's duty to the governed "to effect their safety and happiness." The extraordinary thing is that through the years the two parts of this sentence have not been read together. Adams, who had flatly declared a few months before that "the happiness of society is the end of government," found no fault with Jefferson's version, though he did not hesitate to suggest changes elsewhere in the document.[11]

In view of these circumstances the conclusion seems inescapable that the long-standing misinterpretation of "the pursuit of happiness" should at last be corrected and the history books be rewritten to restore to the celebrated phrase its more emphatic meaning. [327]

---

writings were a major source of patriot inspiration, had used the expression, "the pursuit of happiness," in the sense of "pursuing." For examples see Herbert L. Ganter, "Jefferson's 'Pursuit of Happiness' and Some Forgotten Men," *William and Mary Quarterly*, 2d Ser., XVI (1936), 564.

[9] Hill, *George Mason, Constitutionalist*, 152.

[10] Letter to Timothy Pickering, Aug. 6, 1822, in C. F. Adams, ed., *Works*, II, 513–514n.

[11] Becker, *Declaration of Independence*, 136–138, 152–155.

26

The Declaration as Rhetoric

ROBERT GINSBERG

I. History, Philosophy, and Rhetoric

The Declaration of Independence has been treated historically as a document vital to the American War for Independence, and philosophically as a text whose principles and arguments are timeless and universal. The historical approach [1] focuses on the sources, that is, the evolution of material that went into the document, and on the consequences in action and attitude that resulted from the Declaration. The temptation is to identify the Declaration as the sum of its sources or merely as the source of posterior events. What lies between the antecedents and the consequences, the work itself, containing not only identifiable materials but an organization of them in terms of purposes which may well differ from those preceding and following, is rarely considered.

The philosophic approach [2] focuses on the truth embodied in the Declaration which transcends the particular historical circumstances. Steering clear of all that is stubbornly nonphilosophic in the work, this approach expounds the principles of the Declaration as a recognizable condensation of an elaborate political theory that may be pertinent today. Curiously though, the ideas discovered in the Declaration are open to diverse interpretation, depending on one's own philosophy; and the nonphilosophic parts are often inconsistent with the theory expounded.

Philosopher and historian may join hands to deal with the sources of the *ideas* in the Declaration and with the influence of such ideas

---

[1] Exemplified by John H. Hazelton, *The Declaration of Independence: Its History* (New York: Dodd, Mead and Company, 1906).

[2] Exemplified by Ralph Barton Perry in the essay reprinted in this volume.

WRITTEN especially for this volume and published here for the first time.

on later political speculation and program. Carl L. Becker [3] conducts such a history of ideas in conjunction with a literary analysis, for the Declaration to him is both a philosophic and a literary work. Its implicit philosophy is found in the natural rights theory preceding it, while its literary qualities lie in its style adopted to convince an audience. Most critical appreciation of the Declaration as persuasion has been in terms of its language, this being appropriate to its particular moment in history; while the philosophy embodied may be applicable to all time, or at least, as in Becker's view, to the eighteenth century as a whole. But it is worth examining how philosophic materials serve persuasive rather than philosophic ends in the Declaration, and how such persuasive ends contribute to the form of the work and not just to its expression.

To examine the work as rhetoric is not to neglect the historical, the philosophic, and the literary. The document takes its material from history and aims at affecting its course. Historical information is useful in judging what the terms and issues in the text meant to the eighteenth-century readers it was intended for. But the structure of the text should remain the subject of analysis rather than the historical situation.

A kind of argument plays a prominent role in the text, and one famous passage has a pronounced philosophic aspect calling for analysis of its logic. All that is philosophic is not philosophy, however, and what is argumentative here is not specifically an argument in philosophy. The details of style should be evaluated for their contribution to persuasion, but more important than the language used is the organization given the Declaration by other persuasive resources.

The Declaration of Independence is primarily an effort made by certain men at a given moment to persuade other men to adopt special attitudes and courses of action. Three questions arise in dealing with a work of persuasion: (1) Who is it that is to be persuaded and how is he treated by the persuader? (2) Who is the persuader that undertakes by his character and statements to influence his audience? (3) What reasoning is offered to the listener for the action or the placing of approval and blame that he is urged to? Persuasion presupposes a relationship between what is spoken and to whom and by whom it is spoken, and this relationship may be discovered in the work itself. Determining who the audience was, insofar as it is indicated by the strategy of the speech, and how the speaker represented himself to his audience are different issues than determining the nature of the historical character of the British, Americans, and other parties involved. If the art of rhetoric consists in discovering the best means of persuasion available in a specific case, then the analysis of the Declaration should subordinate the knowledge of the origin of any feature in the text to an appreciation of how it functions in the text. The rhetorical "source" of a device or claim in the Declaration is the requirements of one or more of the powers of persuasion: the appeal to a specific audience, the use of one's specific character to gain goodwill and assent, and the offering of the appearance of a good argument. The rhetorician, having discovered the means of persuasion through these powers, seeks the appropriate language for expression and the effective order for presentation. These too, then, should fall within the scope of our analysis.[4]

II. Audience

Let us take up the question of the audience first since it is the reference point to which the character of the speaker and the shape of his argument must be adjusted. Who is the Declaration made to? The first sentence tells us that *a decent Respect to the Opinions of Mankind* requires the Declaration. More specifically, the Americans aspire to a position *among the Powers of the Earth.* The powers are separate and equal, there is a basis in natural law for them, and they are sanctioned by divine arrangement. There is little that is revolutionary here. The audience as a community of nations is assured that the American uprising is not the beginning of world upheaval. Having offered a characterization of world politics that could hardly be

[4] There are different methods of rhetorical analysis as there are of literary criticism. The conception of rhetoric employed here is borrowed from Aristotle. Wilbur Samuel Howell analyzes the Declaration in an essay reprinted in this volume in terms of eighteenth-century conceptions of rhetoric, the advantage of which lies in exhibiting some ways in which Jefferson and his contemporaries may have thought about rhetoric, and the disadvantage of which lies in the historical connections that have to be made to show Jefferson intended a technically eighteenth-century rhetorical work. Edward Dumbauld, *The Declaration of Independence and What It Means Today* (Norman, Okla.: University of Oklahoma Press, 1950), offers a line-by-line exposition of the Declaration relying upon an ancient method of rhetorical treatment which compiles materials on given topics. Such an approach takes the word as primary and sees the structure as a succession of terms, while neglecting the rationale in the work from which the choice of words and the order of presentation follow.

rejected by their audience as seditious or disrespectful, the Americans may then move themselves up into the world to play a role alongside of the audience.

The manuscript of the Declaration was improved before it reached Congress: *for a people to advance from that subordination in which they have hitherto remained* was altered to *for one People to dissolve the Political Bands which have connected them with another,* removing the image of an ambitious ascension of the colonists into the world of nations. So too in the final paragraph the future tense of the phrase *they shall hereafter have,* mentioning the powers of states accessible to the Americans, was rejected in favor of the present tense *they have*—a stronger yet a less pretentious claim.

To prove its contentions against the King, the Declaration submits facts to the *candid World.* The making public of one's grievances to an impartial judge is an assurance that the speaker has his head about him and that being engaged in a controversy does not weaken his proper attitude towards the rest of the world. A certain weight is also given to what are called "facts," which are then enumerated.

The world must be cautioned against taking advantage of the conflict to stifle the independence of the Colonies; for with their legislative bodies dissolved by the King, the Americans stand in danger of attack from without (accusation vi). But the legislative powers are not to be thought completely abandoned: they revert to the people. Those in a lawless condition may take the law into their own hands to defend themselves. In addition to the British, then, *the rest of Mankind* will be regarded as enemies by the colonists should they offer hostility. The implied warning in accusation vi is followed in accusation vii by the revelation of a friendly, welcoming attitude to foreigners, again offset by the cruelty of the King. He, not the colonists, is the one who has inhibited the coming of settlers to America. The Americans want to share their lands, while the King lacks concern for others. It is the King and his minions who have cut off the colonists' trade with the world (accusation xvi), whereas one of the things the independent state will do is *establish Commerce.*

The King is made out to be a warlord dangerous to nations, while the colonists, who are in rebellion, take on the guise of peacelovers posing no threat to the world. The King, apparently without any need for it, has kept *Standing Armies* in the Colonies (*& ships of war* unfortunately omitted by Congress) (accusation xi). He is depicted as warring on sea, coast, and town, and *transporting large Armies of* *foreign Mercenaries* (accusations xxiv, xxv). He has turned prisoners against their countrymen, incited insurrections against the citizenry of the Colonies, and made use of wild savages, encouraging them to uncivilized acts of war (accusations xxvi, xxvii). If the King acts thus with his innocent subjects, then he is no friend of the audience. Indeed, he is not to be counted among the company of civilized rulers, having done things *totally unworthy the Head of a civilized Nation* (accusation xxv) and being *unfit to be the Ruler of a free People* (¶ III)—which refers to the Americans as well as to others in the British Empire.

By making the King guilty of all the offenses, the Declaration does not respect the truth, but there is something other than proof to be achieved in so formulating these "facts" for third parties. What is a war between peoples, or a war between segments of one people, takes on the appearance of the mistreatment of one people by one man. The plausibility of that man mistreating other peoples is established; therefore it is in the interests of others to aid the Americans in frustrating the aggressive King. Even if one knew the truth, it would be easier to work against England if such work was, as in the case of France, one's traditional penchant, given this public portrayal of the King as an enemy of mankind. The appeal to the audience, then, is made in an opposition of attitudes—the King malevolent, the Americans civil and proper—and in the suggestion of political and commercial advantages that follow from acting in accordance with such attitudes.

Although a number of things are declared in the Declaration of Independence, there is a purpose that distinguishes this work from other declarations and deeds. Independence itself may have been announced by such acts as the nullification of the British governorships, the rejection of Parliamentary supremacy, the institution of a revolutionary Congress, the taking up of arms, and the issuance of numerous pamphlets and resolutions. John Adams was particularly fond of arguing that independence had been declared before the Declaration penned by his rival Jefferson. But these prior steps had not openly called for the participation of the outside world. The declaration of war had been made in the state paper on taking up arms, yet this document stressed the defensive nature of the insurrection and called for reconciliation. War was resorted to as a last avenue to obtain redress without extinction. A pertinent distinction was drawn by James Macpherson, in his reply to the Declaration of

Taking up Arms,[5] between warring independent states that "endeavour to impress the World with a favourable opinion of their own cause" and those people who are in rebellion within a state to whom the "opinions of mankind" are invariably opposed. What was necessary in facing the world's greatest military power in 1776 was, precisely, the outside help that would follow from the goodwill of mankind. Aware of the distinction that Macpherson drew, Congress exercised this reasoning in its deliberations in early June, 1776, as recorded by Jefferson:[6] The irreconcilable conflict with England cannot be successfully concluded without foreign aid; foreign aid depends upon re-opening trade; trade with nations cannot be opened, due to "European delicacy," except as an independent power; hence, a Declaration of Independence is necessary. What the text of the Declaration of Independence distinctively declares, in accordance with this historical situation, is the appropriateness of foreign aid to the American revolution.

Sensitivity to the reaction of the audience to the decisive juridical act seems to be more important in the Declaration than the proclamation of the act itself. Thus the colonists only *declare* independence in the last paragraph, while in the first paragraph they announce that they are required to *declare* its causes. In the title of what was to be universally known as the "Declaration of Independence," Jefferson had curiously restrained himself from using those specific words, having originally written *of* after *Declaration* only to replace it with *by* and the identification of the speaker rather than the subject.

Are the neutral nations of the world the only audience addressed by the Declaration? The historical situation provides other possibilities for persuasion: one may speak to the enemy, warning that the fight is in earnest; one may speak to sympathetic elements among the enemy to gain them over to the rebellion's cause; one may address the people in one's own ranks hesitant to fight against the mother country. But each address must be made with an eye to the primary audience: vituperation against the enemy is to be avoided, as is the suggestion of disunity among the Americans, while brotherly sentiments for the British people will be appreciated.

[5] *The Rights of Great Britain Asserted Against the Claims of America: Being an Answer to the Declaration of the General Congress,* 2d edit. ([London?]: 1776), p. 1.
[6] *The Papers of Thomas Jefferson,* ed. Julian P. Boyd, I (Princeton, N. J.: Princeton University Press, 1950), pp. 312–313.

The long series of grievances, by being formulated in terms of the King, avoids fraternal insult and points out a common enemy to proper British ways of life. Instead of monarchy it is the present *King of Great-Britain* (Adams introduced this phrase in place of the reference to *his majesty*) that is vilified. What he is doing in America, he may try elsewhere in the Empire. He is already responsible for *abolishing the free System of English Laws in a neighbouring Province* (accusation xx). What some people took to be the forethought and generosity of the British in the Canadian question is here treated as the despotic destruction of the rights of British subjects. After all, if Britain had recently been magnanimous and just in Canada, a conquered province, then there would be reason to believe she would behave the same towards the neighboring Americans after their rebellion is crushed. The charge of establishing an *arbitrary Government* in Canada is deftly accompanied by another claim that would draw sympathy from the British people and from anyone generally: the boundaries of Canada have been enlarged to the detriment of the bordering Colonies. Some treatment of the Canadian question in the Declaration seems advisable, though it was an afterthought in Jefferson's draft, since the Americans had already invaded that province, having failed to win its support. There is the germ here of the principle that a revolution must liberate those suppressed by the evil power even if they are reluctant to contribute to their own liberation.

The first sentence had informed us that *Political Bands* are to be dissolved, just as *political Connection* is dissolved in the last paragraph. There is no racial enmity expressed, and the argument does not contend that one people as a nation should perforce be independent of any other people, though this may be a principle of modern nationalist movements. Following the charges against the King, the Americans represent their addresses to the British people, showing reverence for *the Ties of common Kindred*. The British possess *native Justice and Magnanimity* (it is magnanimous to say so), but they have been *deaf to the Voice of Justice and of Consanguinity*. There is an improbability here, and to argue the case is to stoop to contention of questionable taste. It is not argued, however, but given the semblance of probability by being placed after the list of cruelties perpetrated by the King. If the ruler of a civilized nation can commit such acts and if his legislators, with whom he has combined, can commit them, then it may also be the case that the people, despite their virtue, are neglectful of natural obligations in these matters. The British are in the wrong not because of their character, which is praiseworthy, but because of mistaken judgment. A double hand is offered to the British, then, open in friendship if they come to their senses, closed in hostility if they do not.

But the appeal in the Declaration is not phrased directly to the British nor is it in the present tense. The explanation is still made to a third party, recounting a series of *We have dones*. One continues to pay respect to mankind by setting all grievances before it rather than lashing out at one's opponent or pleading with him. The question, If you have had trouble with the King, why have you not appealed to the people? is thus answered without tarnishing the speaker's character.

Jefferson was at odds with Congress over the treatment of the British:

> The pusillanimous idea that we had friends in England worth keeping terms with, still haunted the minds of many. For this reason those passages which conveyed censures on the people of England were struck out, lest they should give them offence.[7]

In the passages struck out, Jefferson had made explicit what in the final version is left to the reader's inference: the people's share of guilt in the acts committed by the King (*they are permitting their chief magistrate to send over* troops) and by his representatives (*they have by their free election re-established them in power*). An undignified slap at British dignity was also suppressed (*a communication of grandeur and of freedom, it seems, is below their dignity*), as was the phrase *unfeeling brethren*. Though Jefferson may have been right that once the break had come there would be little hope of eliciting support within Britain, there remained the advantage of receiving approbation from others for fraternal propriety.

The colonists themselves are given a view of their present struggles. The Declaration stimulates solidarity among the Americans. In its title the official name *UNITED STATES OF AMERICA* is established. The Americans are *one People* distinguishable and separable from others. They have suffered together at the hands of the King. He has invaded their rights; endangered their state; harassed them with officers; subverted their civil authority; exposed them to murder; deprived them of trial; threatened their boundaries; wrecked their charters, laws, and forms of government; and waged

---

[7] Jefferson's Notes on the Proceedings of Congress, reprinted in this volume.

war against them. Common sufferance invites mutual identification and joint action. The charges advance from interference with legislation (the first 13 accusations) to deeds of extreme violence. The natural response to the upsetting of law is to set up one's own legislative and representative bodies. The answer to deeds of war is to wage war.

The Americans have done their duty towards the British people. If anyone is guilty of turning brother against brother, it is the King (accusation xxvi). One may rebel against a king if he himself has *abdicated Government* (accusation xxiii) and is unfit to rule *a free People*. The American people are an important, if secondary, audience who cannot be alienated by the terms of the appeal made in their name to the foreigners. The American image will be embellished both for American and foreign eyes by the characterization the speaker presents of himself.

III. Speaker

Who is the *speaker*, that is, the one making the Declaration? It is not Thomas Jefferson, nor the people of the United States, but, as the title informs, the *Representatives of the UNITED STATES*. One wonders about the motives, character, and capacities of such men, for these will influence one's acceptance of the import and validity of what they say. In the first sentence a third-person reference to the collective speaker, *they should declare,* identifies him as spokesman for the American people. Again, in the final paragraph the speaker claims his official capacity as *the Representatives of the UNITED STATES OF AMERICA, in GENERAL CONGRESS, Assembled,* acting *in the Name, and by Authority of the good People of these Colonies.* But how can one pretend to represent both state and people when assemblies and legislative bodies are subject to the King's will? The people have a fundamental right to representation (accusation vi).

The famous self-evident truths are not presented as self-evident truths. To do such would obviate the necessity of saying one believes in them. The approach used reflects favorably on the speaker: *We hold these* truths to be self-evident. Modesty rather than dogmatism is suggested, because one is stating what one believes rather than making a categorically true statement, though it enhances one's character to believe something that others too must believe as self-evident. If the unobtrusive connection of the speaker's viewpoint with lofty ideas is desirable, the explicit connection of his honesty with the facts he lists is undesirable. Facts unlike truths are not self-evident; they must be *submitted* by someone as evidence. Their objective veracity is felt by simply calling them "facts" rather than attesting to them. Congress improved the text by dropping out a phrase that disadvantageously linked the speaker's character and the "facts": *for the truth of which we pledge a faith yet unsullied by falsehood.*

In the first sentence the speaker shows that he has a *decent* respect for mankind. He reserves *prudence* for himself and his countrymen in the craftily arranged sentence that opens with that word:

Prudence, indeed, will dictate that Governments long established should not be changed for light and transient Causes; and accordingly all Experience hath shewn, that Mankind are more disposed to suffer, while Evils are sufferable, than to right themselves by abolishing the Forms to which they are accustomed. [¶ II]

In the second half of the sentence he shows his understanding of human nature and experience, an understanding reflected in the first sentence of the Declaration and whenever events in human history are mentioned. The arrangement of these universal pronouncements accrues authority and dignity to the speaker.

There is a certain care in keeping the attention of the audience away from the speaker in the first part of the text and instead onto his noble words. A dispassionate tone of explanation is the beguiling fruit of that care. Even when the bill of charges is raised, there is no direct self-reference, only *these States* (accusation vii), until accusation x where the compounding of sufferings initiates a flood of first-person plural references to call forth the sympathy of the audience. The word *our* occurs twenty-two times from its first appearance in the text in accusation x to the end of ¶ IV.[8] *Us* occurs ten times from its first appearance in accusation xi to the end of the list of grievances. This passivity is followed by a string of nominative *wes*, of which eight occur from the conclusion of the accusations to the end of ¶ IV, stressing actions taken by the speaker and those he represents to ameliorate the sufferings undergone. *We* is then used dramatically in the final official proclamation. The presence of the speaker progressively gains power, culminating in the heroic pledge of the closing words.

---

[8] Congress struck out an *our* before *Judges* in accusation ix, and also rearranged accusation viii leaving out *these states.*

If the colonists have suffered, theirs has been a *patient Sufferance* rather than one accompanied by rash revindication. If the King has made inroads on the people's rights, representative assemblies have counteracted with *manly Firmness.* Wronged, the colonists have asked for redress *in the most humble Terms* at *every stage of these Oppressions.* The Americans have *warned, reminded, appealed to,* and *conjured* their British brethren, hoping to retain blood ties but forced at last to break them.

The speaker appeals to the *Supreme Judge of the World* (a Congressional insertion) for the rectitude of his intentions. What better appeal is there for a revolutionary party? They are God-fearing men who rely upon the *Protection of divine Providence* (again, added by Congress). The rebellion against a King does not negate the divine foundations of kingship, but since divine right can be argued on the King's side, it is well to call upon it in behalf of rebellion. The assurances, perhaps overdone, of respect for the Divinity dispel any fears of third parties that the rebels adhere to revolutionary doctrines. The references to the Divinity are sufficiently varied and vague to permit anyone to make Him over into the image of his own God. *Laws of Nature and of Nature's God* is especially ingenious since it covers the cases of a mechanical universe actively run by God, a mechanical universe operating without God, or a God and nature independent but harmonious in their operation. If God judges men, he must find for the Americans. If God provides for and guides men, he must intercede for the Americans. If God created men, he has created Americans with rights worth defending. If God is the ruling principle of nature, the Americans act according to nature. The heterogeneous religious tradition of the Americans is taken account of in the reiterated affirmation of an unspecified Divinity—here is a means to unite men of different persuasion.

The Representatives pledge not only their lives and fortunes but their *sacred Honor* which, morally, is more valuable. Lives are pledged because men are dying and are going to die in the war, and fortunes too, for war lives on money. The rebels are practical men as well as idealists.

IV. Argument

The argument is arranged in three sections: (1) a number of principles laid down at the start concerning the rights of men and the nature of states, (2) a catalogue of facts which make up the main body of the proof, (3) the final decisions the colonists are led to. This syllogistic arrangement sports the cloak of necessity; it is logic applied to history whereby men must do certain things given certain ideals and facts. If anything condemnable is enacted—what is more condemnable than rebelling against one's country and inviting the collaboration of its traditional enemies?—it is not because one wants to do it but because one has to. This necessity is signaled from the first sentence: *necessary for one People, causes which impel them.* Following the apparent major premises, we have: *such is now the Necessity which constrains them.* The breaking of connections with the British people *would inevitably* occur (changed, properly, by Congress from *were likely to*). The Americans *must acquiesce in the Necessity* which proclaims their separation. It does not suffice in political argument that a chosen course of action seem necessary, it must also seem good. It is not only the *Right* of the people to rebel but their *Duty.*

The colonists must rebel. Hence, the right to rebellion is postulated: it is proper for people *to alter or to abolish* any form of government destructive of certain ends. Alteration of an existing government and the abolition of it are, of course, different things. A variety of other phrasings is offered for what is intended: *dissolution, change, throwing off, separation.* The selection of the proper word for rebellion had apparently been a delicate matter, more alterations being made in the composition and editing of the Declaration on this score than on any other. Jefferson originally wrote of the Colonies moving *in a separate state* (changed to *separately*) from England, but the phrase *apart from them* was substituted; the passage, however, was finally dropped by Congress. Before Congress received the draft, *advance from that subordination* was replaced by *dissolve* the bands, *independant* by *separate,* and *to the change* by *to separate,* then by *to the separation.*[9] These alterations all occurred in the first sentence. In the last paragraph *dissolve & break off all political connection* was shortened to *dissolve.* At the hands of Congress *expunge their former systems of government* was changed to *alter,* a passage containing *renounce forever* was omitted, and *reject and renounce* all allegiance was turned into *are absolved from.* However one chooses to call it, the goal of such revolution is to *institute new Government.* What the powers of a new government are we only learn later. If a new government may replace one

---

[9] Jefferson's final choice of wording was excellent, for the very act of *separation* from Britain is the attainment of a *separate* position among nations generally.

run afoul of its ends, the proper ends of government should be stated. Governments are instituted to protect certain rights. What are these rights, and where do they come from? They include *Life, Liberty, and the Pursuit of Happiness*, men being *endowed by their Creator* with them. Finally, how do the Americans know these are rights? It is self-evident to them. But then it is self-evident generally and the truth of these matters is undeniable.

This order of the general principles in terms of the persuasive goals is the reverse of the actual order of presentation which is a philosophic one. The presentation, however, offers as a truth something not logically necessary to the series: *all Men are created equal.* This may be taken as qualifying the following truth, so that *all* men, being *created*, are *endowed* with certain *Rights*, but it does not assert that all men have equal rights. The quantity, limitation, or precedence of the rights is not specified here, fortunately. There is a significant difference between the claims of the first and second truths: in the second it is stipulated that the rights given by the Creator are inalienable, whereas in the first there is no mention of rights and it is not stated that equality cannot be renounced. There is room, then, for the interpretation that some men can lose their equality after birth and thence enjoy lesser, though still inalienable, rights than others, just as there is room for the interpretation that equality is a fundamental right or an inalienable characteristic of rights. The Declaration on this point, as on others, is adamantly silent. The reader has the opportunity to make a favorable interpretation along his own lines.

In Jefferson's early draft there *was* a connection between the two celebrated truths:

(1) *from that equal creation they derive rights inherent & inalienable* (Jefferson had started to write *inherent* before *rights*), *among which are . . .*

This next was changed to read:

(2) *they are endowed by their creator with equal rights, some of which are inherent & inalienable, among which are . . .*

But by the time the draft reached Congress, it had been radically altered to:

(3) *they are endowed by their creator with inherent & inalienable rights; that among these are . . .*

The *equal creation* and derived *rights* of the original became *equal rights* endowed by a Creator in the second version, which was at once clearer, simpler, and more dramatic, though the rest of the sentence was rendered more awkward. The excising of the word *equal* in the third version involved more than a question of style, though the continued presence of the terms *inherent & inalienable* still hinted that the rights derived from the preceding equal creation. Congress went a step further; getting rid of *inherent*, it was content to speak of *certain inalienable* (printed by Dunlap as *unalienable*) *Rights*. Whatever the original intentions of the author, or the traditional doctrine of natural rights philosophy, the egalitarian conception of human rights is not explicit in the completed Declaration's principles.

In the early draft there had been another manner for presenting the egalitarian view, in addition to the linking of the truths. The first sentence made mention of nations being *equal & independant;* in the second sentence it was announced that all men were created *equal & independant*. In the last paragraph of the work the powers of *INDEPENDENT STATES* and that which they *may of right do* is, in part, listed. Similarly, the rights of men were partially listed in the Declaration. Now, if it is by virtue of their independence and their equality that states have certain powers, then the parallel case might be presumed whereby men have rights because of their equality and independence. Furthermore, since the realm of states, which has divine sanction, is designed to serve the rights of men, which are God-given, it appears that the proposition *all men are created equal & independant* is the necessary premise of the argument urged for American independence. In the subsequent editing of the text the parallel formulation was suppressed, and the proposition no longer filled a logical role. We have noticed how the phrase *equal & independant* in the first sentence bowed out in favor of *separate and equal,* possibly because of the desire to have a single word do extra duty; but the second occurrence of the phrase was also altered—the *& independant* being dropped.[10] States and men alike may be equal, according to the public version of the document, but states take their powers from being *FREE AND INDEPENDENT*, and those powers are just if used in harmony with the rights of men,

[10] Becker, *op. cit.,* p. 198, thought of this alteration in Jefferson's text in terms of literary qualities: "I suspect that he erased '& independent' because, having introduced 'self-evident,' he did not like the sound of the two phrases both closing with 'dent.' "

while men receive their rights not from their independence nor even from their equality but from their Creator. *Free* is used in conjunction with *independent* in talking about states, but to have asserted that all men are created *free* would have been begging for trouble since half a million Americans were slaves.

The rights of *Life* and *Liberty* are presumably rights to safeguard one's life and liberty; indeed Jefferson first specified *the preservation of life & liberty*, only to elect the more general expression. *Pursuit of Happiness* is one of the splendid phrases in the Declaration. Along with the notion that happiness is desirable is the indication that men must work for it. *Pursuit*, though, is ambiguous, meaning *exercise of*, as Arthur M. Schlesinger argues, or *seeking after*, as in George Mason's phrase in the Virginia Bill of Rights: *pursueing and obtaining Happiness and Safety*.[11] The usual triad of rights in the natural rights literature was "life, liberty, and property." *Pursuit of Happiness* could easily include property as a means. Those who had no property and who might have to shoulder muskets were still left with the dream of happiness. It sounds better too, to concern oneself with human qualities, such as happiness, rather than material possessions if the latter is what property consists of, though for John Locke it included life and human pursuits. In any case, the embarrassing question of how numerous Americans could be the property of their fellow men was avoided.

The power of these phrases to win goodwill is attested to by their reverent repetition by men everywhere. *All Men are created equal* is as commanding an utterance as men may make. It is pious, philosophic, fraternal. Who would not hesitate to go on record against *Life, Liberty, and the Pursuit of Happiness*? These stirring words beg to be filled in with particular meanings by the hearers, establishing agreement with the speaker. They are rhetorical *commonplaces* rather than philosophical *terms*; the former being topical formulas held to no fixed meaning but admitting of opposing particularizations, the latter being signs defined in a certain way and resisting contradictory interpretations. Thus, whether you will take *all Men are created equal* as your motto or reject it as a self-evident falsehood depends on what meanings you recognize for *Men, created,* and *equal*. Does *Men* include women, children, slaves, Indians? Is *created* the same as born, designed, adjudged? Are men *equal* in physique, wealth, dignity, rights?

[11] Schlesinger's article is reprinted in this volume. Mason's wording is taken from his draft of the Virginia Bill of Rights in the Library of Congress.

The words *Consent of the Governed* have also given rise to generous interpretation. Although the just powers of government are
derived from the consent of the governed, it does not follow that the
specific acts of the government must meet with popular approval,
nor that only self-government in which governed and governor are
identical is just, nor that governors must be chosen by the people. If
consent consists in being governed with certain ends in view, then a
monarchy, even an absolute one, in fulfilling those ends would have
as much claim to just exercise of power as a democracy or a republic, or an insurrectional body. It was unwise in the Declaration to
come out for or against distinct forms of government since the colonists had hardly agreed to a permanent form of confederation. At
the heart of their positions leading up to independence was the
insistence upon a proper observance of the rule of British constitutional monarchy. To argue against the acts of the particular King
and against monarchy at the same time was to jeopardize one's case.
The Declaration of Independence is not a document of ideological
warfare. The criterion for revolution lies not in the form of the government in question but in the practice. It is, moreover, a criterion
set forth in negative terms, for its concern is with the destruction of
ends rather than the maximum realization of goals. If there is any
revolutionary theory in the Declaration, it appears in conservative
form.

The *self-evident Truths* in the Declaration are generally taken to
refer to the first three truths dealing with equality and rights, but
the two other truths dealing with government also fall under this
category. If the self-evident [12] is that which is so clear and undeniable in itself that it requires no argument to be seen as true, then the
first three truths, once their meanings are conceived favorably, are
easily acknowledged to be of this kind, but there is no such clarity
and indubitability in the remaining truths. A government's *deriving*
power, is, as just argued, inexplicit, while a good part of the world
would contend that instead of the consent of the people it is the
wisdom of the Creator or of the governor which is the source of the
state's just powers. That the people have a right to overthrow any
kind of destructive government is not immediately acceptable to
everyone. There is a deductive movement of the propositions from

---

[12] *Sacred & undeniable truths* was Jefferson's original wording. *Self-evident*
avoided the emotive character of the first qualification while not diminishing
the force of the second, since what is self-evident is undeniable. It rather increased the force of the claim, for what is undeniable, such as demonstrated
conclusions, need not be self-evident.

that which is harmlessly acceptable to the pertinent issue that in isolation would be debatable. The qualification of self-evidence as applied to all five truths here, though logically suspect, has its persuasive virtues. In one sense the qualification allows the important contentions to follow from indisputable ones, and in another sense it gives a blanket justification to the important truths, not as conclusions reached but as principles that are discoverable. The author of the document and the printers of it tried various punctuation devices to exhibit the relationship of the five truths each beginning with *that,* the ambiguity being best illustrated by the broken dash followed by a capital *T* in the first Dunlap broadside (¶ II).

The second section of the argument is the list of facts. They are rigged to tell against the King. The admission in Jefferson's draft that

we had adopted one common king, . . . but that submission to their parliament was no part of our constitution, nor ever in idea, if history may be credited,

was essential in justifying his unusual formulation of the charges. Congress, however, taking the bolder tack of ignoring Parliament altogether, expunged it. The reference to the British people's chance to elect a conciliatory Parliament was also dropped, and the dissolution of political connection between the colonists and *the people or parliament of Great Britain* was corrected in the last paragraph to read *the State of Great-Britain.* Though there are references to parliament in the final text, they are made to tell against either the King or the people: *He has combined with others* subjecting the Americans to a *Jurisdiction foreign* to their constitution, *giving his Assent to their Acts of pretended Legislation* (accusation xiii); the people have been warned, but without heed, of the *Attempts by their Legislature to extend an unwarrantable Jurisdiction* over the Americans (*unwarrantable* added by Congress). In rejecting Jefferson's more cautious strategy, Congress erred. What it gained in remaining strongly consistent in its constitutional position —not recognizing the jurisdiction of Parliament—it lost in compounding a fictive history that easily put in doubt the clearheadedness and honesty of the speaker. On the other hand it would have been unseemly for the representatives of one people to swing into attack against the representatives of another. Argumentatively, the personification employed does add a probability to the facts if one is not familiar with the history. A cause is given—the viciousness of a despot—which explains why the host of sufferances were imposed. Congress omitted a passage that may have raised a doubt detrimental to the colonists' purposes: the suggestion that *future ages will scarce believe that the hardiness (audacity* experimented with) *of one man, adventured* what he did in a short period.

The acts of an historical agent are focused upon. Given some deeds and the motives lying behind them, the agent can be accused of future evil deeds, such as using the Canada policy as an instrument against the Colonies (accusation xx). The argument makes much of history, dealing with the *Course of human Events* and with what *Experience hath shewn,* exposing sufferances endured, and concluding with a step taken in history. Appropriate to an historical account, Jefferson had assigned a beginning to the train of abuses *at a distinguished period,* but Congress deleted this reference; none of its *facts,* after all, are assigned to a distinguished time or place in history.

The more emotional grievances involving violence are put after the legalistic claims, as a natural consequence of them. The barbarous acts of war mentioned in accusations xxiv–xxvii follow a villain's declaration of war (accusation xxiii), which is a consequence of giving military powers undue supremacy over civil ones (accusations xi, xii, xiv, xv), which in turn results from a disregard for the civil offices (accusations viii–x), which follows upon the harassment of representative legislation (accusations i–vii). But there is also something logically improper about the military facts that is best hidden by placing them last in the consequential series. For when the Americans complain, *He has plundered our Seas, ravaged our Coasts, burnt our Towns, and destroyed the Lives of our People* (accusation xxiv), they are talking about acts of violence made in answer to the war waged by the colonists themselves. Men, it would appear, if one insists on extracting political philosophy from the Declaration, have the right to rebel but not to quell rebellion—a self-defeating principle. A commentator upon the Declaration, referring to the British military maneuvers to crush the rebellion, asks, "By what kind of logic then are these acts ranked in the class of grievances?" [13] The persuasive value of the inclusion of the charges supersedes their improper logic. To have left out proof of armed conflict would have caused third parties to waver, since reconciliation would be possible. The Americans leave no doubt in the reader's

---

[13] [John Lind,] *An Answer to the Declaration of the American Congress,* 5th edit. (London: T. Cadell, 1776), p. 130.

mind that they are at war, and that the acts directed against them
are not merely defensive police measures but full-scale military operations. Who fired the first shot is not, in the long run, information
essential to the nations of the world calculating their own interests,
so long as the shot is heard.

If a certain number of facts stack up against the King, are there
other circumstances which mitigate the proof? Jefferson had em-
phatically asserted, *no one fact stands single or solitary to contradict
the uniform tenor of the rest.* The wording was improved before it
reached Congress, but that body rejected the statement. The possibility of the King's having done good has nothing to do with the
point that he has done sufficient evil to merit rebellion. Congress
qualified other universal claims forestalling the offering of contradictory evidence: *he has suffered the administration of justice totally
to cease in some of these states* was changed to read simply *He has
obstructed the Administration of Justice* (accusation viii). The
charge of deprivation of jury trial in accusation xviii had *in many
Cases* inserted into it. The charge of dissolution of representative
houses *repeatedly & continually* (accusation v) was tempered by
dropping *continually,* just as in the second paragraph *unremitting*
injuries was softened to *repeated.*

The historical facts contain no dates, pinpoint no places, name no
names. A specific case may have extenuating features which the
enemy can argue in his behalf. Specific cases might even be reme-
died if proved to be blatant injuries, but it is unreasonable to believe
that a general tendency would be corrected. Arguing from the general in each accusation implies a motivation lying behind its instances, and in turn this motivation can be identified as a universal
behind all the kinds of grievance: the desire to establish *an absolute
Tyranny* which is the *direct Object* of *all* the abuses. The general
gives the sense of numerous violations as does repeated use of the
word *repeated.* The lack of dates keeps from view the immense
difference between sufferances endured passively and those brought
on oneself by rebellion.

The third part of the argument is the conclusion which presumably cannot be questioned if the premises and facts have been accepted. America becomes an independent state and has the *full
Power to levy War* (*full* an excellent insertion in the early draft).
But there are certain other things listed which the new nation may
of right do, including the contracting of *Alliances* and the establishment of *Commerce.* These are precisely the conclusions that must be

made public to third parties, yet they are arrived at circuitously. Since these are extensions of a state's powers, they should have been argued in the theoretical portion of the text. That portion had already reached the justification of a kind of war, rebellion, but it did not argue the right of a people in rebellion to solicit outside aid. Rebellion is a war against a government, raging from within, and it does not qualify as an international war until the rebellious side is independent. The theoretical section could simply have concluded: an independent state has the right to seek aid in its conflict with the mother country it has just rebelled against. Though this *is* the point, it surely would not do stated in such candor, for it makes clear the opportunistic purport of the Americans' political theorizing. The list of grievances is interposed, breaking off the theory before it goes too far, and showing that there is no way the Americans can live under present rule. The force of circumstances drives them to independence. The prerogatives of independence are now spelled out. In the last paragraph, then, the grounds are laid bare for building co-operation between the Americans and others in the current war. The grounds seem firm, coming as they do after the intricate factual details and arising calmly out of the pomposity of the paragraph's official wording. And the conclusion is not unexpected; the first paragraph had shown the colonists seeking a place among nations. Between the opening and the conclusion, the task of the Declaration is to make clear that receiving aid is necessary for the Americans and giving it is advantageous to the other nations.

V. *Style*

When one considers the three aspects of the persuasion separately, it becomes apparent that certain passages perform a double service. The order of analysis may have little to do with the author's process of invention or with the order of the sentences in the finished work. The persuasive artist like the poetic artist imagines, discovers, invents, fuses, and expresses. Knowing what the persuasive situation is does not produce the result. Rhetoric is a practical art; its aim is to affect men through language, and not merely to please them as do the poetic arts. Hence the verbalization of the persuasive appeals and their presentation in the speech are important.

The variety of style in the Declaration is striking—by turns abstract, dispassionate, passionate, and officious. This matches the rich content which includes a miniature history, an outline of political theory, a mass of grievances, and a juridical act. These variations upon reiterated themes—*injury, usurpation, tyranny, rights, people, power*—hold the attention of the reader while his mind and heart are worked upon. He is engaged from the first sentence, itself a paragraph, with its interwoven strands of persuasiveness: respect for the audience, dignity of the speaker, necessity of the action. The second paragraph disinterestedly commences, treading cautiously with philosophic gravity into the issue at hand. Then come the facts in bold and massive accusation. Thirteen sentences are lined up beginning *He has.* A variation is achieved in the nine clauses beginning *For.* Two miscellaneous claims have been slipped in here, that is, they are not principally matters of law and justice or of military activity. These acts of pretended legislation are couched in economic terms, treating of trade and taxes (accusations xvi, xvii). The former is pertinent to foreign eyes, while the latter is of local interest, since, as Lind suggested,[14] men generally do not like to pay taxes. The *For*s are looser in organization than the *He*s, and vaguer in causation. Actually they are a subclass of accusation xiii. That one accusation can be expanded into subcharges suggests the same may be done elsewhere in the list. The return to five *He* sentences, one of which—it may go unnoticed—is not in the past tense (accusation xxv), attaches the greatest onus to the King.

The techniques by which the facts are presented were exposed by John Lind who sought to refute them. He showed how acts of omission are phrased as acts of commission, how temporary measures are spoken of as permanent, how specialized cases are set in general terms, how violent means are portrayed as ends, how future and present acts are treated in the same language as past cases. The aim, he claims, is "to *confuse* where they could not hope to *convince.*"[15] The logician will find that the eighteen *He* accusations are not simple singular propositions; there are at least sixty accusations entailed. Combination of charges, as in the Canadian question, served to conceal weaknesses of individual claims.

The dry statement of the early legalistic facts gives way to swelling passion expressed in vivid language. There is revulsion in *Swarms* of officers that *eat out* the substance of the people. A string of verbs of violence—*plundered, ravaged, burnt, destroyed*—is impressively spread in one sentence to catch the pity of the reader. So too, *Works of Death, Desolation, and Tyranny* chill the bones and call for pro-

---

[14] *Ibid.,* pp. 64–65.   [15] *Ibid.,* p. 10. Italics are Lind's.

test, especially since they are accompanied by *circumstances of Cruelty and Perfidy, scarcely paralleled in the most barbarous Ages* (the last seven words added by Congress). Congressional editing brought to the fore as the last accusation an evocation of the wildest desolation accessible to the European imagination: the *merciless Indian Savages* have been brought on, *whose known Rule of Warfare, is an undistinguished Destruction, of all Ages, Sexes and Conditions.*

The grotesque is left aside for the sentimental as in paragraph IV the colonists dilate on their fraternal feeling. The solemnity of the final paragraph keeps before us the fact that the government of a new state is speaking. Congress had reworked this passage, placing the declaration of independence of the Colonies before the absolution from Britain, removing a distracting reference to future British Kings, and sprinkling in some holy words. The purport of this editing was to include in the Declaration the Resolution of Independence passed on July 2.

Commentators have taken much trouble to indicate the debt owed by the wording of the Declaration to other works, generally proceeding on the assumption that the meaning of the words remained the same. In the Declaration there is no citation of any treatise or bill. That its terms should be the current and reiterated ones Jefferson recognized.[16] It is expressed in the American political language. This language also was part of the fundamental British tradition. It is wise to justify oneself in terms taken over from or shared with the other party in a dispute. The American ways are more properly British in the final analysis, it is implied, than those of the British. But if the persuasive work makes use of a tradition of thought in order to command assent and of a manner of phrasing things appropriate to the occasion, it does not follow that in this case it accepts the full tradition, that it is a recognizable, consistent affirmation of natural rights philosophy. It sounds like Locke, but it isn't.

VI. Revision

If what is found in the text can be understood for what it contributes to convincing certain audiences about certain issues, that which was rejected for appearance in the final version or changed about may also be assessed for its persuasive significance. Evaluating the

---

[16] Cf. Letters to James Madison, August 30, 1823, and Henry Lee, May 8, 1825, reprinted in this volume.

rhetoric of textual omissions and alterations is not to claim that they were made for persuasive reasons. Why a particular phrase or topic was ultimately added or deleted, whether in rhetoric or poetry, is perhaps always beyond the scholar even when the author or editor proffer testimony. What matters is not the intention in the mind of the corrector but the character of the change in the text.

About 25 percent of the version submitted to Congress was eliminated, while some 15 percent of the Rough Draft never made the public light. The Congressional tendency to shorten included the effort, common to the earlier revision, to simplify, to broaden, to curtail details and explanations. The connections and specifics that were left out could have posed issues the colonists were not ready to debate. References to the speaker's veracity; the relationship between the British people, the Parliament, and the King; the mention of specific time intervals; and the attack upon slavery were thus dropped.

The slavery accusation, the longest in the Jeffersonian list, the most vituperative, and as such the final one in his original series, would have been the strongest accusation of human rottenness to be leveled against the King had it been allowed to remain. But, alas, it was a species of rottenness that the revolutionary collaborators were themselves tainted with:

> The clause too, reprobating the enslaving the inhabitants of Africa, was struck out in complaisance to South Carolina & Georgia, who had never attempted to restrain the importation of slaves, and who on the contrary still wished to continue it. Our Northern brethren also I believe felt a little tender under those censures; for tho' their people had very few slaves themselves yet they had been pretty considerable carriers of them to others.[17]

The string of war charges in the Declaration reached their acme in the King's warring *against human nature itself* by carrying on the slave trade. The charges of legislative interference also culminated in his suppression of *every legislative attempt to prohibit or to restrain this execrable commerce*. The domestic horror of slave rebellion was

---

[17] Jefferson's Notes on the Proceedings of Congress. There are two curious points revealed by this passage: first, that ceasing to import slaves would have been more detrimental to the mercenary interests in the North, since the South would be able to continue the trade of home-bred slaves; second, that though Jefferson clearly knew that some Colonies had never done anything to prevent importation, he made it sound in the Rough Draft as if the Americans as a whole were against it.

greater than the Indian menace mentioned as twenty-sixth in a list of twenty-nine charges.[18]

In addition to capping the train of facts, the slavery paragraph crystallized the argument and attitude central to the Declaration. The *sacred rights of life & liberty* are those belonging to a people, and the King has suppressed them. In this case he is threatening the *lives* of one people (the Americans) by offering to another (the Africans) the *liberties* he deprived them of. The Africans *never offended him*, just as the Americans are his innocent victims. This kind of warfare does not befit a proper *Christian king*.

Before the patriots are exonerated for not printing their proper moral stand on the question of slavery because the contrary views of a few made it inexpedient, it is pertinent to observe what is not present in that stand. What chiefly is missing is a condemnation of slavery, that is, of one man's owning another. The act of enslaving a people is denounced. The carrying on of a market for the selling of men is execrated. The freeing of slaves to attack their masters is protested. But there is no suggestion that Americans should give up their slaves, or that slaves have the right to be free. Indeed, the only road open to freedom for them is murderous rebellion. It was best not to declare this publicly. Had the paragraph been allowed to remain, there would have been no choice in the eyes of the world but immediate and total emancipation. Americans, including one such as Thomas Jefferson, though they would rather die free men than live slaves themselves, were not ready for that. The slavery charge amplified the King's guilt but carried with it the echo of American guilt. It could not fool anyone. The nation whose initiation was heralded by the phrase *all Men are created equal* simply accepted a goodly number of men as slaves.

[18] In the version submitted to Congress accusation xxv (the mercenaries) and accusation xxvi (the Indians) were grouped together as cases of outsiders invading the Americans, while accusation xxvii (dealing with the *treasonable insurrections of our fellow-citizens*—words that could be applied to the rebels as well as to the counter-revolutionaries), accusation xxviii (sea prisoners), and accusation xxix (slavery) follow as cases of the incitement to internecine strife. Accusation xxvii, which ill-advisedly mentioned *allurements of forfeiture & confiscation of property* by those opposing the rebellion, was dropped, and the vague words *domestic Insurrections* were surreptitiously inserted at the beginning of the charge about Indians. The rejection of accusation xxix on slavery, leaving the one on sea prisoners as last, did away with any series of internecine conflict. Congress then shuffled the charges, mixing domestic and external gestures of war, to come up with the most frightful accusation available—the Indians—as the final one in the list.

VII. *Evaluation*

The charge will be made that an analysis of this kind reduces to propaganda what is a noble document replete with the courageous expression of ideals that serve as a foundation stone of the American way of life and a landmark for all men, free or otherwise. The displeasure with such a reduction may spring from the low repute in which rhetoric as an art has fallen. Thus, parts of the Declaration have been tossed off by critics as "mere" rhetoric, or "pure" rhetoric, or "only" rhetoric, implying that such parts cannot be taken seriously as offering arguments, as shaping facts, or as expressing genuine feelings. But rhetoric is essential in the affairs of men, so long as action and judgment are amenable to discussion. The crucial movements of war and peace demand that men take a part. The path to be chosen is often open to debate. Political rhetoric does not aim at the truth, which may be objective and abstract, but at that which is more urgent and important in politics, decision and action in particular circumstances. The problem in 1776 for America, Britain, Europe was one of *doing*; and the significance of the Declaration is in its contrivance as persuasion to commitment.

The criterion of excellence of a persuasive work is not whether you are convinced by it or agree with what it claims, for the work was not addressed to you, nor whether it achieved its purposes upon its intended audience; for in the responses to the work it is difficult to tell if the persuasive powers have been operative rather than something fortuitous. The compilation of the reactions of those to whom the rhetoric has been applied is never the test of persuasion. The judgment of whether the action urged was a good one, whether effectuated or not, belongs to ethics and politics rather than to rhetorical critique. The utility that can be found for the persuasive work is an index not of its rhetorical worth but of the imagination and purposes of those who use it. Re-creation of the Declaration or borrowing from it has long been a convenience in gaining authority for the credo of individuals or groups. Despite the reputation of the Declaration and the uses we make of it, what we can judge as rhetoric is whether the work made use in the best way of what was available to it in order to achieve its goals.

Could the Declaration have been still more persuasive if it had been given another form, that is, another exercise of the appeal to the audience conjoined with a representation of the speaker's character and method of argument? Given its form, could any alteration in its presentation, that is, the ordering, combining, and verbal expression of its materials, have increased its persuasiveness? To answer these questions is to see how good the Declaration is and *what* it is as an encounter of creativity with the pressures of actions, ideals, and feelings. Its genius, though directed uniquely to July 4, 1776, is accessible to the appreciation of men aware of the perpetual play of circumstance and aspiration in the course of human events.

The too literal historian, his eye caught by materials that have a prior and later history, will not ask such questions, nor will the too abstract philosopher, his eye caught by ideas that have a place in political theory. The too ambitious patriot, if he asks questions, generally will raise "rhetorical questions," that is, ones that have no answer other than his own programs, so that the appreciation of the Declaration as rhetoric is often obstructed by rhetoric itself.

Appendices

ᥱᕇᗱᐱ I ᘏᥱ

Chronology

1763. Conclusion of French and Indian War. England acquires Canada. New policy of taxing the Colonies directly for support of an army in America.

1765. Stamp Act. Quartering Act.

1766. Repeal of Stamp Act. Declaratory Act, asserting the right of Parliament to "bind the Colonies in all cases whatsoever."

1767. Townshend Acts, taxing imports.

1770, March 5. Boston Massacre. Repeal of Townshend Acts, except for tax on tea.

1773, December 16. Boston Tea Party.

1774, March–June. Coercive Acts chastizing Massachusetts, including closing of the Port of Boston.

August. Jefferson's *Summary View of the Rights of British America* published.

September. The First Continental Congress meets at Philadelphia, prepares a Declaration of Rights and Grievances.

1775, March 22. Edmund Burke's Speech in Parliament on Conciliation with the Colonies.

April 19. Battles of Lexington and Concord.

June 15. Washington named Commander-in-Chief of the Continental Army.

June 17. Battle of Bunker Hill.

July 6. The Second Continental Congress issues a Declaration of the Causes and Necessity of Taking up Arms.

August 23. George III declares the Colonies in rebellion.

November 7. Gov. Dunmore of Virginia declares that slaves who rebel against their masters will be set free.

December 22. Parliament prohibits all trade with the Colonies.

December 31. American invasion of Canada fails with defeat at Quebec.

1776, January 10. Paine's *Common Sense* appears; thousands of copies sold in the succeeding months.

May 15. Virginia instructs its delegates to Congress to propose independence.

June 7. Richard Henry Lee moves the Resolution for Independence.

June 11. Congress appoints a Committee of Five, comprising Thomas Jefferson, John Adams, Benjamin Franklin, Roger Sherman, and Robert R. Livingston, to draft a Declaration of Independence, in case one is required.

June 11–28. Jefferson prepares the draft of the Declaration in consultation with Adams and Franklin.

June 12. Bill of Rights drafted by George Mason adopted by Virginia.

June 28. The draft of the Declaration submitted to Congress by the Committee of Five.

July 2. After debate the Lee Resolution is adopted.

July 2–4. Debate by the Congress as a whole on the text of the Declaration.

July 4. The Declaration of Independence adopted.

July 4–5. The Declaration printed as a broadside. Copies dispatched to military and civilian leaders.

July 19. The New York delegation having been newly instructed to vote for independence, Congress orders the now unanimous Declaration engrossed on parchment and signed.

August 2. Parchment Copy signed.

1777, January 18. Congress orders publication of the Declaration under a new title reflecting its unanimity, and with the names of the signers attached.

1778, February 6. France signs treaties of commerce and alliance with the United States.

1783, September 3. Definitive Treaty of Peace with England, recognizing the independence of the United States.

1823. Facsimile of Parchment Copy distributed under the direction of John Quincy Adams.

July 4. Oration by Timothy Pickering provokes controversy over the originality of the Declaration.

1826, July 4. Jubilee celebration. Death of Jefferson and Adams.

1829. Autobiography of Jefferson appears, containing his Notes on the Congressional Proceedings and a facsimile of the Rough Draft.

1858. Lincoln and Douglas debate the equality clause in the Declaration.

1876. Centennial celebration. Exposition at Philadelphia and orations throughout the country.

1906. Compendious documentary study of the Declaration published by John H. Hazelton.

1922. Carl L. Becker publishes influential analysis of the Declaration in terms of history of ideas and literary art.

1926. Sesquicentennial speeches.

1947. Compositional Fragment of the Declaration unearthed in the Library of Congress.

Revolutionary Documents

A Declaration of Rebellion *

We are reduced to the alternative of chusing an unconditional submission to the tyranny of irritated ministers, or resistance by force—The latter is our choice.—We have counted the cost of this contest, and find nothing so dreadful as voluntary slavery.—Honor, justice, and humanity forbid us tamely to surrender that freedom which we received from our gallant ancestors, and which our innocent posterity have a right to receive from us. We cannot endure the infamy and guilt of resigning succeeding generations to that wretchedness which inevitably awaits them, if we basely entail hereditary bondage upon them.

Our cause is just. Our union is perfect. Our internal resources are great, and if necessary, foreign assistance is undoubtedly attainable.—We gratefully acknowledge, as signal instances of the Divine favour towards us, that his Providence [11] would not permit us to be called into this severe controversy, until we were grown up to our present strength, had been previously exercised in warlike operations, and possessed of the means of defending ourselves. —With hearts fortified with these animating reflections, we most solemnly, before GOD and the world declare, that, exerting the utmost energy of those powers, which our beneficent Creator hath graciously bestowed upon us, the arms we have been compelled by our enemies to assume, we will, in defiance of every hazard, with unabating firmness and perseverance, employ for the preservation of our liberties, being with one mind resolved, to dye Free-men rather than to live Slaves.

Lest this declaration should disquiet the minds of our friends and fellow subjects in any part of the empire, we assure them, that we

* FROM A Declaration by the Representatives of the United Colonies of North-America, Now Met in General Congress at Philadelphia, Seting Forth the Causes and Necessity of Their Taking up Arms (Philadelphia: William and Thomas Bradford, 1775), pp. 11–13.

mean not to dissolve that Union which has so long and so happily subsisted between us, and which we sincerely wish to see restored. —Necessity has not yet driven us into that desperate measure, or induced us to excite any other nation to war against them.—We have not raised armies with ambitious designs of separating from Great-Britain, and establishing independant states.—We fight not for glory or for conquest. We exhibit to mankind the remarkable spectacle of a people attacked by unprovoked enemies, without any imputation, or even suspicion, of offence. They boast of their privileges and civilization, and yet proffer no milder conditions than servitude or death.—[12]

In our own native land, in defence of the freedom that is our birthright, and which we ever enjoyed till the late violation of it—for the protection of our property, acquired solely by the honest industry of our fore-fathers and ourselves, against violence actually offered, we have taken up arms. We shall lay them down when hostilities shall cease on the part of the aggressors, and all danger of their being renewed shall be removed, and not before.

With an humble confidence in the mercies of the supreme and impartial Judge and Ruler of the universe, we most devoutly implore his divine goodness to conduct us happily through this great conflict, to dispose our adversaries to reconciliation on reasonable terms, and thereby to relieve the empire from the calamities of civil war. [13]

The Conclusions of Common Sense *

THOMAS PAINE

To conclude, however strange it may appear to some, or however unwilling they may be to think so, matters not, but many strong and striking reasons may be given, to shew, that nothing can settle our affairs so expeditiously as an open and determined declaration for independance. Some of which are,

First.—It is the custom of nations, when any two are at war, for some other powers, not engaged in the quarrel, to step in as mediators, and bring about the preliminaries of a peace: but while Amer-

* FROM *Common Sense: Addressed to the Inhabitants of America,* enl. ed. (Philadelphia: W. and T. Bradford, [1776]), pp. 36–37, 43–44. Published anonymously.

ica calls herself the Subject of Great-Britain, no power, however well disposed she may be, can offer her mediation. Wherefore, in our present state we may quarrel on for ever.

Secondly.—It is unreasonable to suppose, that France or Spain will give us any kind of assistance, if we mean only, to make use of that assistance for the purpose of repairing the breach, and strengthening the connection between Britain and America; because, those powers would be sufferers by the consequences.

Thirdly.—While we profess ourselves the subjects of Britain, we must, in the eye of foreign nations, be considered as rebels. The precedent is somewhat dangerous to *their peace,* for men to be in arms under the name of subjects; we, on the spot, can solve the paradox: but to unite resistance and subjection, requires an idea much too refined for common understanding.

Fourthly.—Were a manifesto to be published, and despatched to foreign courts, setting forth the miseries we have endured, and the peaceable methods we have ineffectually used for redress; declaring, at the same time, that not being able, any longer, to live happily or safely under the cruel disposition of the British court, we had been driven to [36] the necessity of breaking off all connections with her; at the same time, assuring all such courts of our peaceable disposition towards them, and of our desire of entering into trade with them: Such a memorial would produce more good effects to this Continent, than if a ship were freighted with petitions to Britain.

Under our present denomination of British subjects, we can neither be received nor heard abroad: The custom of all courts is against us, and will be so, until, by an independance, we take rank with other nations.

These proceedings may at first appear strange and difficult; but, like all other steps which we have already passed over, will in a little time become familiar and agreeable; and, until an independance is declared, the Continent will feel itself like a man who continues putting off some unpleasant business from day to day, yet knows it must be done, hates to set about it, wishes it over, and is continually haunted with the thoughts of its necessity. [37]

· · · · ·

I shall conclude these remarks, with the following timely and well intended hints, We ought to reflect, that there are three different ways, by which an independancy may hereafter be effected; and that *one* of those *three,* will one day or other, be the fate of America, viz. By the legal voice of the people in Congress; by a military power; or by a mob: It may not always happen that our soldiers are citizens, and the multitude a body of reasonable men; virtue, as I have already remarked, is not hereditary, neither is it perpetual. Should an independancy be brought about by the first of those means, we have every opportunity and every encouragement before us, to form the noblest purest constitution on the face of the earth. We have it in our power to begin the world over again. A situation, similar to the present, hath not happened since the days of Noah until now. The birthday of a new world is at hand, and a race of men, perhaps as numerous as all Europe contains, are to receive their portion of freedom from the event of a few months. The Reflexion is awful—and in this point of view, How trifling, how ridiculous, do the little, paltry cavellings, of a few weak or interested men appear, when weighed against the business of a world.

Should we neglect the present favorable and inviting period, and an Independance be hereafter effected by any other means, we must charge the consequence to ourselves, or to those rather, whose narrow and prejudiced souls, are habitually opposing the measure, without either inquiring or reflecting. There are reasons to be given in support of Independance, which men should rather privately think of, than be publicly told of. We ought not now to be debating whether we shall be independant or not, but, anxious to accomplish it on a firm, secure, and honorable basis, and uneasy rather that it is not yet began upon. Every day convinces [43] us of its necessity. Even the Tories (if such beings yet remain among us) should, of all men, be the most solicitous to promote it; for, as the appointment of committees at first, protected them from popular rage, so, a wise and well established form of government, will be the only certain means of continuing it securely to them. *Wherefore,* if they have not virtue enough to be WHIGS, they ought to have prudence enough to wish for Independance.

In short, Independance is the only BOND that can tye and keep us together. We shall then see our object, and our ears will be legally shut against the schemes of an intriguing, as well, as a cruel enemy. We shall then too, be on a proper footing, to treat with Britain; for there is reason to conclude, that the pride of that court, will be less hurt by treating with the American states for terms of peace, than with those, whom she denominates, "rebellious subjects," for terms of accommodation. It is our delaying it that encourages her to hope for conquest, and our backwardness tends only to prolong the war.

As we have, without any good effect therefrom, withheld our trade to obtain a redress of our grievances, let us *now* try the alternative, by *independantly* redressing them ourselves, and then offering to open the trade. The mercantile and reasonable part in England, will be still with us; because, peace *with* trade, is preferable to war *without* it. And if this offer be not accepted, other courts may be applied to.

On these grounds I rest the matter. And as no offer hath yet been made to refute the doctrine contained in the former editions of this pamphlet, it is a negative proof, that either the doctrine cannot be refuted, or, that the party in favour of it are too numerous to be opposed. WHEREFORE, instead of gazing at each other with suspicious or doubtful curiosity, let each of us, hold out to his neighbour the hearty hand of friendship, and unite in drawing a line, which, like an act of oblivion shall bury in forgetfulness every former dissention. Let the names of Whig and Tory be extinct; and let none other be heard among us, than those of *a good citizen, an open and resolute friend, and a virtuous supporter of the* RIGHTS *of* MANKIND *and of the* FREE AND INDEPENDANT STATES OF AMERICA. [44]

Resolutions Respecting Independence *

[JUNE 7, 1776]
Resolved

That these United Colonies are, and of right ought to be, free and independent States, that they are absolved from all allegiance to the British Crown, and that all political connection between them and the State of Great Britain is, and ought to be, totally dissolved.

That it is expedient forthwith to take the most effectual measures for forming foreign Alliances.

That a plan of confederation be prepared and transmitted to the respective Colonies for their consideration and approbation.

[JUNE 10, 1776]

Resolved that it is the opinion of this Com tha[t] the first Resolution be postponed to this day three weeks and that in the mean time [1] a committee be appointed to prepare a Declaration to the effect of the said first resolution.

[1] Least any time sh.ᵈ be lost in case the Congress agree to this resolution.

* FROM MS in the National Archives, Washington. The Resolutions of June 7 are in the hand of Richard Henry Lee.

Resolutions Concerning the Declaration *

[JULY 4, 1776]

Ordered That the declaration be authenticated & printed

That the committee appointed to prepare the declaration superintend & correct the press.

That copies of the declaration be sent to the several assemblies, conventions & committees or councils of safety and to the several commanding officers of the continental troops that it be proclaimed in each of the united states & at the head of the army.

* FROM the Rough Journal of the Continental Congress, National Archives.

Composition and Revision
of the Declaration

THOMAS JEFFERSON

First Ideas on the Constitution of Virginia *

Whereas George   Guelph King of Great Britain & Ireland and Elector of Hanover, heretofore entrusted with the exercise of the kingly office in this government hath endeavored to pervert the same into a detestable & insupportable tyranny

1. by *neg* [1] his negative on laws the most wholesome & necessary for the public good [2]
2. by denying to his governors permission to pass laws of *the most* immediate & pressing importance, unless suspended in their operation for his *consent,*[3] &, when so suspended, neglecting *for m* to attend to them for many years:
3. by refusing to pass certain other laws, unless the persons to be benefited by them would relinquish the inestimable *rights* [4] of representation in the legislature: [5]
4. by dissolving legislative assemblies repeatedly & continually for opposing with manly firmness his invasions on the rights of the people:
5. when dissolved, by refusing to call others for a long space of

---

[1] "Putting."

[2] Line inserted: *"has kept some colonies without judiciary establmts."*

[3] "Assent."   [4] "Right."   [5] Line inserted: *"judges dependant."*

* FROM MS in the Library of Congress. Wording that Jefferson rejected is printed in *italics,* and later wording is listed in the notes. The marginal numbers and letters were added by Jefferson to reorder the contents for his Rough Draft of the Declaration of Independence. The title is adapted from Jefferson's endorsement of the MS.

time, thereby leaving the political system *in a state of dissolu-tion* without any legislative *body*.[6]

6. by endeavoring to prevent the population of our country *by* [7] obstructing the laws *for the naturalization* [8] of foreigners & rais-ing the conditions of *appropriating lands*: [9]

7. by keeping among us in times of peace standing armies & ships of war:

8. by affecting to render the military independent of & superior to the civil power:

9. by combining with others to subject us to a foreign jurisdiction giving his *consent* [10] to their pretended acts of legislation *for imposing taxes on us without our consent*

   a. for quartering large bodies of armed troops among us: [11]

   b. for cutting off our trade with all parts of the world:

   c. for *depriving us of* imposing taxes on us without our consent:

   d. for depriving us of the benefits of trial by jury:

   e. for transporting us beyond seas to be tried for pretended of-fences: [12]

   f. for suspending our own legislatures & declaring themselves invested with power to legislate for us in all cases whatsoever

16.

10. by plundering our seas, ravaging our coasts, burning our towns, *de* [13] destroying the lives of our people:

14. 13.

11. by inciting insurrections of our fellow *subjects* [14] with the allure-ments of forfeiture & confiscation:

12. by prompting our negroes to rise in arms among us; those very negroes whom he hath [15] *from time to time* refused us permis-sion to exclude by law:

13. by endeavoring to bring on the inhabitants of our frontiers the merciless Indian savages whose known rule of warfare is an un-distinguished destruction of all ages, sexes, & conditions: [16]

14. by transporting at this time a large army of foreign mercenaries

[6] "Head."   [7] "& for that purpose."   [8] "Encouraging the importn."
[9] *"Appropriating new lands."* Then: "new appropriations of lands." Lines in-serted: "refused judiciary establmts to some without unjust & partial
  judges dependant
  erected swarms of offices."
[10] "Assent."   [11] Inserted: "& protectg them &c—murders."
[12] Line inserted: "for taking away our charters & altering fundamentally the forms of our governments."
[13] "&."   [14] "Citizens."   [15] Inserted: "by an inhuman use of his negative."
[16] Inserted: *"of life."* Then: "of existence."

to compleat the works of death, desolation, & tyranny already begun *in a stile* [17] so unworthy *a ci* [18] head of a civilized *people:* [19]

15. by answering our repeated petitions [20] *against this repeated injury* [21] *with accumulation of new injury* [22]

And by various other acts of tyranny too often enumerated to need repetition, and too cruel for the reflection of those who have felt them.

Compositional Fragment *

re-established them in po[wer . . .] [1]

this conduct and at this [2] time [3] are permitting their *sovereign* [4] [to] send over not [5] soldiers of our *own* [6] blood but [7] foreign mercenaries to *destroy us.*[8] *this is too much to be borne even by relations! enough* [9] *be it to say, we are now done with them!* [10] we must endeavor to forget our former love for them and to hold them, as [11] the rest of mankind, enemies in war, in peace friends. we might have been a *great & a happy* [12] people together, but [13] *communicated* [14] *of happiness & of grandeur* [15] it seems is *beneath* [16] their dignity. *we will climb then the roads to glory & happiness apart.* be it so, since they will have it: the road to *glory & to happiness* [17] is open to us too, we will climb it *in a separate state,*[18] & acquiesce in the necessity which *pronounces* [19] our *everlasting Adieu.*[20]

these facts have given the last stab to agonizing affection, & manly spirit bids us to renounce for ever these unjust [21] *brethren.*

---

[17] "With circumstances of cruelty & perfidy."   [18] "The."   [19] "Nation."
[20] Inserted: "for redress."
[21] "*Against these repeated injuries.*" Then: "with a repetition of injuries."
[22] ¶ inserted: "16. and finally by abandoning the helm of government & [deleted and reinserted] declaring us out of his allegiance & protection."

---

[1] The fragment is torn here.   [2] Inserted: "very."
[3] Inserted: "too, they."   [4] "Chief magistrate."   [5] Inserted: "only."
[6] "Common."   [7] Inserted: "Scotch &."
[8] "Invade and deluge us in blood."   [9] Inserted: "*then.*"
[10] Inserted: "these facts have given the last stab to agonizing affection, & manly spirit bids us to renounce for ever these unfeeling brethren."
[11] Inserted: "we hold."   [12] "Free & a great."   [13] Inserted: "a."
[14] "Communication."   [15] "[G]randeur & of freedom."   [16] "Below."
[17] "Happiness & to glory."   [18] "Apart from them."   [19] "Denounces."
[20] "Eternal separation."   [21] "*Unfeeling.*"

* FROM MS in the Library of Congress. Wording that was struck out by Jefferson is in *italics,* and the notes contain later wording.

this time too they are permitting their chief magistrate to send over not only soldiers of our common blood but Scotch & foreign mercenaries to invade & destroy us. this is too much to be borne even by relations. enough then be it to say we [could?] endeavor to forget our former love for them, and to hold them, as the rest of mankind, enemies in war, in peace friends. we might have been a free & a happy people together; but a communication of grandeur & of happiness it seems is below their dignity. be it so, since they will have it: the road to happiness & to glory is open to us too; we will climb it apart from them, and acquiesce in the necessity which denounces our eternal separation.

these facts have given the last stab to agonizing affection, and manly spirit bids us to renounce for ever these unfeeling brethren.

Original Rough Draught of the
Declaration of Independence *

A Declaration *of* [1] the Representatives of the UNITED STATES
OF AMERICA, in General Congress assembled.

When in the course of human events it becomes necessary for *a* [2]
people to *advance from that subordination in which they have hith-*
erto remained, & to [3] assume among the powers of the earth the *equal*
& independant [4] station to which the laws of nature & of nature's god
entitle them, a decent respect to the opinions of mankind requires
that they should declare the causes which impel them *to the*
change.[5]

We hold these truths to be *sacred & undeniable;* [6] that all men are
created equal *& independant;* that *from that equal creation they*
derive in rights [7] *inherent &* [8] inalienable,[9] among *which* [10] are *the*
preservation of life, *&* liberty, & the pursuit of happiness; that to
secure these *ends,*[11] governments are instituted among men, deriving their just powers from the consent of the governed; that whenever any form of government *shall become* [12] destructive of these
ends, it is the right of the people to alter or to abolish it, & to
institute new government, laying it's foundation on such principles, &
organising it's powers in such form, as to them shall seem most
likely to effect their safety & happiness. prudence indeed will dictate
that governments long established should not be changed for light &
transient causes: and accordingly all experience hath shewn that
mankind are more disposed to suffer while evils are sufferable, than
to right themselves by abolishing the forms to which they are accus-

[1] "By." [2] "One."
[3] "Dissolve the political bands which have connected them with another
["other" inserted and then rejected], and to."
[4] "Separate and equal." [5] *"To separate."* Then: "to the separation."
[6] "Self-evident."
[7] "They are endowed by their creator with *equal rights, some of which are.*"
[8] "Certain." [Cong] [9] Inserted: "rights; that." [10] "These."
[11] "Rights." [12] "Becomes."

* FROM the four-page MS in the Library of Congress. The earliest wording is
reprinted here, with passages that were struck out, bracketed, erased, or written
over printed in *italics,* and changes of wording listed in the notes. Alterations
attributed by Jefferson in his marginal notes to John Adams [JA] and Benjamin
Franklin [BF] are so indicated here, and those changes that we can attribute
to Congress [Cong] are also signaled. The other revisions in the text are presumably those of Jefferson himself. The title is derived from Jefferson's endorsement of the MS.

tomed. but when a long train of abuses & usurpations, *begun at a distinguished period,* &[13] pursuing invariably the same object, evinces a design to *subject*[14] them *to arbitrary power,*[15] it is their right, it is their duty, to throw off such government & to provide new guards for their future security. such has been the patient sufferance of these colonies; & such is now the necessity which constrains them to *expunge*[16] their former systems of government. the history of *his present majesty,*[17] is a history of *unremitting*[18] injuries and usurpations, *among which no one fact stands single or solitary*[19] *to contradict the uniform tenor of the rest,*[20] *all of which have*[21] in direct object the establishment of an absolute tyranny over these states. to prove this, let facts be submitted to a candid world, *for the truth of which we pledge a faith yet unsullied by falsehood.*[22] [1]

he has refused his assent to laws the most wholesome and necessary for the public good:

he has forbidden his governors to pass laws of immediate & pressing importance, unless suspended in their operation till his assent should be obtained; and when so suspended, he has *neglected utterly*[23] to attend to them.

he has refused to pass other laws for the accomodation of large districts of people unless those people would relinquish the right of representation;[24] a right inestimable to them, & formidable to tyrants *alone:*[25]

[he] has dissolved Representative houses repeatedly & *continually*[26] for opposing [with] manly firmness his invasions on the rights of the people:

[*when*[27]] *dissolved,* he has refused for a long *space of time*[28] to cause others to be elected, whereby the legislative powers, incapable of annihilation, have returned to the people at large for their exercise, the state remaining in the mean time exposed to all the dangers of invasion from without, &, convulsions within:

[13] Deleted by Congress.　　　[14] "Reduce."
[15] *"Under absolute power."* Then: "under absolute Despotism." [BF]
[16] "Alter." [Cong]　　　[17] "The present King of Great Britain." [JA]
[18] "Repeated." [Cong]　　[19] *"Among which appears no solitary fact."*
[20] "Among which . . . the rest" deleted by Congress.
[21] *"But all possess."* Then: "all having." [Cong]　　[22] Deleted by Congress.
[23] "Utterly neglected." [Cong]　　[24] Inserted: "in the legislature."
[25] "Only." ¶ inserted: "he has called together legislative bodies at places unusual, unco[mfortable, & distan]t from the depository of their public records, for the sole purpose of fatigui[ng them into compl]iance with his measures."
[26] Deleted by Congress.　　　[27] Possibly: "he has."
[28] Inserted: "after such Dissolutions." [JA]. Then "space of time" shortened o "time."

he has endeavored to prevent the population of these states; for that purpose obstructing the laws for naturalization of foreigners; refusing to pass others to encourage their migrations hither; & raising the conditions of new appropriations of lands:

he has *suffered* [29] the administration of justice *totally to cease in some of these colonies*,[30] refusing his assent to laws for establishing judiciary powers:

he has made *our* [31] judges dependant on his will alone, for the tenure of their offices, and *amount* [32] of their salaries:

he has erected a multitude of new offices *by a self-assumed power*,[33] & sent hither swarms of officers to harrass our people & eat out their substance:

he has kept among us in times of peace [34] standing armies & *ships of war:* [35]

he has affected to render the military, independent of & superior to the civil power:

he has combined with others to subject us to a jurisdiction foreign to our constitutions and unacknoleged by our laws; giving his assent to their *pretended acts of legislation*,[36] for quartering large bodies of armed troops among us;

> for protecting them by a mock-trial from punishment for any murders [37] they should commit on the inhabitants of these states;

> for cutting off our trade with all parts of the world;

> for imposing taxes on us without our consent;

> for depriving us [38] of the benefits of trial by jury;

> for transporting us beyond seas to be tried for pretended offences: [39] [2]

> for taking away our charters,[40] & altering fundamentally the forms of our governments;

[29] "Obstructed." [Cong]

[30] *States.* Then the entire phrase replaced by: "by." [Cong]

[31] Deleted by Congress.   [32] "The amount & payment." [BF]

[33] Deleted by Congress.   [34] Inserted: *"without our consent."*

[35] Inserted: *"without our consent."* Then: "without the consent of our legislatures." "& ships of war" deleted by Congress.

[36] "Acts of pretended legislation."   [37] Inserted: "which."

[38] Inserted: "in many cases." [Cong]

[39] ¶ inserted: "for abolishing the free system of English laws in a neighboring province, establishing therein an arbitrary government and enlarging it's boundaries so as to render it at once an example & fit instrument for introducing the same absolute rule into these *colonies.*" The last word replaced by: *"states."* Then: "colonies." [Cong]

[40] Inserted: "abolishing our most *important* [then: "valuable"] Laws." [BF

for suspending our own legislatures & declaring themselves invested with power to legislate for us in all cases whatsoever:

he has abdicated government here, *withdrawing his governors, & declaring us out of his allegiance & protection:* [41]

he has plundered our seas, ravaged our coasts, burnt our towns & destroyed the lives of our people:

he is at this time transporting large armies of [42] foreign mercenaries to compleat the works of death, desolation & tyranny, already begun with circumstan[ces] of cruelty & perifidy [43] unworthy the head of a civilized nation: [44]

he has [45] endeavored to bring on the inhabitants of our frontiers the merciless Indian savages, whose known rule of warfare is an undistinguished destruction of all ages, sexes, & conditions *of existence:* [46]

he has incited treasonable insurrections of our fellow-subjects,[47] *with the allurements of forfeiture & confiscation of our property:* [48]

he has waged cruel war against human nature itself, violating it's most sacred rights of life & liberty in the persons of a distant people who never offended him, captivating & carrying them into slavery in another hemisphere, or to incur miserable death in their transportation thither. this piratical warfare, the opprobrium of *infidel powers, is the warfare of the* C HRISTIAN *king of Great Britain. determined to keep open a market where MEN should be bought & sold* [49] *he has prostituted his negative for suppressing every legislative attempt to prohibit or to restrain this execrable commerce:* [50] *and that this assemblage of horrors might want no*

[41] "By declaring us out of his protection & waging war against us." [Cong]

[42] Inserted: "Scotch and other."

[43] Inserted: "scarcely paralleled in the most barbarous ages and totally." [Cong]

[44] Line inserted: "he has constrained c⁵." [Cong]

[45] Inserted: "excited domestic insurrections amongst us and has." [Cong]

[46] Deleted by Congress.   [47] "Fellow-citizens."

[48] "He has incited . . . our property" deleted by Congress. ¶ inserted: "he has constrained others *falling into his hands* [then: *"taken captives,"* finally: "taken captive"] on the high seas to bear arms against their country & *to destroy & be destroyed by the brethren whom they love."* The closing words replaced by: "to become the executioners of their friends & brethren or to fall themselves by their hands."

[49] "Determined . . . sold" bracketed and "and" inserted, then these changes rejected.

[50] Inserted and then deleted: "determining to keep open a market where MEN should be bought & sold."

fact of distinguished die, he is now exciting those very people to rise in arms among us, and to purchase that liberty of which he has deprived them, by murdering the people upon whom he also obtruded them; thus paying off former crimes committed against the liberties of one people, with crimes which he urges them to commit against the lives of another.[51]

in every stage of these oppressions we have petitioned for redress in the most humble terms; our repeated petitions have been answered [52] by repeated *injury*.[53] a prince whose character is thus marked by every act which may define a tyrant, is unfit to be the ruler of a *people who mean to be free.*[54] *future ages will scarce believe that the hardiness* [55] *of one man, adventured within the short compass of 12* [56] *years only, on so many acts of tyranny without a mask,*[57] *over a people fostered & fixed in principles of liberty.*[58] [3]

Nor have we been wanting in attentions to our British brethren. we have warned them from time to time of attempts by their legislature to extend *a* [59] jurisdiction over *these our states.*[60] we have reminded them of the circumstances of our emigration & settlement here, *no one of which could warrant so strange a pretension: that these were effected at the expence of our own blood & treasure, unassisted by the wealth or the strength of Great Britain: that in constituting indeed our several forms of government, we had adopted one common king, thereby laying a foundation for perpetual league & amity with them: but that submission to their [parliament was no part of our constitution, nor ever in idea, if history may]* be credited: and [61] we [62] appealed to their native justice & magnanimity, *as well as to* [63] the ties of our common kindred to disavow these usurpations which *were likely to* [64] interrupt our *correspondence & connection.*[65] they too have been deaf to the voice of justice & of consanguinity,[66] *& when occasions have been given them, by the regular course of their laws, of removing from their*

---

[51] Entire ¶ deleted by Congress.   [52] Inserted: "only." [BF]   [53] "Injuries."
[54] "Free people." [Cong]   [55] "Audacity" inserted and then rejected.
[56] "Twelve."
[57] "On so many . . . a mask" replaced by: "to lay [then: "build"] a foundation so broad & undisguised, for tyranny."
[58] "Freedom." The passage, "future ages . . . principles of freedom," deleted by Congress.
[59] Inserted: "an unwarrantable." [Cong]   [60] "Us." [Cong]
[61] "No one . . . credited: and" deleted by Congress.
[62] Inserted: "have." [Cong]   [63] "& we have conjured them by." [Cong]
[64] "Would inevitably." [Cong]   [65] "Connection & correspondence."
[66] Line inserted: "We must therefore." [Cong]

councils the disturbers of our harmony, they have by their free election re-established them in power. at this very time too are [67] *permitting their chief magistrate to send over not only soldiers of our common blood, but Scotch & foreign mercenaries to invade & deluge us in blood.* [68] *these facts have given the last stab to agonizing affection, and manly spirit bids us to renounce for ever these unfeeling brethren. we must endeavor to forget our former love for them, and to hold them as we hold the rest of mankind, enemies in war, in peace friends. we might have been a free & a great people together; but a communication of grandeur & of freedom it seems is below their dignity. be it so, since they will have it: the road to glory & happiness* [69] *is open to us too; we will* [70] *climb* [71] *it in a separate state,* [72] *and* [73] *acquiesce in the necessity which pronounces* [74] *our everlasting Adieu!* [75]

We therefore the representatives of the United States of America in General Congress assembled [76] do, in the name & by authority of the good people of these *states,* [77] *reject and renounce all allegiance & subjection to the kings of Great Britain & all others who may hereafter claim by, through, or under them; we utterly dissolve & break off* [78] *all political connection which may have heretofore* [79] *subsisted between us & the people or parliament of Great Britain; and finally we do assert and declare these colonies to be free and independant states,* [80] and that as free & independant states they *shall hereafter* have [81] power to levy war, conclude peace, contract alliances, establish commerce, & to do all other acts and things which independant states may of right do. And for the support of this declaration we mutually pledge to each other our lives, our fortunes, & our sacred honour. [4]

[67] *"They are."*   [68] In place of "deluge us in blood": *"destroy us."* [BF]
[69] *"To happiness & to glory."*   [70] "Must" inserted and then rejected.
[71] *"Tread."*
[72] In place of "in a separate state": *"separately."* Then: *"apart from them."*
[73] The passage, "& when occasions . . . apart from them, and," deleted by Congress. Line inserted: *"We must theref."*
[74] *"Denounces."*
[75] Inserted: *"eternal* [deleted by Congress] *separation!"* Then inserted: "and hold them as we hold the rest of mankind enemies in war, in peace friends." [Cong]
[76] Inserted: "appealing to the supreme judge of the world for the rectitude of our intentions." [Cong]
[77] "Colonies." [Cong]   [78] "& break off" deleted by Jefferson.
[79] *"Heretofore have."*
[80] "Reject and renounce . . . independent states" deleted by Congress from the final text and, as Jefferson notes, "a different phraseology inserted."
[81] Inserted: "full."

Bibliography

The Bibliography is arranged in four parts: A. A brief list of background materials, including pamphlets, collections of documents, and special studies, helpful in understanding the political controversy of the American Revolution. B. A descriptive list of the manuscripts of the Declaration. C. A list of significant editions of the text of the Declaration. D. An extensive compilation of articles and books dealing with the Declaration in critical, philosophic, historical, and bibliographical ways.

A. Background

ADAMS, RANDOLPH G. *Political Ideas of the American Revolution: Britannic-American Contributions to the Problem of Imperial Organization, 1765 to 1775*, 3rd ed., with Commentary by Merrill Jensen. New York: Barnes & Noble, Inc. (paperback), 1958.

BELOFF, MAX (ed.), *The Debate on the American Revolution, 1761–1783*. New York: Harper & Row, Publishers Incorporated (paperback), 1965.

BEMIS, SAMUEL FLAGG. *The Diplomacy of the American Revolution*. Bloomington, Ind.: Indiana University Press (paperback), 1957.

BURKE, EDMUND. *On the American Revolution: Selected Speeches and Addresses,* ed. Elliott Robert Barkan. New York: Harper & Row, Publishers, Incorporated (paperback), 1966.

CLOUGH, WILSON OBER (ed.), *Intellectual Origins of American National Thought: Pages from the Books Our Founding Fathers Read,* 2d ed. New York: Corinth Books (paperback), 1961.

COMMAGER, HENRY STEELE, and MORRIS, RICHARD B. (eds.), *The Spirit of 'Seventy-Six: The Story of the American Revolution as Told by Participants,* Vol. I. Indianapolis: The Bobbs-Merrill Company, Inc., 1958.

FORD, WORTHINGTON CHAUNCEY (ed.), *Journals of the Continental Congress,* Vols. I–V. Washington: Government Printing Office, 1904–1906.

JEFFERSON, THOMAS. *The Political Writings: Representative Selections,* ed. Edward Dumbauld. Indianapolis: The Bobbs-Merrill Company, Inc. (paperback), 1955.

KRIEGEL, LEONARD (ed.), *Essential Works of the Founding Fathers*. New York: Bantam Books, Inc. (paperback), 1964.

LOCKE, JOHN. *Two Treatises of Government*, with Robert Filmer's *Patriarcha*, ed. Thomas I. Cook. New York: Hafner Publishing Company, Inc. (paperback), 1947. Originally published in 1690.

[MACPHERSON, JAMES.] *The Rights of Great Britain Asserted Against the Claims of America: Being an Answer to the Declaration of the General Congress*, 2d ed. [London?]: 1776. This was written in answer to the Declaration of Taking up Arms of 1775.

MORISON, SAMUEL ELIOT (ed.), *Sources and Documents Illustrating the American Revolution, 1764–1788, and the Formation of the Federal Constitution*, 2d ed. New York: Oxford University Press (paperback), 1965.

MORRIS, RICHARD B. *The American Revolution: A Short History*. Princeton, N.J.: D. Van Nostrand Company, Inc. (paperback), 1955.

PADOVER, SAUL K. *Thomas Jefferson and the Foundations of American Freedom*. Princeton, N.J.: D. Van Nostrand Company, Inc. (paperback), 1965.

PAINE, THOMAS. *Common Sense* and *The Crisis*. Garden City, N.Y.: Doubleday & Company, Inc. (paperback), 1960. Originally published separately, the first in 1776 and the second from 1776 to 1783. Selections from *Common Sense* are reprinted in this volume, pp. 251–254.

PICKERING, DANBY (ed.), *The Statutes at Large*, Vols. XXVI–XXXI. Cambridge, Eng.: Printed by Joseph Bentham [later John Archdeacon] for Charles Bathurst, 1764–1775. These volumes contain Acts of Parliament dealing with America.

B. Manuscript Versions and Copies of the Declaration

1. First Ideas on the Constitution of Virginia in Jefferson's hand. Library of Congress. List of grievances drawn up before June 13, 1776, and utilized in the Rough Draft. Reprinted in this volume, pp. 256–258.
2. Compositional Fragment in Jefferson's hand. Library of Congress. Statement of attitudes towards the British people, composed in June, 1776, and utilized in the Rough Draft. Reprinted in this volume, p. 258, and reproduced, p. 259.
3. Rough Draft in Jefferson's hand, with corrections written in by Adams and Franklin. Library of Congress. On the document Jefferson recorded the changes made in the course of its adoption. Some of his annotations were made later than July, 1776. Reprinted in this volume, pp. 260–265.
4. Copy of Jefferson's draft in the hand of John Adams. Massachusetts Historical Society, Boston. Prepared in June, 1776, from the Rough Draft before it was submitted to Franklin.

5. Copy of version as reported by the Committee of Five in Jefferson's hand, with indications of corrections and deletions in the hand of Arthur Lee. American Philosophical Society, Philadelphia. Sent by Jefferson to Richard Henry Lee, July 8, 1776, but possibly copied before July 4.

6. Copy of version as reported by the Committee of Five in Jefferson's hand, with indications in an unidentified hand of deletions made by Congress. New York Public Library. Sent to George Wythe in July, 1776, [formerly known as the Cassius F. Lee Copy] and perhaps copied before July 4.

7. Copy of version as reported by the Committee of Five in Jefferson's hand, without indication of any changes made by Congress. Massachusetts Historical Society. The MS, known as the Washburn Copy, is incomplete. It may have been prepared by Jefferson in July, 1776, and sent to one of his associates.

8. Copy of version as approved by the Continental Congress written out by its Secretary, Charles Thomson, in the Corrected Journal. Library of Congress. July, 1776.

9. Copy of version as reported by the Committee of Five in Jefferson's hand, with his indications of the Congressional corrections and deletions, in his Notes of the Proceedings of the Continental Congress. Library of Congress. Written between July 4, 1776, and June 1, 1783, but probably in 1776. Jefferson inserted this copy with his Notes in his Autobiography.

10. Copy of version as approved by Congress, engrossed on parchment, perhaps by Timothy Matlack, with corrections in Jefferson's hand, and signed by the members of Congress. National Archives, Washington. The Parchment Copy was ordered on July 19, 1776, and signed on Aug. 2.

11. Copy of version as reported by the Committee of Five with indications of Congressional corrections and additions, prepared in Jefferson's hand from his Notes (No. 9 above). Library of Congress. Sent to James Madison, June 1, 1783.

C. Editions and Reproductions of the Declaration

1. Under the title "A Declaration by the Representatives of the United States of America, in General Congress Assembled." First broadside edition published in Philadelphia by John Dunlap, July 4, 1776. Reprinted in this volume, pp. 1–5. Reproduced as the frontispiece.

2. In *The Pennsylvania Evening Post* (Philadelphia), July 6, 1776. First newspaper appearance.

3. In *The Genuine Principles of the Ancient Saxon, or English Constitution: Carefully Collected from the Best Authorities, with Some Observations on Their Peculiar Fitness for the United Colonies in*

General, and Pennsylvania in Particular, by Demophilus. Philadelphia: Robert Bell, 1776. First appearance in a book.

4. Under the title "The Unanimous Declaration of the Thirteen United States of America." Broadside published in Baltimore by Mary Katharine Goddard under Congressional order of Jan. 18, 1777.

5. Facsimile of the Parchment Copy. An engraving printed by W. J. Stone, 1823.

6. In Memoir, Correspondence, and Miscellanies, from the Papers of Thomas Jefferson, ed. Thomas Jefferson Randolph, Vol. I. Charlottesville, Va.: F. Carr and Co., 1829.

7. In The Writings of Thomas Jefferson, ed. Paul Leicester Ford, Vol. II. New York: G. P. Putnam's Sons, 1893.

8. In John H. Hazelton, The Declaration of Independence: Its History. New York: Dodd, Mead & Company, Inc., 1906.

9. In Carl L. Becker, The Declaration of Independence: A Study in the History of Political Ideas. New York: Harcourt, Brace and Company, Inc., 1922; Alfred A. Knopf, Inc. (paperback), 1958.

10. In The Declaration of Independence: The Evolution of the Text as Shown in Facsimiles of Various Drafts by Its Author. Washington: The Library of Congress, 1943. Actual size photographic reproductions of the following manuscripts as listed in Part B of this Bibliography: Nos. 1, 3, 4, 5, 6, 7, 11.

11. In The Papers of Thomas Jefferson, ed. Julian P. Boyd, Vol. I. Princeton, N.J.: Princeton University Press, 1950.

12. In The Jefferson Drafts of the Declaration of Independence in Facsimile, comp. Gerald Force. Washington: Colortone Press, 1963.

D. Works on the Declaration

ADAMS, JOHN. Works, ed. Charles Francis Adams. Boston: Charles C. Little and James Brown, 1850–1856. Vol. II, pp. 513–514, note; Vol. VII, pp. 396–397. Reprinted in this volume, pp. 26–27, 22–23, respectively.

———. Diary and Autobiography, ed. L. H. Butterfield, Vol. III. "The Adams Papers." Cambridge, Mass.: The Belknap Press of Harvard University Press, 1961, pp. 335–337; Atheneum (paperback), 1964. Reprinted in this volume, pp. 23–25.

ADAMS, JOHN QUINCY. Memoirs, ed. Charles Francis Adams, Vol. VIII. Philadelphia: J. B. Lippincott & Co., 1876, pp. 281–283. Written in Jan. 1831.

APTHEKER, HERBERT. The American Revolution, 1763–1783, Part II of A History of the American People: An Interpretation. New York: International Publishers Co., Inc. (paperback), 1960, pp. 100–110. Reprinted in this volume, pp. 184–193.

ARENDT, HANNAH. On Revolution. New York: The Viking Press, Inc., 1963.

AUBREY, JOSEPH. *Our Republic: An Historical and Critical Essay on the Declaration of Independence*. Utica, N.Y.: T. J. Griffiths, 1891.

BALDWIN, M. M. "The Declaration of Independence," *Magazine of American History*, XX (Dec. 1888), 479–484.

BANCROFT, GEORGE. *History of the United States*, Vol. VIII. Boston: Little, Brown & Company, 1860, pp. 472–475.

BASLER, ROY P. "As One Southerner to Another: Concerning Lincoln and the Declaration of Independence," *South Atlantic Quarterly*, XLII (Jan. 1943), 45–53.

BEARD, CHARLES A. *The Republic: Conversations on Fundamentals*. New York: The Viking Press, Inc., 1943, pp. 17–20.

BECK, JAMES M. "The Triumph of Democracy," *May It Please the Court*, ed. O. R. McGuire. Atlanta: The Harrison Company, 1930, pp. 181–199. Speech delivered July 4, 1926.

BECKER, CARL L. *The Declaration of Independence: A Study in the History of Political Ideas*. New York: Harcourt, Brace and Company, Inc., 1922; Alfred A. Knopf, Inc. (paperback), 1958. Ch. V is reprinted in this volume, pp. 139–153.

————. "Declaration of Independence," *Encyclopaedia of the Social Sciences*, ed. Edwin R. A. Seligman, Vol. V. New York: The Macmillan Company, 1937, pp. 45–47. Another version appears in *Dictionary of American History*, 2d ed., ed. James Truslow Adams, Vol. II. New York: Charles Scribner's Sons, 1940, pp. 120–121.

BELISLE, D. W. "Remarks on the Declaration," *History of Independence Hall*. Philadelphia: James Challen & Son, 1859, pp. 128–133.

BENNETT, JESSE LEE. "The [Characteristic American Political] Ideas as Expressed in or by the Declaration of Independence and the Federal and State Constitutions," *The Essential American Tradition*. New York: George H. Doran Company, 1925, pp. 61–83.

BERGEN, FRANK. *The Other Side of the Declaration of Independence: A Lecture*, 4th ed. Newark, N.J.: Baker Printing Co., 1898.

BERGER, CARL. *Broadsides and Bayonets: The Propaganda War of the American Revolution*. Philadelphia: University of Pennsylvania Press, 1961, pp. 218–223.

BEVERIDGE, ALBERT J. "Sources of the Declaration of Independence," *Pennsylvania Magazine of History and Biography*, L (4th Quarter, 1926), 289–315.

BISCHOFF, HENRY, JR. *An Essay on the American Declaration of Independence*. New York: 1871.

BLACK, R. M. "The Ethics of the Declaration of Independence," *Annals of the American Academy of Political and Social Science*, II (July 1891), 138–144. Reprinted in this volume, pp. 78–82.

BLEDSOE, ALBERT TAYLOR. "The Seventeenth Fallacy of the Abolitionist;

or, The Argument from the Declaration of Independence," *An Essay on Liberty and Slavery*. Philadelphia: J. B. Lippincott & Co., 1856, pp. 102–137.

BOORSTIN, DANIEL J. *The Genius of American Politics*. Chicago: The University of Chicago Press, 1953, pp. 81–85.

BOYD, JULIAN P. *The Declaration of Independence: The Evolution of the Text as Shown in Facsimiles of Various Drafts by Its Author, Thomas Jefferson*. Princeton, N.J.: Princeton University Press, 1945.

————. "New Light on Jefferson and His Great Task," *New York Times Magazine*, Apr. 13, 1947, pp. 17, 64–65, 67–70.

————. "Jefferson's Final Testament of Faith," *New York Times Magazine*, Apr. 10, 1949, pp. 11, 33–35, 37, 39.

————. Editorial and Textual Notes, *The Papers of Thomas Jefferson*, Vol. I. Princeton, N. J.: Princeton University Press, 1950, pp. 299–308, 328, 413–417, 419–420, 421–423, 427–428, 433.

BRUCKBERGER, R. L. *Image of America*, trans. by C. G. Paulding and Virgilia Peterson. New York: The Viking Press, Inc. (paperback), 1964, pp. 79–108, 272–277.

BUCHANAN, ROBERDEAU. *Observations on the Declaration of Independence, with a Critical Examination of the Facts Attending Its Attestation.* Lancaster, Pa · Inquirer Printing Company, 1890. Revised from *Life of the Hon. Thomas McKean, LL.D.*, 1890.

BUCK, ELIZABETH HAWTHORN. "The Declaration as a Document," *Manuscripts*, X (Sum. 1958), 2–10, 37.

BURNETT, EDMUND C. "Launching the National Ship: The Declaration of Independence," *The Continental Congress*. New York: W. W. Norton & Company, Inc. (paperback), 1964, pp. 170–197.

B[URR], W[ILLIAM] H[ENRY]. *The Declaration of Independence, A Masterpiece: But How It Got Mutilated!* [Washington?]: 1881.

————. "The Authorship of the Declaration of Independence," *Thomas Paine: Was He Junius?*, 2d ed. Washington: n.d., pp. 17–26. Originally published in 1890.

BUTLER, NICHOLAS MURRAY. "The Declaration of Independence, 1776–1926," *Looking Forward*. New York: Charles Scribner's Sons, 1932, pp. 319–335. Speech delivered July 5, 1926.

BUTTERFIELD, L. H. "The Jubilee of Independence, July 4, 1826," *Virginia Magazine of History and Biography*, LXI (Apr. 1953), 119–140.

CALHOUN, JOHN C. Speech on the Oregon Bill, June 27, 1848, *Appendix to the Congressional Globe*, 30th Cong., 1st Sess. Washington: Blair & Rives, 1848, p. 872. Reprinted in this volume, pp. 57–58.

CARR, JOHN FOSTER. *The Declaration of Independence and the Colonies*. New York: Immigrant Publication Society, Inc., 1924.

CHAFEE, ZECHARIAH, JR. "How Human Rights Got into the Constitution," Preface, *Documents on Fundamental Human Rights*, Vol. I. New York: Atheneum (paperback), 1963, pp. 11–18.

CHAMBERLAIN, MELLEN. "The Authentication of the Declaration of Independence, July 4, 1776," *Proceedings of the Massachusetts Historical Society*, 2d Ser., I (Nov. 1884), 273–298. Reprinted in *John Adams . . . with Other Essays and Addresses*. Boston: Houghton, Mifflin and Company, 1898, pp. 97–133.

CHANNING, EDWARD. *A History of the United States*, Vol. III. New York: The Macmillan Company, 1912, pp. 200–208.

CHIDSEY, DONALD BARR. *July 4, 1776: The Dramatic Story of the First Four Days of July, 1776*. New York: Crown Publishers, Inc., 1958.

CHINARD, GILBERT. *Thomas Jefferson: The Apostle of Americanism*, 2d ed. Ann Arbor, Mich.: The University of Michigan Press (paperback), 1957, pp. 69–85.

———. *La Déclaration des droits de l'homme et du citoyen et ses antécédents américains*. Washington: Institut Français, 1945.

CLASON, A. W. "The Fallacy of 1776," *Magazine of American History*, XIII (May 1885), 445–456.

COMMAGER, HENRY STEELE. "The Declaration Is for Today!" *New York Times Magazine*, July 1, 1951, pp. 5, 29.

———. *The Great Declaration: A Book for Young Americans*. Indianapolis: The Bobbs-Merrill Company, Inc., 1958.

CONDORCET, MARQUIS DE. *De l'influence de la révolution de l'Amérique sur l'Europe, Œuvres complètes*, ed. Garat and Cabanis, Vol. XI. Paris: Fuchs, An IX [1800–1801], p. 249. Originally published in 1786. Translated in this volume, p. 20.

COOLIDGE, CALVIN. "The Inspiration of the Declaration," *Foundations of the Republic: Speeches and Addresses*. New York: Charles Scribner's Sons, 1926, pp. 439–454.

CORWIN, EDWARD S. and PELTASON, JACK W. *Understanding the Constitution*, 3rd ed. New York: Holt, Rinehart and Winston, 1964, pp. 2–11.

D. D. "London Newspapers of 1776 and the Declaration of Independence," *The Nation*, LXVI (Feb. 17, 1898), 127–128.

DANA, WILLIAM F. "The Declaration of Independence," *Harvard Law Review*, XIII (Jan. 1900), 319–343. Reprinted in this volume, pp. 102–126.

DARLING, ARTHUR B. *A Historical Introduction to the Declaration of Independence*. New Haven, Conn.: Quinnipiack Press, Inc., 1932.

"The Declaration and Its Sesquicentennial," *Constitutional Review*, X (July 1926), 182–185.

"Déclaration des droits de l'homme & du citoyen, décrétée par l'assemblée nationale, & sanctionnée par le roi, comparée avec les lois de plusieurs peuples anciens & modernes, & principalement avec les déclarations des États-unis de l'amérique," *L'Ami de la révolution*, 12th "Philippique." Paris: Champigny [1790], pp. 238–239, 242–243. Translated in this volume, p. 21.

"The Declaration of Independence (Emmet Collection)," *Bulletin of the New York Public Library*, I (Dec. 1897), 351–364.

A Declaration of Independence Published by the Congress at Philadelphia in 1776, with a Counter-Declaration Published at New-York in 1781, appended to *Paris Papers, or Mr. Silas Deane's Late Intercepted Letters.* New York: Reprinted by James Rivington [1782].

DENSLOW, VAN BUREN. "Thomas Paine," *Modern Thinkers*. Chicago: Belford, Clarke & Co., 1884, pp. 156–163.

DESHLER, CHARLES D. "How the Declaration Was Received in the Old Thirteen," *Harper's New Monthly Magazine*, LXXXV (July 1892), 165–187.

DETWEILER, PHILIP F. "The Declaration of Independence in Jefferson's Lifetime," *Tulane University Bulletin, The Graduate School: Abstracts of Dissertations and Theses*, 55th Ser., No. 14 (Dec. 1, 1954), 49–52.

———. "Congressional Debate on Slavery and the Declaration of Independence, 1819–1821," *American Historical Review*, LXIII (Apr. 1958), 598–616.

———. "The Changing Reputation of the Declaration of Independence: The First Fifty Years," *William and Mary Quarterly*, 3rd Ser., XIX (Oct. 1962), 557–574.

DEWEY, JOHN. *The Living Thoughts of Thomas Jefferson Presented by John Dewey*. New York: Longmans, Green and Co., Inc., 1940; Fawcett Publications, Inc. (paperback), 1963. A selection is reprinted in this volume, pp. 162–165.

DONOVAN, FRANK. "The First Fourth," *The Thomas Jefferson Papers*. New York: Dodd, Mead & Company, Inc. (paperback), 1963, pp. 1–30.

DOUGLAS, WILLIAM O. *An Almanac of Liberty*. Garden City, N.Y.: Doubleday & Company, Inc. (paperback), 1954, pp. 24–27.

DRAKE, ALICE HUTCHINS. "The Declaration of Independence: The Why and the Wherefore," *Daughters of the American Revolution Magazine*, LXVIII (July 1934), 417–421.

DUMBAULD, EDWARD. *The Declaration of Independence and What It Means Today*. Norman, Okla.: University of Oklahoma Press, 1950.

DUNNING, WILLIAM A. "An Historic Phrase," *Annual Report of the American Historical Association for the Year 1902*, I, 82–85. Reprinted in *Truth in History, and Other Essays*. New York: Columbia University Press, 1937, pp. 56–59.

ECHEVERRIA, DURAND. "French Publications of the Declaration of Independence and the American Constitutions, 1776–1783," *Papers of the*

Bibliographical Society of America, XLVII (4th Quarter, 1953), 313–338.

VON ECKARDT, URSULA M. *The Pursuit of Happiness in the Democratic Creed: An Analysis of Political Ethics.* New York: Frederick A. Praeger, Inc., 1959.

ELIOT, CHARLES W. *The Independence of 1776 and the Dependence of 1911.* City of Boston Document No. 96. Speech delivered July 4, 1911.

ELLIS, GEORGE E. "Remarks on the Declaration of Independence," *Unitarian Review and Religious Magazine*, VI (July 1876), 1–24.

————. "The Sentiment of Independence, Its Growth and Consummation," *Narrative and Critical History of America*, ed. Justin Winsor, Vol. VI. Boston: Houghton, Mifflin and Company, 1888, pp. 231–274.

An Englishman. Remarks on the Declaration of Independence, *The Scots Magazine*, XXXVIII (Aug. 1776), 433–434. Also appeared in *The Gentleman's Magazine*, XLVI (Sept. 1776), 403–404. Reprinted in this volume, pp. 6–8.

FAŸ, BERNARD. *The Revolutionary Spirit in France and America*, trans. by Ramon Guthrie. New York: Harcourt, Brace and Company, Inc., 1927, pp. 78–81.

FINDLAY, BRUCE ALLYN and ESTHER BLAIR. *Your Magnificent Declaration.* New York: Holt, Rinehart & Winston, Inc. (paperback), 1961.

FISHER, SYDNEY GEORGE. "The Twenty-Eight Charges Against the King in the Declaration of Independence," *Pennsylvania Magazine of History and Biography*, XXXI (3rd Quarter, 1907), 257–303. Selections are reprinted in this volume, pp. 127–135.

————. *The Struggle for American Independence*, Vol. I. Philadelphia: J. B. Lippincott Company, 1908, pp. 460–465.

FISKE, AMOS K. "Some Consecrated Fallacies," *North American Review*, CLXIX (Dec. 1899), 821–828.

FITZPATRICK, JOHN C. *The Spirit of the Revolution: New Light from Some of the Original Sources of American History.* Boston: Houghton Mifflin Company, 1924. Chs. I–III. Appeared originally in the *Daughters of the American Revolution Magazine.*

FORCE, PETER. *The Declaration of Independence, or Notes on Lord Mahon's History of the American Declaration of Independence.* London: G. Willis, 1855. Another version appears in *Littell's Living Age*, 2d Ser., XLIV (Feb. 17, 1855), 387–407.

FORD, JOHN C. "The Natural Law and the 'Pursuit of Happiness,'" *Notre Dame Lawyer*, XXVI (Spr. 1951), 429–461.

FRIEDENWALD, HERBERT. *The Declaration of Independence: An Interpretation and an Analysis.* New York: The Macmillan Company, 1904. Appeared originally in *The International Monthly.*

FRIEDRICH, CARL J. and McCLOSKEY, ROBERT G. "The Roots of American Constitutionalism," *From the Declaration of Independence to the Con-*

stitution. Indianapolis: The Bobbs-Merrill Company, Inc. (paperback),
1954, pp. vii–lxvi.

FROTHINGHAM, RICHARD. *The Rise of the Republic of the United States.*
Boston: Little, Brown, and Company, 1872, pp. 555–560.

FURNESS, W. H. *The Declaration of Independence: A Discourse Delivered
in the First Congregational Unitarian Church.* Philadelphia: C. Sherman
& Son Printers, 1862.

GANTER, HERBERT LAWRENCE. "Jefferson's 'Pursuit of Happiness' and
Some Forgotten Men," *William and Mary Quarterly*, 2d Ser., XVI
(July 1936), 422–434; (Oct. 1936), 558–585.

GARVER, FRANK HARMON. "The Declaration of Independence," *What
Made the United States Great: Essays in American History Written for
the Los Angeles Times.* Los Angeles: University of Southern Cali-
fornia Press, 1953, pp. 79–98.

GOEBEL, JULIUS. "Christian Wolff and the Declaration of Independence,"
*Jahrbuch der deutsch-amerikanischen historischen Gesellschaft von
Illinois,* XVIII–XIX (1918–1919), 69–87. Reprinted as "Jus Connatum
and the Declaration of the Rights of Man," *Journal of English and
Germanic Philology,* XIX (1920), 1–18. A selection is reprinted in
this volume, pp. 136–138.

GOFF, FREDERICK R. "A Contemporary Broadside Printing of the Declaration of Independence," *The Library of Congress Quarterly Journal,*
V (Nov. 1947), 12–16.

GREGG, JARVIS. "Declaration of American Independence," *American Quarterly Observer,* II (Jan. 1834), 48–89.

GROGAN, FRANCIS J. "The Traditional Background of the Declaration of
Independence," *Fordham University Dissertations Accepted for Higher
Degrees in the Graduate School of Arts and Sciences,* XVII, Pt. II
(1950), 119–124.

HALL, EDWARD HAGAMAN. "Notes Concerning the Declaration of Independence, Including the Correction of Some Popular Errors," *American Scenic and Historic Preservation Society Annual Report,* XVIII
(1913), 467–483.

HARNETT, ROBERT C. "The Declaration of Independence," *The Great
Books: A Christian Appraisal; A Symposium on the First Year's Pro-
gram of the Great Books Foundation,* ed. Harold C. Gardiner. New
York: The Devin-Adair Company, 1949, pp. 1–7.

HARVEY, RAY FORREST. *Jean Jacques Burlamaqui: A Liberal Tradition in
American Constitutionalism.* Chapel Hill, N.C.: The University of
North Carolina Press, 1937, pp. 119–140.

HAWKE, DAVID. *A Transaction of Free Men: The Birth and Course of the
Declaration of Independence.* New York: Charles Scribner's Sons, 1964.

HAYS, I. MINIS. "A Note on the History of the Jefferson Manuscript Draught of the Declaration of Independence in the Library of the American Philosophical Society," *Proceedings of the American Philosophical Society,* XXXVII (1898), 88–107.

———. "A Contribution to the Bibliography of the Declaration of Independence," *Proceedings of the American Philosophical Society,* XXXIX (1900), 69–78.

HAZELTON, JOHN H. *The Declaration of Independence: Its History.* New York: Dodd, Mead & Company, Inc., 1906.

———. "The Declaration of Independence," *Case and Comment,* XXIV (July 1917), 87–91.

HELLER, BERNARD. *Syllabus for Teachers on Basic Religious Ideas in American Documents: Declaration of Independence,* experimental ed. New York: Jewish Education Committee of New York, 1947.

HETTICH, ERNEST L. "Exhibition Commemorating the 150th Anniversary of the Adoption of the Declaration of Independence, 1776–1926," *Bulletin of the New York Public Library,* XXXI (Oct. 1927), 806–825; (Nov. 1927), 904–939.

HILL, MABEL (ed.), *Liberty Documents, with Contemporary Exposition and Critical Comments Drawn from Various Writers.* New York: Longmans, Green and Co., Inc., 1901, pp. 182–203.

HIRST, FRANCIS W. *Life and Letters of Thomas Jefferson.* New York: The Macmillan Company, 1926, pp. 118–129.

A History of the Origin of the Appellation Keystone State, as Applied to the Commonwealth of Pennsylvania: Together with Extracts from Many Authorities Relative to the Adoption of the Declaration of Independence by the Continental Congress. Philadelphia: Claxton, Remsen & Haffelfinger, 1874.

VON HOLST, H[ERMANN E.] *The Constitutional and Political History of the United States,* trans. by John J. Lalor and Alfred B. Mason, Vol. I. Chicago: Callaghan and Company, 1877, pp. 5–8.

HOMMEL, RUDOLF. "Early Imprints of the Declaration of Independence," *Hobbies: The Magazine for Collectors,* LIV (Jan. 1950), 138–139.

HOWELL, WILBUR SAMUEL. "The Declaration of Independence and Eighteenth-Century Logic," *William and Mary Quarterly,* 3rd Ser., XVIII (Oct. 1961), 463–484. Reprinted in this volume, pp. 194–215.

HUGHES, AGNES LOCKHART. "The Makers of the Declaration of Independence," *Overland Monthly,* 2d Ser., LVIII (July 1911), 69–76.

HUGHES, CHARLES E. "The Declaration of Independence," *American Bar Association Journal,* XI (Aug. 1925), 532–534.

HUNT, GAILLARD. "The Virginia Declaration of Rights and Cardinal Bellarmine," *Catholic Historical Review,* III (Oct. 1917), 276–289.

[HUTCHINSON, THOMAS.] *Strictures upon the Declaration of the Congress at Philadelphia: In a Letter to a Noble Lord,* ed. Malcolm Freiberg.

"Old South Leaflets." Boston: The Old South Association, 1958. Originally published in 1776.

INGERSOLL, ROBERT G. "The Meaning of the Declaration," *Our National Centennial Jubilee: Orations, Addresses, and Poems Delivered on the Fourth of July, 1876, in the Several States of the Union,* ed. Frederick Saunders. New York: E. B. Treat, 1877. A selection is reprinted in this volume, pp. 68–70.

JAFFA, HARRY V. *Equality and Liberty: Theory and Practice in American Politics.* New York: Oxford University Press, 1965.

JEFFERSON, THOMAS. *The Jeffersonian Cyclopedia: A Comprehensive Collection of the Views of Thomas Jefferson,* ed. John P. Foley. New York & London: Funk & Wagnalls Company, 1900. Entries 2105–2133.

JONAS, MANFRED. *Die Unabhängigkeitserklärung der Vereinigten Staaten.* "Schriftenreihe der niedersächsischen Landeszentrale für politische Bildung." Hanover: 1964.

KALLICH, MARTIN and MACLEISH, ANDREW (eds.), "On American Affairs, July–December, 1776," *The American Revolution Through British Eyes.* New York: Harper & Row, Publishers, Incorporated (paperback), 1962, pp. 92–97.

KITE, ELIZABETH S. "How the Declaration of Independence Reached Europe," *Daughters of the American Revolution Magazine,* LXII (July 1928), 405–413.

KOCH, ADRIENNE. *Power, Morals, and the Founding Fathers: Essays in the Interpretation of the American Enlightenment.* Ithaca, N.Y.: Cornell University Press (paperback), 1961, pp. 25–31.

LANCASTER, BRUCE and PLUMB, J. H. *The American Heritage Book of the Revolution.* New York: Dell Publishing Co., Inc. (paperback), 1963, pp. 141–152.

LANE, ROBERT E., BARBER, JAMES D., and GREENSTEIN, FRED I. *An Introduction to Political Analysis: Problems in American Government,* 3rd ed. Englewood Cliffs, N.J.: Prentice-Hall, Inc. (paperback), 1962, pp. 1–7.

LATHAM, EARL (ed.), *The Declaration of Independence and the Constitution,* 2d ed. Boston: D. C. Heath and Company (paperback), 1956.

LEFFMANN, HENRY. *The True Story of the Declaration of Independence.* Philadelphia: Publication of the City History Society of Philadelphia, Vol. II (1917), pp. 23–35.

LENGYEL, CORNEL. *Four Days in July: The Story Behind the Declaration of Independence.* Garden City, N.Y.: Doubleday & Company, Inc., 1958.

"Lettre d'un banquier de Londres à M. ———, à Anvers," *Affaires de l'Angleterre et de l'Amérique*, Vol. II. Aug. 16, 1776, p. 88; Sept. 2, 1776, pp. 89–92. Translated in this volume, pp. 18–20.

LEWIS, JOSEPH. *Thomas Paine: Author of the Declaration of Independence*. New York: Freethought Press Assn., 1947. A selection is reprinted in this volume, pp. 174–176.

———. "Thomas Paine: Author of the Declaration of Independence," *The Age of Reason Magazine*, XXXIV (July–Aug. 1965), 1–16.

LINCOLN, ABRAHAM. *The Collected Works*, ed. Roy P. Basler. New Brunswick, N.J.: Rutgers University Press, 1953–1955. Speech at Springfield, Ill., June 26, 1857, Vol. II, pp. 403–407. Speech at Lewistown, Ill., Aug. 17, 1858, Vol. II, pp. 546–547 (reprinted in this volume pp. 64–65). Speech at Columbus, Ohio, Sept. 16, 1859, Vol. III, pp. 423–425. Speech at Independence Hall, Philadelphia, Feb. 22, 1861, Vol. IV, pp. 240–241.

LINCOLN, ABRAHAM and DOUGLAS, STEPHEN A. *The Illinois Political Campaign of 1858: A Facsimile of the Printer's Copy of His Debates with Senator Stephen Arnold Douglas as Edited and Prepared for Press by Abraham Lincoln*. [Washington:] The Library of Congress, [1958]. Selections are reprinted in this volume, pp. 59–63, 65–67.

[LIND, JOHN.] *An Answer to the Declaration of the American Congress*, 5th ed. London: T. Cadell, 1776. The closing section of this work is reprinted in this volume, pp. 9–17.

LIVERMORE, GEORGE. *An Historical Research Respecting the Opinions of the Founders of the Republic on Negroes as Slaves, as Citizens, and as Soldiers*, 4th ed. Boston: A. Williams and Company, 1863, pp. 15–26.

LONGSHORE, JOS. S. and KNOWLES, BENJAMIN L. *The Centennial Liberty Bell, Independence Hall: Its Traditions and Associations; The Declaration of Independence and Its Signers.* . . . Philadelphia: Claxton, Remsen & Haffelfinger, 1876.

LOSSING, B[ENSON] J. *Biographical Sketches of the Signers of the Declaration of American Independence, the Declaration Historically Considered* . . . . New York: George F. Cooledge & Brother, 1848.

———. "Our National Anniversary," *Harper's New Monthly Magazine*, III (July 1851), 145–160.

———. "Signing of the Declaration of Independence," *Potter's American Monthly*, V (Oct. 1875), 754–756.

MCANDREW, WILLIAM. "The Declaration and the Schools," *School and Society*, XXIV (July 31, 1926), 121–125.

MADISON, JAMES. *Letters and Other Writings*, Vol. III. New York: R. Worthington, 1884, pp. 336–337. Letter to Jefferson, Sept. 6, 1823.

MAHON, LORD. *History of England*, 3rd ed., Vol. VI. Boston: Little, Brown, and Company, 1853, pp. 96–99.

MALAGÓN, JAVIER (ed.), *Las Actas de independencia de América*. Washington: Unión Panamericana, 1955. Includes a comparative study by Charles C. Griffin.

MALONE, DUMAS. "Herald of Freedom," *Jefferson the Virginian*, Vol. I of *Jefferson and His Time*. Boston: Little, Brown and Company, 1948, pp. 215–231. Adapted as Introduction, *Autobiography of Thomas Jefferson*. New York: Capricorn Books (paperback), [1959], pp. 1–18.

———. *The Story of the Declaration of Independence*. New York: Oxford University Press, 1954.

MARSH, DANIEL L. "The Second Gospel of Americanism: The Declaration of Independence," *Methodist Review*, 5th Ser., XLII (July 1926), 512–530.

MATTHEWS, ALBERT. "Thomas Paine and the Declaration of Independence," *Proceedings of the Massachusetts Historical Society*, XLIII (Jan. 1910), 241–253. Revised from *Notes and Queries*, 10th Ser., XII (Dec. 4, 1909), 441–443.

MEARNS, DAVID C. *The Declaration of Independence: The Story of a Parchment*. Washington: The Library of Congress, 1950.

MENCKEN, H. L. "The Declaration of Independence in American," *A Mencken Chrestomathy*. New York: Alfred A. Knopf, Inc., 1962, pp. 583–587.

MESSENGER, NORTH OVERTON. "Our Lost Declaration of Independence," *The Independent*, LV (July 2, 1903), 1562–1564.

MICHAEL, WILLIAM H. *The Declaration of Independence: Illustrated Story of Its Adoption, with the Biographies and Portraits of the Signers and of the Secretary of the Congress*. Washington: Government Printing Office, 1904.

MIRABEAU, COMTE DE. *Des lettres de cachet et des prisons d'état, Œuvres*, Vol. VII. Paris: Lecointe et Pougin, 1835, pp. 239–240. Originally published in 1782. Translated in this volume, p. 20.

MONAGHAN, FRANK. "Thomas Jefferson's 'Rough Draft' of the Declaration of Independence," *Heritage of Freedom: The History & Significance of the Basic Documents of American Liberty*. Princeton, N.J.: Princeton University Press, 1947, pp. 17–19.

[MOODY, JOEL.] "An Examination of the Declaration of Independence," *Junius Unmasked: Or, Thomas Paine the Author of the Letters of Junius and the Declaration of Independence*. Washington: John Gray & Co., Publishers, 1872, pp. 201–278.

MORRIS, NELLIE HESS. "The Birth of the American Republic, Ninety-Nine Years Ago," *Potter's American Monthly*, V (July 1875), 491–504.

———. "The Signing of the Declaration of Independence—August 2, 1776," *Potter's American Monthly*, V (Sept. 1875), 648–650. This article is followed by a contribution of the editors entitled "The Declaration of Independence—Statements of Thomas McKean and Thomas Jefferson Compared," pp. 650–652.

MOSES, ERNEST CURTIS. "The Signing of the Declaration, with Docu-

mental History," *American Monthly Magazine* [of the Daughters of
the American Revolution], XXIII (Aug. 1903), 107–110.

MUZZEY, DAVID SAVILLE. *Thomas Jefferson.* New York: Charles Scribner's
Sons, 1918, pp. 40–51.

MYERS, HENRY ALONZO. *Are Men Equal? An Inquiry into the Meaning of
American Democracy.* Ithaca, N.Y.: Cornell University Press (paperback), 1959.

NUGENT, ARTHUR F. "The Constitution and the Declaration," United
States Catholic Historical Society, *Historical Records and Studies,*
XXXIV (1945), 137–174.

O'BRIEN, EDWARD C. "The Declaration of Independence," *Lawyer and
Banker, and Central Law Review* (New Orleans), XXI (Sept.–Oct.
1928), 297–309.

ONCKEN, WILHELM. *Das Zeitalter Friedrichs des Großen, Allgemeine
Geschichte,* 3rd Ser., Vol. VIII, Pt. II. Berlin: G. Grote'sche Verlags-
buchhandlung, 1882, pp. 719–726. Translated in this volume, pp. 71–
77.

PADOVER, S. K. "Jefferson's Prose Poem: The Declaration of Independence," *American Mercury,* LIV (Feb. 1942), 165–171.

PARKS, SAMUEL C. "A Defense of the Declaration of Independence,"
Arena, XXX (Aug. 1903), 152–158.

PEATTIE, DONALD CULROSS. "The Declaration of Independence—America's Gospel," *Reader's Digest,* LIII (July 1948), 21–26.

PERRY, RALPH BARTON. *Puritanism and Democracy.* New York: The
Vanguard Press, 1944; Harper Torchbook (paperback), 1964. A selection is reprinted in this volume, pp. 166–173.

PETERSON, MERRILL D. *The Jefferson Image in the American Mind.*
New York: Oxford University Press (paperback), 1962.

PHILLIPS, W. ALISON. "The Declaration of Independence," *Edinburgh
Review,* CCXLIV (July 1926), 1–17.

PICKERING, TIMOTHY. *Observations Introductory to Reading the Declaration of Independence at Salem, July 4, 1823.* Salem, Mass.: Warwick
Palfray, Jun., 1823. Reprinted in Charles W. Upham, *The Life of
Timothy Pickering,* Vol. IV. Boston: Little, Brown, and Company,
1873, Appendix D.

PITTMAN, R. CARTER. *Equality v. Liberty: The Eternal Conflict.* [Rich-
mond, Va.:] Virginia Commission on Constitutional Government (paperback), [1960]. Reprinted from *American Bar Association Journal,*
XLVI (Aug. 1960), 873–880.

POOKE, FLORENCE A. *Fountain-Sources of American Political Theory: A
Study of the Origin and Meaning of the Democratic Political Theories*

in the American Declaration of Independence. New York: Lewis Cope-
land and Company, 1930.

Powell, J. H. *The Books of a New Nation: United States Government
Publications, 1774–1814*. Philadelphia: University of Pennsylvania
Press, 1957, pp. 53–60.

Prince, L. Bradford. "The Declaration of Independence: Its Principle
and Its Power," *Journal of American History*, XI (1st Quarter, 1917),
108–112, 129–132.

"The Principles of the Fathers," *Outlook*, LXII (May 20, 1899), 147–
150.

*The Pro-Slavery Argument, as Maintained by the Most Distinguished
Writers of the Southern States*. Philadelphia: Lippincott, Grambo, &
Co., 1853. Chancellor Harper, pp. 5–6, 10–12. W. Gilmore Simms, pp.
250–260.

Purcell, Richard J. "Background of the Declaration of Independence,"
Democracy: Should It Survive?, issued by the William J. Kerby Foundation. Milwaukee: The Bruce Publishing Company, 1943, pp. 19–31.

Rager, John Clement. *Democracy and Bellarmine: An Examination of
Blessed Cardinal Bellarmine's Defense of Popular Government and the
Influence of His Political Theory upon the American Declaration of
Independence*. Shelbyville, Ind.: Qualityprint Inc., 1926. Originally
entitled *Political Philosophy of Blessed Cardinal Bellarmine*. A Doc-
toral Dissertation published by the Catholic University of America,
1926.

Randall, Henry S. *The Life of Thomas Jefferson*, Vol. I. New York:
Derby & Jackson, 1858, pp. 164–193.

Raynal, Abbé. *The Revolution of America*. Philadelphia: Robert Bell,
1782, pp. 40–42.

[Richards, George.] *The Declaration of Independence: A Poem*. Boston: 1793. Reprinted in *The Magazine of History*, XXXVIII, Extra
No. 150 (1929), 93–114.

Richards, George W. "The Declaration of Independence," *Reformed
Church Review*, 4th Ser., XV (Apr. 1911), 204–230.

Robinson, Stewart M. *"And . . . We Mutually Pledge . . .": The
Spirit of the Declaration of Independence, and the Writings of the
Colonial Clergy Which Are Reflected Therein*. New Canaan, Conn.:
The Long House, Inc. (paperback), 1964.

Rodríguez Demorizi, Emilio. *El Acta de la separación dominicana y el
acta de independencia de los Estados Unidos de América*. Ciudad
Trujillo: Imprenta "La Opinion," 1943.

Ross, J. Elliot. " 'We hold these Truths . . . ,' " *Religious Education*,
XXXVIII (Mar.–Apr. 1943), 110–115.

Ross, Ralph, Berryman, John, and Tate, Allen. *The Arts of Reading*.
New York: Thomas Y. Crowell Company, 1960, pp. 39–48.

SCHAFF, DAVID S. "The Bellarmine-Jefferson Legend and the Declaration of Independence," *Papers of the American Society of Church History,* 2d Ser., VIII (1928), 239–276.

SCHLESINGER, ARTHUR M. "The Lost Meaning of 'The Pursuit of Happiness,' " *William and Mary Quarterly,* 3rd Ser., XXI (July 1964), 325–327. Reprinted in this volume, pp. 216–218.

SCOTT, JOHN A. "Thomas Jefferson and the Declaration of Independence," *Living Documents in American History.* New York: Washington Square Press, Inc. (paperback), 1964, pp. 163–168.

[SELDEN, RICHARD ELY.] *Criticism on the Declaration of Independence as a Literary Document,* by Mon Droit. New York: 1846. Selections are reprinted in this volume, pp. 37–56.

SMITH, PAGE. *John Adams,* Vol. I. Garden City, N.Y.: Doubleday & Company, Inc., 1962, pp. 265–274.

SMITH, T. V. *The American Philosophy of Equality.* Chicago: The University of Chicago Press, 1927.

SMITH, WILLIAM RAYMOND. "The Rhetoric of the Declaration of Independence," *College English,* XXVI (Jan. 1965), 306–309.

SMYTH, THOMAS. *The True Origin and Source of the Mecklenburg and National Declaration of Independence.* Columbia, S.C.: I. C. Morgan, 1847.

SNOW, ALPHEUS HENRY. "The Declaration of Independence as the Fundamental Constitution of the United States," *The American Philosophy of Government.* New York: G. P. Putnam's Sons, 1921, pp. 35–66. Paper read in 1906.

SNYDER, ALFRED J. *America's Purpose.* Philadelphia: The Declaration Press, 1937.

SOTO PAZ, RAFAEL. *No es de Jefferson la declaración de independencia.* Havana: Editorial Lex, 1947.

STILLÉ, CHARLES J. "Pennsylvania and the Declaration of Independence," *Pennsylvania Magazine of History and Biography,* XIII (4th Quarter, 1889), 385–429.

STONE, WILLIAM L. "The Declaration of Independence in a New Light," *Harper's New Monthly Magazine,* LXVII (July 1883), 208–212.

STORRS, R. S. *Oration on the Declaration of Independence and the Effects of It.* New York: Anson D. F. Randolph & Company, 1876.

SULLIVAN, JAMES. "The Antecedents of the Declaration of Independence," *Annual Report of the American Historical Association for the Year 1902,* I, 67–81.

————. "United States: The Declaration of Independence," *Encyclopedia Americana,* Vol. XXVII. New York: Americana Corporation, 1932, pp. 331–333.

SUMNER, CHARLES. "Promises of the Declaration of Independence, and Abraham Lincoln," *Works,* Vol. IX. Boston: Lee and Shepard, 1875, pp. 367–428. Eulogy delivered June 1, 1865.

Taney, Chief Justice Roger B. *Dred Scott v. Sandford, Reports of Cases Argued and Adjudged in the Supreme Court of the United States*, by Benjamin C. Howard, Vol. XIX (Dec. Term, 1856). New York: The Banks Law Publishing Co., 1903, pp. 409–410.

Tarbell, Ida M. "The Story of the Declaration of Independence," *Mc-Clure's Magazine*, XVII (July 1901), 223–235.

Thompson, Charles O. F. *A History of the Declaration of Independence: A Story of the American Patriots Who Brought about the Birth of the Nation*. Bristol, R.I.: Published by the author, 1947.

Trevelyan, George Otto. *The American Revolution*, 2d ed., Vol. II. New York: Longmans, Green and Co., Inc., 1922, pp. 160–171.

Tyler, Benjamin Owen. *Declaration of Independence: A Candid Statement of Facts in Answer to an Unwarrantable Denunciation of My Publication of the Declaration of American Independence Made by Mr. John Binns*. Washington: 1818.

Tyler, Moses Coit. *The Literary History of the American Revolution, 1763–1783*, Vol. I. New York: G. P. Putnam's Sons, 1897, pp. 498–521. Reprinted in this volume, pp. 83–101. Tyler's essay originally appeared in *North American Review*, CLXIII (July 1896), 1–16. *The Literary History* has been reprinted by Frederick Ungar Publishing Co., New York, 1957.

U.S. Department of Health, Education, and Welfare. *The Declaration of Independence and Its Story*. Washington: Government Printing Office, 1953.

Vail, R. W. G. "The Unique Declaration of Independence Printed by Hugh Gaine," *New-York Historical Society Quarterly*, XXXII (July 1948), 220–224.

Van Der Weyde, William M. *Who Wrote the Declaration of Independence?* New York: Thomas Paine National Historical Association, n.d. Also appears in *Americana [American Historical Magazine]*, VI (Jan. 1911), 8–15.

Van Zandt, Roland. *The Metaphysical Foundations of American History*. The Hague: Mouton & Co., 1959, pp. 105–108.

Vossler, Otto. *Die amerikanischen Revolutionsideale in ihrem Verhältnis zu den Europäischen: Untersucht an Thomas Jefferson*. Munich & Berlin: Verlag von R. Oldenbourg, 1929, pp. 79–86. Translated in this volume, pp. 154–161. An abstract of Vossler's book has been published in English by R. R. Palmer, "A Neglected Work: Otto Vossler on Jefferson and the Revolutionary Era," *William and Mary Quarterly*, 3rd Ser., XII (July 1955), 462–471.

[Waites, Alfred.] *A Brief Account of John Milton and His Declaration of Independence*, limited ed. Worcester, Mass.: Gilbert G. Davis, 1903.

APPENDIX 4

WALL, A. J. "New York and the Declaration of Independence," *New-York Historical Society Quarterly Bulletin*, X (July 1926), 43–51.

WALSH, MICHAEL J. "Contemporary Broadside Editions of the Declaration of Independence," *Harvard Library Bulletin*, III (Win. 1949), 31–43.

WARREN, CHARLES. "Fourth of July Myths," *William and Mary Quarterly*, 3rd Ser., II (July 1945), 237–272.

WARREN, WINSLOW. *The Declaration of Independence: An Address*. Boston: 1904.

WASHBURN, CHARLES G. "Who Was the Author of the Declaration of Independence?" *Proceedings of the American Antiquarian Society*, New Ser., XXXVIII (Apr. 1928), 51–62.

WEBSTER, DANIEL. *A Discourse in Commemoration of the Lives and Services of John Adams and Thomas Jefferson*. Boston: Cummings, Hilliard and Company, 1826. A selection is reprinted in this volume, pp. 35–36.

WELSH, EDWARD BURGETT. "Some Presbyterian Backgrounds of the Declaration of Independence," *Western Pennsylvania Historical Magazine*, XXIV (Dec. 1941), 261–267.

WHITNEY, PETER. *American Independence Vindicated: A Sermon Delivered September 12, 1776 at a Lecture Appointed for Publishing the Declaration of Independence*. Boston: E. Draper, 1777.

WHITTLESEY, WALTER LINCOLN. "The First Great American Publicity Job," *Survey*, LVI (July 1, 1926), 405–407.

WILSON, WOODROW. "The Author and Signers of the Declaration of Independence," *North American Review*, CLXXXVI (Sept. 1907), 22–33.

WINTHROP, ROBERT C. *Oration . . . July 4, 1876*. Boston: Printed by order of the City Council, 1876.

WISHY, BERNARD. "John Locke and the Spirit of '76," *Political Science Quarterly*, LXXIII (Sept. 1958), 413–425.

ZYSKIND, HAROLD. "The Declaration of Independence," *Promoting Growth Toward Maturity in Interpreting What Is Read*, ed. William S. Grey, *Supplementary Educational Monographs*, XIII, No. 74 (Nov. 1951), 7–12. Reprinted in this volume, pp. 177–183.

⊱ 5 ⊰

Problems for Study
and Writing

A. *Problems for Discussion and Expository Writing*

1. What do these terms and phrases mean in the Declaration: *unalienable Rights, Pursuit of Happiness, to secure these Rights, Consent of the Governed, the Necessity which denounces our separation?*

2. How many "self-evident truths" are listed in the Declaration? How are they interrelated? Is their meaning self-evident? Are they true?

3. According to the Declaration what powers and limitations do states and governments have? What is the difference between a state and a people? After breaking the ties with England, were there thirteen sovereign states in America or one?

4. Explain the right of revolution embodied in the Declaration. Suppose most people in a country are unhappy: do they have the right to overthrow their government? Do the people have the right to overthrow a benevolent despot?

5. What conception of history is employed throughout the Declaration? How do character, duty, and necessity enter into this conception?

6. Restate in a few sentences what is expressed in the first sentence of the Declaration. What is peculiar about that sentence?

7. Into what groupings do the accusations in the Declaration fall? Are there more than twenty-seven charges? How do you account for inclusion of accusation xiv when the issue it raises has been dealt with in accusation xi?

8. How is paragraph IV on the British people organized? What does it contribute to the Declaration? Is its emotional appeal out of place?

9. What changes took place in the composition and revision of the

285

final paragraph of the Declaration? Compare Jefferson's original wording with Richard Henry Lee's Resolution.

10. Write an analysis of all the commentaries in this book on the line, *We mutually pledge to each other our Lives, our Fortunes, and our sacred Honor*.

11. Give a detailed skeletal outline of the Declaration showing the place of all its parts.

12. Reconstruct the text of the Declaration as it stood when submitted to Congress.

13. What is declared in the Declaration? Why is it declared in a few hundred words rather than in a few words?

14. Does the Declaration of Independence contradict the Declaration of Taking up Arms?

15. To what extent are Thomas Paine's conclusions concerning independence applicable to the Declaration?

16. What conception of the Declaration did John Adams have? List the faults he found in it and Jefferson's replies.

B. *Problems for Critical Study and Writing*

1. Explain the political theory embodied in the Declaration; and evaluate its clarity, completeness, consistency, and practicality.

2. What consequences does the political philosophy of the Declaration have for ethics, theology, and theory of nature?

3. What kind of argument is present in the Declaration? What appeals does it make in order to convince? Whom is it meant to win over? Can you find major and minor premises and a conclusion drawn from them?

4. How are we to understand the statement, *all Men are created equal*? What role does it play in the Declaration? Compare the major interpretations of the statement by the critics.

5. Examine the merits of both sides of this contention: The great weakness in the Declaration is its vilification of the King as exclusive cause of all the trouble.

6. Judge the appropriateness of the attack on slavery to the Declaration. What significant changes were made in the anti-slavery passage from its appearance in the First Ideas on the Constitution of Virginia to the version submitted by the Committee of Five? What would have been the consequences of leaving it in the final text?

7. Give an account of the changes the material in the Composi-

tional Fragment was to undergo. What insight do such changes afford into the purpose and organization of the Declaration?

8. Trace the transformations in order and content of the grievances from the First Ideas on the Constitution of Virginia to the final Declaration.

9. Making use of the Rough Draft, write a critical judgment, supported by examples, of the Congressional editing of the Declaration. Are there any changes made by Congress that are apparent in the final text which Jefferson did not enter onto his Rough Draft?

10. The writing in the Declaration is sloppy, awkward, vague, ungrammatical, repetitious, and pretentious. Evaluate the justice and pertinence of these judgments.

11. Write a defense of the originality of the Declaration.

12. According to Jefferson what was the purpose of the Declaration? What steps did he take to fulfill it? How successful was he?

13. Compare the contemporary reactions to the Declaration by "An Englishman" and "Un Banquier de Londres." What would each have to say of the other's comments?

14. What differences of method and preoccupation underlie the discussion of the Declaration's style by Selden, Becker, Lewis, and Ginsberg? What should one look for in assessing the style of the Declaration?

15. What are the main distinctions of logic and rhetoric that Howell and Ginsberg draw in their articles, and how pertinent are such distinctions to the particular problems raised by the Declaration?

16. Compare the discussions by Oncken, Dana, Vossler, and Aptheker of the Declaration as a political act. What conception of political events does each author employ, and what conception do you think is most applicable to the Declaration?

17. Write a detailed reply to Lind's answer to the Declaration and then a brief rebuttal on his behalf.

18. Was the Declaration designed primarily with the French in mind? Did French reception of it shape the conception of the Declaration that was to become prevalent among American commentators? What changes in reaction are noticeable in France between 1776 and 1790?

19. Evaluate the scholarly methods by which Dana clarifies the meaning of the Declaration's principles. Are his conclusions justified?

20. Write a sequel to Zyskind's article, extending the inquiry he

pursues into further detail and into areas you believe require fresh study.

21. Write a study of the Declaration in the Light of Modern Criticism, starting from Tyler's article and using the essays in this casebook.

22. Draw up a catalogue of all the errors and misconceptions concerning the Declaration you can find in this book. Explain how the various types of error are arrived at and how they are to be avoided.

23. What is there to the Declaration that is not limited to the time and circumstances of its origin but is universal and enduring?

24. What light do philosophy, history, and literary study each throw on the Declaration? In which of these fields, if any, is the principal understanding and appreciation of the Declaration to be arrived at?

25. What standards can one use to judge the greatness of the Declaration? How should the criticism and evaluation of it differ from criticism and evaluation of a fictional work or a philosophic treatise?

26. Assess the greatness of the Declaration.

C. Problems for Research

1. Study the political thought of one of the following in conjunction with the ideas embodied in the Declaration: John Locke, Jean-Jacques Rousseau, Cardinal Bellarmine, Thomas Paine, George Mason, Jean-Jacques Burlamaqui, Richard Price, Christian Wolff, William Molyneux. What changes does the Declaration make in theory? What significance is there to the particular wording used in the Declaration for previous ideas? What evidence is there that the Declaration was influenced by such ideas?

2. Study the Declaration in the context of the political writings of Thomas Jefferson. In what sense is the Declaration (or the Rough Draft) the key to his own philosophy?

3. Select a manuscript available in facsimile or an early printed edition of the Declaration and give a full account of its relationship to the first printed edition. What light do its textual variants throw upon the composition or significance of the Declaration?

4. Make a critical study of the various discussions of the role of religious thought in the Declaration, using works listed in the Bibliography.

5. Select one of the grievances in the Declaration, collect the historical materials appropriate to it, summarize the views of commentators upon it, and offer your own judgment of its inclusion in the Declaration as fact and as accusation.

6. Present a comparative study of the Declaration and one of the following works: Pericles' Funeral Oration as recorded by Thucydides, *The Communist Manifesto* by Marx and Engels, Lincoln's Gettysburg Address. Specify the genre of writing they belong to, and judge the success of each in that genre.

7. Making use of writings listed in the Bibliography, explore the shifts in the popular conception of the Declaration evidenced at each jubilee (1826, 1876, 1926).

8. Take one of the following problems in American history: slavery, states' rights, secession, women's rights, imperialism, civil rights, and analyze it in terms of principles or paradoxes that are involved in the Declaration. Give a careful account of how the Declaration has been interpreted in terms of the issue you select.

9. Compile a bibliography of the revolutionary manifestoes, such as those of France (1789), Santo Domingo (1844), Viet-Nam (1945), and Rhodesia (1965), which borrow from the Declaration of Independence. Supply a commentary pointing out any insights such employ gives into the original document and signaling the shifts in emphasis upon the Declaration that have occurred in the course of revolutionary events.

10. Study the orations listed in the Bibliography and then write a Fourth of July speech of your own addressed to a popular audience and true to the significance of the Declaration.